media

MANUAL

digital video camerawork

MANUAL

media

MANUAL

digital video camerawork

peter ward

Focal Press

OXFORD AUCKLAND BOSTON JOHANNESBURG MELBOURNE NEW DELHI

Focal Press is an imprint of Elsevier
Linacre House, Jordan Hill, Oxford OX2 8DP, UK
30 Corporate Drive, Suite 400, Burlington, MA 01803, USA

First edition 2000
Reprinted 2001, 2002, 2003, 2004, 2005, 2006

Notice
No responsibility is assumed by the publisher for any injury and/or damage to persons
or property as a matter of products liability, negligence or otherwise, or from any use
or operation of any methods, products, instructions or ideas contained in the material
herein. Because of rapid advances in the medical sciences, in particular, independent
verification of diagnoses and drug dosages should be made

British Library Cataloguing in Publication Data
A catalogue record for this book is available from the British Library

Library of Congress Cataloging-in-Publication Data
A catalog record for this book is available from the Library of Congress

ISBN–13: 978-0-240-51605-9
ISBN–10: 0-240-51605-2

For information on all Focal Press publications
visit our website at www.focalpress.com

Printed and bound in *Great Britain*

06 07 08 09 10 10 9 8 7

Working together to grow
libraries in developing countries

www.elsevier.com | www.bookaid.org | www.sabre.org

ELSEVIER   BOOK AID International   Sabre Foundation

Contents

Acknowledgements

The author wishes to acknowledge the help and assistance in compiling this manual from many television colleagues and equipment manufacturers. In particular, Alan Bermingham for his help on many sections, Roger Laycock and Chris Wherry for their help on the section on sound, Anton/Bauer Inc., Avid Technology, Cannon (UK) Ltd., Neil Burtonshaw, Colin Green, Vas Nathwani, JVC, OpTex, Panasonic, Sony Corporation, Thomson Broadcast Systems, Vinten Broadcast Ltd. Diagrams reprinted from Focal Press manuals include *The Video Studio*, A. Bermingham, M. Talbot-Smith, Ken Angola-Stephens, Ed Boyce; *Sound and Recording: An Introduction*, Francis Rumsey and Tim McCormick; *The Gaffer's Handbook*, Harry C. Box, edited by Brian Fitt. My thanks for their help and cooperation, especially to my wife Sue for her help and support and Tom Barcley for his close interest.

Introduction

This is a manual about digital camerawork techniques used in television or video production. Within this context, television applies to the system of broadcasting programmes by terrestrial transmitters, satellites or cable to an audience who can watch the production at the time of transmission or record for future viewing. Video usually describes a production which is intended to be sold and used as a cassette. Confusingly, it also describes programme making using video cameras as opposed to film production.

We are in a period of transition between analogue and digital acquisition/recording formats. The price of equipment is an overriding factor in an industry that is forced to become more competitive chasing fewer viewers scattered across a greater number of channels. This requires smaller programme budgets, cheaper equipment, and has generated interest in DVCPro, Digital-S, DVCam, and DV format cameras. However, the existing format competition may be a false battle as all the present competing formats are tape. Disk cameras are in production but it is not only a format battle, there is also a compression battle.

'Digital' is sometimes mistakenly used as an adjective for quality, but picture quality is dependent on a number of factors. How the signal is digitalized, the amount of compression employed and the affect of coding/decoding several times along a signal path will have an impact on picture quality. The initials *DV* can stand for digital video and are also used to identify 'DV', a recording format. In this manual the initials are restricted to the DV recording format. Most digital formats are covered except Digi beta and BetacamSX which are discussed in *Basic Betacam Camerawork* in the Media Manual series.

With such a diversity of recording formats and camera design, choosing the appropriate camera/recorder format will depend on budget and the production requirements. Technique is dependent on technology and therefore an understanding of different production techniques and the variation in shooting styles is required for each genre. Each production type requires some specialist technique and possibly a specific format. It is essential to have an understanding of all the controls on the camera and how to record a technically acceptable image (e.g. exposure, gain, shutter, etc.). Also the programme making importance of camera peripherals such as batteries, camera mounts, microphones and tape.

The digital camera has become a computer. Data manipulation before recording is similar to the action of a computer, and can be applied to video because the signal is in a digital form. Digital manipulation of the image allows customizing the image through the camera menu and an expansion of automatic facilities such as exposure zones, speed of iris response, precise control of face tone, the removal of blemishes and picture zones. Digital manipulation also allows selective contouring, and softer transitions between auto functions. We can also expect the growth of specialized software that can be loaded into the camera for specific needs or to expand the camera's facilities. Disk recording allows in-camera digital manipulation of the image after recording. This includes loop recording; editing on disk; position and shot size; editing in the field. Good production technique is understanding and exploiting the basic skills of camerawork, lighting and sound to serve the specific needs of a production. Providing a story structure and shot variety, to enable flexibility in editing, are basic standard techniques required from the ENG/EFP cameraman. Editing in the field based on the low-cost DV format is a useful time-saver for news bulletins, as is SNG. There is an essential need to shoot with editing in mind and to have a working knowledge and familiarity with different production styles and their requirements.

The manual does not assume that the reader will have had extensive analogue camerawork experience or a knowledge of TV engineering fundamentals. With low-price digital formats available, DV working may be the first experience many people have of television camerawork and therefore an account of perennial camerawork technique is included.

The responsibility for acquiring and editing television material often rests with a number of people. Sometimes a single person will shoot and cut an item. On other programmes there will be many more people involved in getting the material 'on-air'. Traditionally there has been a division of 'production' labour shared between different crafts skills. In this manual, camerawork and editing are descriptions of production activities and need not necessarily refer to a particular craft skill. Throughout the manual, terms such as 'cameraman' are used without wishing to imply that any production craft is restricted to one gender. 'Cameraman' for example is the customary title to describe a job practised by both men and women and 'he', where it occurs, should be read as 'he/she'.

Technique and technology

There is an urban myth of an American tourist hiring a car in a foreign land and driving 200 miles in first gear. When the engine eventually overheated and seized up he was asked if did he not suspect somewhere along the journey that something was wrong. He said he thought it was noisy and slow compared to his own car with automatic transmission back home, but having never driven a car with a manual gear change he had no way of comparing the car's performance.

A basic knowledge of television technology is required to avoid a similar foul-up when new to programme making. Technology is simply a means to an end; the end being a programme that communicates with its audience. Without an understanding of the camera equipment employed or an over-reliance on automatic features, the end result may be less than satisfactory.

In 1888 the Kodak camera was launched as an easy, simple method of taking photographs. 'You press the button, we do the rest', was a sales slogan to demystify the arcane process of photography. In the early days of the craft, would-be photographers had to prepare their own glass plates, and then develop them in a combined camera/darkroom. After 1888, anybody could press a button and the camera and the chemist would do the rest. Training in photographic competence was condensed to the few minutes required to be instructed on which button to press.

Over 100 years later, in response to the needs of the TV industry, the craft of camerawork is promoted as a simple matter of knowing the position of a couple of buttons on the camera. After a very short training period, anybody can become a competent television cameraman. If this was true about photography and broadcast camerawork, there should be no visual difference between a holiday snapshot and an advertising brochure of a resort, or a holiday video and a feature film shot at that resort.

Technology and technique intertwine. How you do something in broadcasting depends on what equipment you are using. It is not simply a question of being told which button to press in order to get a professional result. In television camerawork, an understanding of camera technology plus the ability to exploit and take into consideration the attributes of the camera and the lens characteristics is the basis of practical programme production. Most camera equipment is now wrapped up with auto features in the hope of being user-friendly to technophobic customers, but camera operators should aim to understand what is happening when they are using a camera rather than trust the old slogan of 'you press the button, the equipment will do the rest'.

Simplified figure of a DV camera/recorder

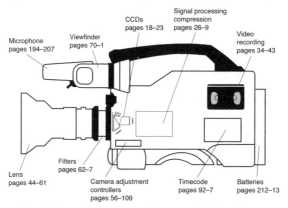

Microphone
pages 194–207

Viewfinder
pages 70–1

CCDs
pages 18–23

Signal processing
compression
pages 26–9

Video
recording
pages 34–43

Lens
pages 44–61

Filters
pages 62–7

Camera adjustment
controllers
pages 56–109

Timecode
pages 92–7

Batteries
pages 212–13

Lens system: The design of the lens affects resolution, image quality, focal length, zoom ratio, exposure and control of zooming. Also important is the lens fitting to allow interchangeability with other lenses.

Charge coupled device: The choice of pick-up sensors (e.g. FIT, HAD, etc.) will determine how light is converted into electricity and will control the quality of image, definition, highlight handling, contrast range and sensitivity.

Television system: How the signal is read from the CCDs will depend on the video system chosen and how it will be seen by its potential audience. Choice of systems range from decisions on colour system (PAL, NTSC, SECAM), line structure (625, 525, 1088, etc.), aspect ratio (4:3 or 16:9), interlace or progressively scanned.

Digital conversion: Choice of sampling rate and how the colour information is sampled will affect how the material is displayed and edited.

Signal processing: How the signal is processed and modified such as knee, linear matrix, gamma will affect the appearance of the final displayed image.

Compression: Digital signals require compression before recording and the compression ratio chosen for the camera and the design and method of compression all affect the signal output.

Video recording format: There are many methods of recording video onto tape or disk (e.g. Betacam SX, DVCPro, DV, Digital-S, etc.). The method and format used in the camera will control the quality of recording and editing format.

Sound: An effective method of recording and monitoring audio levels is needed and the facilities for microphone inputs will affect the final edited audio presentation.

Camera controls: A range of controls are required to achieve a good technical quality image (e.g. white balance, shutter, gain, exposure, menus, set-up cards, built in filters, method of genlocking and monitoring outputs, etc.).

Viewfinder: A quality viewfinder to monitor all aspects of the image output.

Timecode: A method of setting up and recording timecode information on the tape is essential for editing.

Power supplies: Batteries and monitoring the state of charge of batteries is required. Also an input to use an AC adaptor if required.

Pan/tilt head and support system: Adaptor plate on the base of the camera to enable it to be mounted on pan/tilt head and tripod.

Robust mechanical design: A camcorder used for everyday programme production is subjected to much harder wear and tear than a camera used for holidays and family events.

Light into electricity

Light reflected from the subject in view will pass through the lens and be focused on the charge-coupled devices fitted in the camera. The effect of the lens and lens characteristics are discussed later. This page details how light is turned into an electrical signal.

How the eye sees colour

There are many nerve endings in the retina which respond to visible light including red, green and blue receptors which respond to a range of wavelengths. Colours are seen as a mixture of signals from these three types of receptors. Colour television adopts the same principle by using a prism behind the lens to split the light from a scene into three separate channels (see figure opposite).

White balance

In colorimetry it is convenient to think of white being obtained from equal amounts of red, green and blue light. This concept is continued in colour cameras. When exposed to a white surface (neutral scene), the three signals are matched to the green signal to give equal amounts of red, green and blue. This is known as white balance. The actual amounts of red, green and blue light when white is displayed on a colour tube are in the proportion of 30 per cent red lumens, 59 per cent green lumens and 11 per cent blue lumens. Although the eye adapts if the colour temperature illuminating a white subject alters (see Colour temperature, page 64), there is no adaptation by the camera and the three video amplifiers have to be adjusted to ensure they have unity output.

Colour difference signals

To avoid transmitting three separate red, green and blue signals and therefore trebling the bandwidth required for each TV channel, a method was devised to combine (encode) the colour signals with the luminance signal.

The ability of the eye to see fine detail depends for the most part on differences in luminance in the image and only, to a much smaller extent, on colour detail. This allows the luminance (Y) information to be transmitted at high definition and the colour information at a lower definition resulting in another saving on bandwidth. Two colour difference signals are obtained, Er (red) – Ey (luminance) and Eb (blue) – Ey, by electronically subtracting the luminance signal from the output of the red and blue amplifiers. These two colour signals are coded into the luminance signal (Ey) and transmitted as a single, bandwidth-saving signal. Different solutions on how to modulate the colour information has resulted in each country choosing between one of three systems – NTSC, PAL and SECAM. At the receiver, the signal can be decoded to produce separate red, green, blue and luminance signals necessary for a colour picture. A receiver is a television set that derives its signal from an RF (radio frequency) source (e.g. a transmitter). A monitor is a visual display that is fed with a video signal via a coaxial cable (see Monitor termination, page 17).

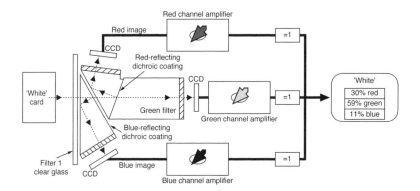

Light into electricity

The amplitude of the three individual colour signals depends on the actual colour in the televised scene. Colours are broadband and the light splitting block divides this 'broad' spectrum into red, green and blue light to produce three optical images on the respective red, green and blue CCDs. The CCD converts the optical image into an electrical charge pattern. A fourth signal, called the luminance signal, is obtained by combining proportions of the red, green and blue signals. It is this signal which allows compatibility with a monochrome display. The amplitude of the signal at any moment is proportional to the brightness of the particular picture element being scanned.

Additive colour

A composite video signal is an encoded combined colour signal using one of the coding standards – NTSC, PAL or SECAM. This can be achieved using the luminance (Y) signal and the colour difference signals of red minus luminance (Er – Ey) and blue minus luminance (Eb – Ey). The signals are derived from the original red, green and blue sources and this is a form of analogue bandwidth compression.

A component video signal is one in which the luminance and the chrominance remain as separate components, i.e. separate Y, R – Y and B – Y signals.

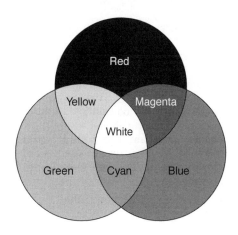

The video signal

Television translates light into an electrical signal and then back into light. In its journey from initial acquisition to the viewer's TV set, the television signal is subjected to adjustments and alterations before it is converted back into a visible image. Like all translations, something is lost along the way and a two-dimensional viewed image can never be an exact visual equivalent of the original. The amount of signal adjustment that occurs in broadcast television is a result of the historical need to ration and allocate transmission bandwidths. These technical restraints set limits to image definition and tonal range. The deliberate subjective creative choices made in creating the programme image also affect the picture viewed by the audience. There are continuing attempts to upgrade the existing various standard TV signals to a higher definition origination and transmission system, but the cost of re-equipping all production and receiving equipment and the lack of agreement on standardization inhibits rapid change.

The technical accuracy of the transmitted image depends on:

■ **Time:** Human vision cannot instantaneously perceive a complex image and intuitively scans a field of view in order to visually understand what is presented. A video camera requires a mechanism to scan a field of view in a precise, repeated line structure.

■ **Detail:** The choice of the number of lines and method of scanning is critical to the definition of the captured image and ultimately is dependent on the method chosen to relay the picture to its intended audience. The shape of the screen, the ratio of picture width to picture height, will determine line structure and resolution.

■ **Movement:** Human perception requires that the repetition rate of each image must exceed approximately 40 pictures per second to avoid flicker and to provide a convincing simulation of smooth movement of any object that changes its position within the frame.

■ **Synchronization:** The displayed image watched by the viewer must have a mechanism to stay in step with the original scanning of the televised image.

■ **Accuracy of the tonal range:** Human perception is able to accommodate a wide range of brightness. The television system is only able to replicate a limited range of tonal gradations.

■ **Colour:** A television electrical signal requires a method of accurately conveying the colour range of the reproduced image. As colour superseded black and white television, the colour system chosen was required to continue to provide compatible pictures for those viewers watching on black and white receivers.

■ **Subjective creative choices:** The final production images can be customized in an almost limitless way to suit the creative requirements of the programme originator. The line structure and synchronization however remain unaltered.

The television scanning principle

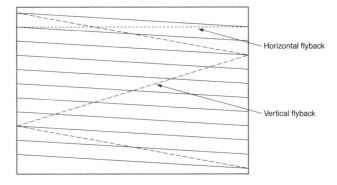

The television picture is made up of a series of lines which are transmitted with synchronizing pulses to ensure that the display monitor scans the same area of the image as the camera. In the PAL 625 line system, each of the 25 frames per second is made up two sets of lines (fields) that interlace and cover different parts of the display. The electrical 'picture' is scanned a line at a time and at the end of each line a new line is started at the left-hand side until the bottom of the picture is reached. In the first field the odd lines are scanned after which the beam returns to scan the even lines. The first field (odd lines) begins with a full line and ends on a half line. The second field (even lines) begins with a half line and ends on a full line.

The television waveform

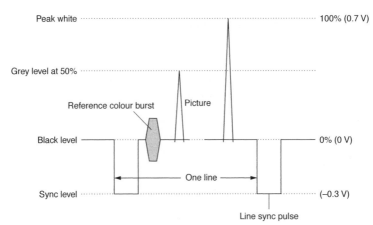

Diagrammatic representation of the signal waveform – not to scale

The waveform of the 1 V television signal divides into two parts at black level. Above black, the signal varies depending on the tones in the picture from black (0 V) to peak white (0.7 V). Below black, the signal (which is never seen) is used for synchronizing the start of each line and frame. A reference colour burst provides the receiver with information to allow colour signal processing.

15

Image quality

Video images are eventually displayed on a television screen. The quality of the screen, how it has been aligned and adjusted, any reflections or ambient light on the surface of the screen, the size of the screen and the distance at which it is viewed will all affect the quality of the image as seen by the viewer. Some compensation can be built into the video signal to mitigate receiver limitations (see Gamma and linear matrix, page 102), but other factors affecting viewing conditions are outside the control of the programme maker.

Unlike film, where the projected image consists of light reflected from a screen, a television tube emits light. The maximum white it can emit depends on its design and how the display has been adjusted. Black is displayed when there is an absence of any signal, but even when the set is switched off, there is never a true black. The glass front surface of the tube, acting like a mirror, will reflect any images or light falling on the screen degrading 'black'. These two aspects of the display, its maximum high intensity white and how much ambient light is reflected from its screen set the contrast range that the display will reproduce independent of its received signal.

Resolution

The size of the display screen and its viewing distance will be one factor in how much detail is discernible in a televised image. Due to the regulation of television transmissions, the design of the system (e.g. number of lines, interlace, etc.) and the permitted bandwidth will affect the detail (sharpness) of the broadcast picture. Bandwidth will determine how much fine detail can be transmitted.

The active number of lines (visible on screen) in a 4:3 PAL picture is 575. However, a subject televised that alternated between black and white, 575 times in the vertical direction would not necessarily coincide with the line structure and therefore this detail would not be resolved. The limit of resolution that can be achieved is deduced by applying the Kell factor which for the above example is typically 0.7. This results in a practical resolution of 400 lines/picture height. The horizontal resolution will be 4/3 of 400 equalling 533. The number of cycles of information/line equals 533/2, resulting in 266.5 taking place in 52 µS (time taken per line). This results in a bandwidth requirement of 266.5/52 µS – approximately 5.2 MHz for 625 4:3 picture transmission.

5.2 MHz bandwidth will be required for each channel broadcast using PAL 625, 4:3 picture origination. Other systems will have different bandwidth requirements such as 1250 HDTV PAL which has twice the resolution and needs 30 MHz. Digital transmission allows some bandwidth reduction using compression (see Compression, page 26).

Slot-mask colour tube

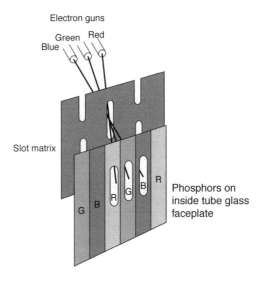

Electron guns

Green Red
Blue

Slot matrix

R G B R
G B

Phosphors on
inside tube glass
faceplate

Colour is created on a TV screen by bombarding three different phosphors (red, green and blue) that glow when energized by an electronic beam. The screen may be one of three designs, shadow mask, aperture grill or slot-mask (illustrated above), depending on how the pattern of phosphor dots are arranged on the inside face of the tube. The slot-matrix vertical slots are arranged so that each beam only strikes its corresponding phosphor line on the screen.

NB: a video monitor refers to a visual display fed with a video signal. A receiver refers to a display fed with a radio frequency signal.

Monitor termination

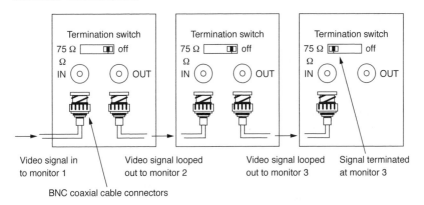

Termination switch
75 Ω   off
Ω
IN   OUT

Termination switch
75 Ω   off
Ω
IN   OUT

Termination switch
75 Ω   off
Ω
IN   OUT

Video signal in
to monitor 1

Video signal looped
out to monitor 2

Video signal looped
out to monitor 3

Signal terminated
at monitor 3

BNC coaxial cable connectors

A video signal fed to a monitor must always be terminated (usual value is 75 Ω) unless it is looped through to another monitor. The last monitor in the chain (monitor 3 above) must be terminated to avoid signal distortion.

Charge-coupled devices

MOS capacitors

A MOS capacitor (see figure opposite) is a sandwich of a metal electrode insulated by a film of silicon dioxide from a layer of P-type silicon. If a positive voltage is applied to the metal electrode, a low energy well is created close to the interface between the silicon dioxide and the silicon. Any free electrons will be attracted to this well and stored. They can then be moved on to an adjacent cell if a deeper depletion region is created there. The ability to store a charge is fundamental to the operation of the charge-coupled device plus a method of transferring the charge.

Charge-coupled device

If a photosensor replaces the top metal electrode, and each picture element (abbreviated to pixel) is grouped to form a large array as the imaging device behind a prism block and lens, we have the basic structure of a CCD camera. Each pixel (between 500 and 800 per picture line) will develop a charge in proportion to the brightness of that part of the image focused onto it. A method is then required to read out the different charges of each of the half a million or so pixels in a scanning order matching the line and frame structure of the originating TV picture. Currently there are three types of sensors in use differing in the position of their storage area and the method of transfer; they are frame transfer, interline transfer and frame interline transfer (see page 20).

- **Frame transfer:** The first method of transfer developed was the frame transfer (FT) structure. The silicon chip containing the imaging area of pixels is split into two parts (see figure opposite). One half is the array of photosensors exposed to the image produced by the lens and a duplicate set of sensors (for charge storage) is masked so that no light (and therefore no build up of charge) can affect it. A charge pattern is created in each picture field which is then rapidly passed vertically to the storage area during vertical blanking. Because the individual pixel charges are passed through other pixels a mechanical shutter is required to cut the light off from the lens during the transfer. An important requirement for all types of CCDs is that the noise produced by each sensor must be equivalent, otherwise patterns of noise may be discernible in the darker areas of the picture.
- **Interline transfer:** To eliminate the need for a mechanical shutter, interline transfer (IT) was developed. With this method, the storage cell was placed adjacent to the pick-up pixel (see figure on page 21), so that during field blanking the charge generated in the photosensor is shifted sideways into the corresponding storage element. The performance of the two types of cell (photosensor and storage) can be optimized for their specific function although there is a reduction in sensitivity because a proportion of the pick-up area forms part of the storage area.

MOS capacitors

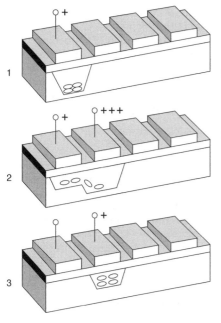

1: After a positive voltage (e.g. 5 V) is applied to the electrode, a low-energy well is created below the oxide/semiconductor surface, attracting free electrons.

2: If 10 V is applied to the adjacent electrode, a deeper low-energy well is created, attracting free electrons which now flow into this deeper bucket.

3: If the voltage on the first electrode is removed and the second electrode voltage is reduced to 5 V, the process can be repeated with the third cell. The charge can be moved along a line of capacitors by a chain of pulses (called a transfer clock) applied to the electrodes.

By replacing the electrode with a light-sensitive substance called a 'photosensor', a charge proportional to the incident light is transferred using the above technique.

Schematic of frame transfer CCD

The imaging area of a frame transfer CCD is exposed to the subject (X) and each photosensor is charged in proportion to the incident light intensity. A mechanical shutter covers the photosensors during vertical blanking and each photosensor transfers its charge to the sensor below until the storage area duplicates the imaging area. The shutter is opened for the next field whilst each sensor in the storage area is horizontally read out in turn. What was a two-dimensional grid of variations in light intensity has been converted into a series of voltage variations.

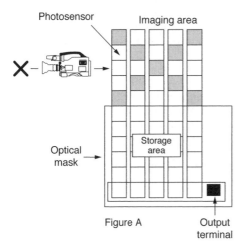
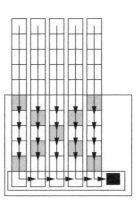

Figure A   Output
                  terminal

Figure B

FIT and HAD CCDs

Vertical smear
One problem with interline transfer is vertical smear. This occurs when a very strong highlight is in the picture and results in a vertical line running through the highlight. It is caused by the light penetrating very deeply into the semiconductor structure and leaking directly into the vertical shift register. Since only longer wavelength light is able to penetrate deeply into the silicon, the vertical smear appears as a red or a pink line.

Frame interline transfer
In an attempt to eliminate the vertical smear the frame interline transfer (FIT) was developed (see figure opposite). This combines the interline method of transferring the charge horizontally to an adjacent storage cell but then moves the charge down vertically at 60 times line rate into a frame store area. The charge is therefore only corrupted for a sixtieth of the time compared to IT CCDs.

Resolution
To reproduce fine detail accurately a large number of pixels are needed. Increasing the number of picture elements in a 2/3-in pick-up device results in smaller pixel size which decreases sensitivity.

Aliasing
Each pixel 'samples' a portion of a continuous image to produce a facsimile of scene brightness. This is similar to analogue-to-digital conversion and is subject to the mathematical rules established by Nyquist which states that if the input signal is to be reproduced faithfully it must be sampled at a frequency which is greater than twice the maximum input frequency. Aliasing, which shows up as a moiré patterning particularly on moving subjects, is caused by a high input frequency causing a low 'beat' frequency. It is suppressed by offsetting the green CCD by half a pixel compared to red and blue. Another technique is to place an optical low pass filter in the light path to reduce the amount of fine detail present in the incoming light.

HAD
The hole accumulated diode (HAD) sensor allows up to 750 pixels per line with an improvement in the photosensing area of the total pick-up (see figure on page 23). Increasing the proportion of the surface of the photosensor that can collect light improves sensitivity without decreasing resolution. The HAD chip also helps to avoid vertical smear. Hyper HAD chips increase the sensitivity of cameras by positioning a tiny condensing lens on each individual pixel. This increases the collecting area of light.

Interline transfer

Photosensor

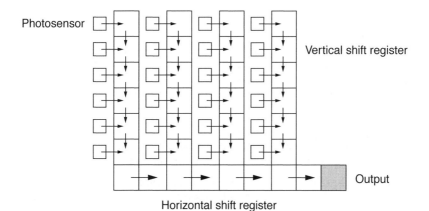

Vertical shift register

Output

Horizontal shift register

Frame interline transfer

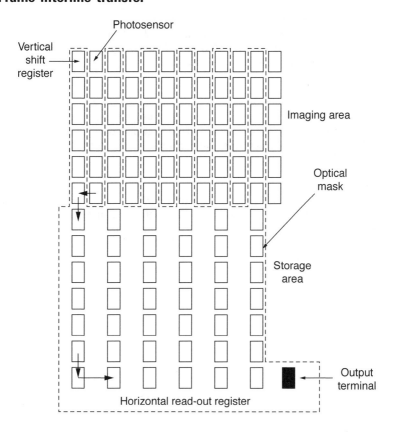

Photosensor

Vertical
shift
register

Imaging area

Optical
mask

Storage
area

Output
terminal

Horizontal read-out register

CCD integration

Switched output integration

A PAL television picture is composed of 625 interlaced lines. In a tube camera, the odd lines are scanned first then the beam returns to the top of the frame to scan the even lines. It requires two of these fields to produce a complete picture (frame) and to synchronize with the mains frequency of 50 Hz, the picture or frame is repeated 25 times a second. CCD frame transfer (FT) devices use the same pixels for both odd and even fields whereas interline transfer (IT) and frame interline transfer (FIT) CCDs use separate pixels with a consequent increase in resolution. There are two methods to read out the stored charge:

- **Field integration:** This reads out every pixel but the signals from adjacent lines are averaged. Although this decreases vertical resolution, motion-blur will be less.

- **Frame integration:** This reads out once every frame (two fields) and therefore will have more motion-blur as the signal is averaged over a longer time span than field integration but may have better vertical resolution on static subjects. Enhanced vertical definition systems offer a higher resolution of frame integration without the same motion blur. It is obtained by blanking off one field with the electronic shutter, reducing camera sensitivity by one stop.

Colorimetry

The transparent polysilicon covering the photosensor of the IT chip progressively filters out the shorter blue wavelength and therefore is less sensitive to the blue end of the spectrum compared to its red response. On HAD sensors there is no polysilicon layer and therefore the spectral response is more uniform.

Flare

Each element in a zoom lens is coated to reduce surface reflections but stray light reaching the prism causes flare, lightening the blacks, and a consequent reduction in contrast of the optical image. Flare is to some extent a linear effect and can be compensated for electronically. Flare can also occur at the surface of CCD devices where light is reflected between layers or scattered by the etched edges of sensor windows.

The Hyper HAD

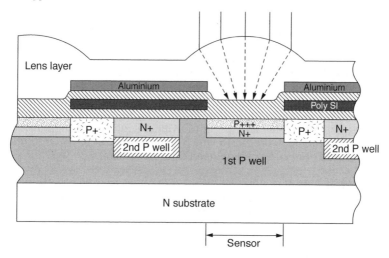

The Hyper HAD has a microlens positioned on each pixel which increases the light-capturing ability of each photosensor area, doubling the camera sensitivity.

Field integration

Field integration (adjacent lines averaged) produces less motion blur than frame integration because the charge is only integrated over one field. Vertical resolution is reduced because two lines are read as one.

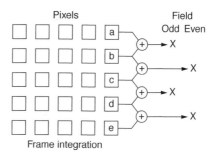

Enhanced vertical definition system

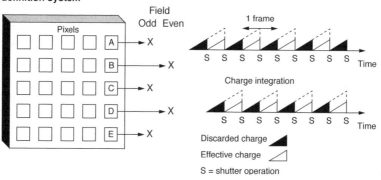

The digital signal

Television broadcasting was originated and developed using an analogue signal – a continuous voltage or frequency varying in time. Over the years, engineering techniques overcame many problems associated with this method but there was a limit to what could be achieved. The analogue signal can suffer degradation during processing through the signal chain, particularly in multi-generation editing where impairment to the signal is cumulative. Digital video is an alternative method of carrying a video signal. By coding the video signal into a digital form, a stream of numbers is produced which change sufficiently often to mimic the analogue continuous signal (see figure opposite).

The digital signal

Whereas an analogue signal is an unbroken voltage variation, a pulse coded modulated (PCM) digital signal is a series of numbers each representing the analogue signal voltage at a specific moment in time. The number of times the analogue signal is measured is called the *sampling rate* or sampling frequency. The value of each measured voltage is converted to a whole number by a process called *quantizing*. These series of whole numbers are recorded or transmitted rather than the waveform itself. The advantage of using whole numbers is they are not prone to drift and the original information in whole numbers is better able to resist unwanted change. The method of quantizing to whole numbers will have an effect on the accuracy of the conversion of the analogue signal to digital. Any sampling rate which is high enough could be used for video, but it is common to make the sampling rate a whole number of the line rate allowing samples to be taken in the same place on every line.

A monochrome digital image would consist of a rectangular array of sampled points of brightness stored as a number. These points are known as picture cells or more usually abbreviated to *pixels*. The closer the pixels are together, the greater the resolution and the more continuous the image will appear. The greater the number of pixels the greater the amount of data that will need to be stored with a corresponding increase in cost. A typical 625/50 frame consists of over a third of a million pixels. A colour image will require three separate values for each pixel representing brightness, hue and saturation for each individual sampled point of the image. These three values can represent red, green and blue elements or colour difference values of luminance, red minus luminance and blue minus luminance. A moving image will require the three values of each pixel to be updated continuously.

Advantages of the digital signal

When a digital recording is copied, the same numbers appear on the copy. It is not a dub, it is a clone. As the copy is indistinguishable from the original there is no generation loss. Digital TV allows an easy interface with computers and becomes a branch of data processing.

Analogue to digital

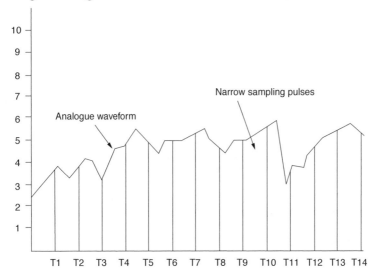

The continuously varying voltage of the TV signal (the analogue signal) is measured (or sampled) at a set number of positions per television line and converted into a stream of numbers (the digital signal) which alters in magnitude in proportion to the original signal.

Storing the signal as binary numbers (ones and zeros) has two advantages. It provides a robust signal that is resistant to noise and distortion and can be restored to its original condition whenever required. Second, it enables computer techniques to be applied to the video signal creating numerous opportunities for picture manipulation and to re-order the digital samples for standards conversion.

Binary counting

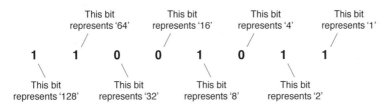

In this 8-bit word called a byte (abbreviated from 'by eight') each bit position in the word determines its decimal equivalent. This binary number's decimal equivalent (reading from left to right) is 128 + 64 + 0 + 0 + 8 + 0 + 2 + 1 = 203.

A 4-bit word has 16 combinations
An 8-bit word has 256 combinations
A 10-bit word has 1024 combinations
A kilobyte (1 Kbyte) of memory contains 1024 bytes
A megabyte (1 Mbyte) contains 1024 kilobytes
A gigabyte contains 1024 megabytes

Why compression is needed

Digital television has many advantages compared to the older analogue system. Equipment is generally cheaper and error correction can compensate for signal degradation introduced along the signal path. As digital television deals only with ones and zeros, circuits do not require the sophistication needed to maintain the quality of the continuously varying voltage of the analogue signal. But working on the principle that there are never any free lunches, digital signal routing and storage is required to handle very large packets of data and this does pose certain problems. For 625 line, 4:3 PAL TV, the active picture is: 720 pixels (Y) + 360 pixels (Cr) + 360 pixels (Cb) = 1440 pixels per line. 576 active lines per picture means 1440 pixels/line × 576 = 829,440 pixels per picture. Sampling at 8 bits, the picture takes 829,440 bytes, or 830 Kbytes, of storage. One second of pictures would require 830 × 25 = 20,750 Kbytes, or 21 Mbytes. Both 625 and 525 line systems require approximately the same amount of storage for a given time. One minute requires 1.26 Gbytes and 1 hour requires 76 Gbytes. Standard video tape capacity can record only a few minutes of material at this density.

Compression

To reduce the large amounts of data digital television generates, a technique was introduced that looked at each video frame and only passed on the difference between successive frames. With this method of coding it is possible to discard a large percentage of information yet still deliver acceptable TV pictures. The original data rate can be compressed to fit the recording storage capability or to reduce the bandwidth needed for transmission. By eliminating selected data, the signal can be passed through a channel that has a lower bit rate. The ratio between the source and the channel bit rates is called the compression factor. At the receiving end of the channel an expander or decoder will attempt to restore the compressed signal to near its original range of values. A compressor is designed to recognize and pass on the useful part of the input signal known as the *entropy*. The remaining part of the input signal is called the *redundancy*. It is redundant because the filtered-out information can be predicted from what has already been received by the decoder. If the decoder cannot reconstruct the withheld data, then the signal is incomplete and the compression has degraded the original signal. This may or may not be acceptable when viewing the received image. Portions of an image may contain elements that are unchanging from frame to frame. Considerable saving in the amount of data transmitted can be achieved if, on a shot change, all of the image is transmitted and then with each successive frame only that which alters from frame to frame is transmitted. The image can then be reconstructed by the decoder by adding the changing elements of the image to the static or unvarying parts of the image. The degree of compression cannot be so severe that information is lost.

Motion compensation

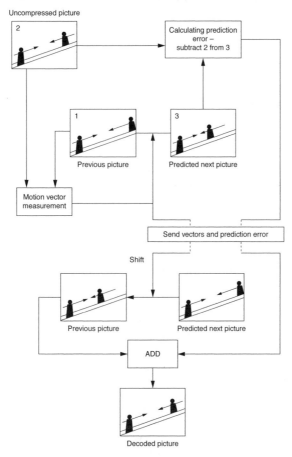

A picture of a passenger travelling on an up escalator is shot with the camera travelling at the same speed as the passenger (2). The only movement in the frame is another passenger travelling on the down escalator. Motion compensation compression attempts to make movement information 'redundant' by measuring successive areas of pictures which contain movement and producing motion vectors. These are applied to the object and its predicted new position (3) reconstructed. Any errors are eliminated by comparing the reconstructed movement with the actual movement of the original image. The coder sends the motion vectors and the discrepancies along the channel to the decoder which shifts the previous picture by the vectors and adds the discrepancies to reproduce the next picture. This allows a saving in the amount of data that needs to be transmitted along a channel, even with movement.

Providing only the difference between one picture and the next means that at any instant in time, an image can only be reconstructed by reference to a previous 'complete' picture. Editing such compressed pictures can only occur on a complete frame. If there is significant movement in the frame there will be very little redundancy and therefore very little compression possible.

Compression standards

Gains

The main benefits of compressing digital material include:

- a smaller quantity of storage is required for a given quantity of source material;
- digital compression reduces the required bandwidth in terrestrial, satellite and cable transmission and allows cheaper use of data transport (e.g. SNG links), interactive services, etc.

4:2:2

A common sampling rate for 625/50 and 525/60 video is chosen to be locked to the horizontal sync pulses. For the luminance signal this is often 13.5 MHz. Only the active lines (576 lines in the 625 system) are transmitted or recorded. Each line consists of 720 pixels. The 49 field blanking lines are ignored and recreated when required.

In many digital formats the colour difference signals have one half the luminance bandwidth and are sampled at half the luminance sample rate of 13.5 MHz (i.e. 6.75 MHz). The lowest practicable sampling rate is 3.375 MHz – a quarter of the luminance rate and identified as 1. Using this code convention:

1 = 3.375 MHz sample rate (3,375,000 samples per second)
2 = 6.75 MHz sample rate (6,750,000 samples per second)
4 = 13.5 MHz sample rate (13,500,000 samples per second)

Most component production equipment uses 4:2:2 sampling which indicates that 13.5 MHz (4) is the sample rate for luminance, 6.75 MHz (2) is the sample rate for red minus luminance and 6.75 MHz (2) is the sample rate for blue minus luminance. Higher compression can be achieved (e.g. 4:1:1 or 4:2:0 sampling). In general, compression can be expected to impose some form of loss or degradation on the picture, its degree depending on the algorithm used as well as the compression ratio (ratio of the data in the compressed signal to the original version) and the contents of the picture itself. Applying greater and greater degrees of compression (i.e. eliminating more of the original) results in artifacts such as fast-moving subjects 'pixilating' or breaking up into moving blocks.

Moving Picture Experts Group (MPEG)

MPEG compiled a set of standards describing a range of bitstreams which decoders must be able to handle. MPEG 1 was an earlier specification that is not adequate for broadcast TV. MPEG 2 recommendations for data compression of moving pictures can be abbreviated to a table containing five profiles ranging from Simple (minimum complexity) to High. Each profile can operate at four resolution levels ranging from 352 × 288 pixel image up to 1920 × 1152 pixels. MPEG 2 is not a decoder technique or a method of transmitting bitstreams but a series of benchmarks specifying different degrees of compression.

Compression and video editing

MPEG 2 interframe compression achieves data reduction by grouping a number of pictures together identified as a GOP (group of pictures). When the MPEG compression process begins, an initial I (intraframe or intrapicture) is coded. This frame is complete and uncompressed and can be displayed without degradation. In the group of pictures associated with this I frame are P (predicted) frames which are based on the I frame and cannot exist without the I frame. Interleaved between the I frame and the P frames are B (Bi-directional) frames which are assembled from interpolated data from the closest I and P frames. A new I frame is usually created in response to a change of pixels in the incoming frames although this can occur without change every approximately half second. Compression is achieved because only the I frames require data to be forwarded.

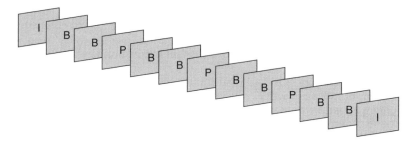

Because only I frames carry complete picture information, an edit point that occurs between a P and a B frame will start with a frame that cannot reconstruct itself as its reference I frame is missing. It is desirable for efficient compression to have the longest practical group of pictures before a new I frame is included whereas flexibility in deciding which frame to cut on requires the smallest practical GOP and still achieves some degree of compression. Dynamic random access memory (DRAM) chip sets perform I, P and B frame searches to identify an I frame edit.

Concatenation

Along the signal path from acquisition, up and down links, format change, editing and then transmission a video signal can be coded and decoded several times. There are many different types of data compression. Degradation of the digital signal can occur if it is repeatedly coded and decoded whilst passing through two or three different manufacturer's processors.

Metadata

Metadata is the data that goes along with video and audio as it is networked digitally. Each clip can carry with it detail of where and when it was shot, what format it was in, how it has been processed or compressed, who has the rights to it, when and where it has been transmitted, and any other information that might be needed. This information can be downloaded into an archive database to allow indexing and searches.

The digital camera

A very basic specification for a digital camera suitable for general programme production could include:

- the ability to interchange the lens (designed for manual focusing/zoom as well as the option of servo control);
- a camera that allows manual adjustment of a number of facilities (e.g. white balance, timecode, audio level, shutter speed) as well as the option of auto control;
- a digital recording format with 4:2:2 video sampling plus audio and timecode tracks.

Essentially all three, lens, camera and recorder components, need to be of broadcast quality (see below), but in addition to their engineering specification, they must have the operational facilities required to cover a range of production techniques from initial acquisition to edited master.

Broadcast quality
What is 'broadcast quality' will ultimately depend on the broadcaster. Digital acquisition and recording allows variation in sampling (see page 28) and a range of compression ratios. Year on year, technological innovation provides new recording formats. Some, such as the mini DV format, were initially designed for the consumer market but are often used in programme making. A minimum quality benchmark is generally agreed to be 4:2:2 sampling, basically because it allows more flexibility in post-production compositing. But the variety of compression systems introduced into the programme chain also has a significant effect on the final picture quality.

It has always been notoriously difficult to achieve standardization of operational features between different makes of broadcast camera. A simple mechanical device such as the tripod adaptor plate needed to mount the camera/recorder on a pan and tilt head appears to exist in as many versions as there are camera manufacturers. From a cameraman's point of view, how the production peripherals of a new camera design (batteries, lens, etc.) dovetail with existing equipment is an important practical (and economic) consideration. Broadcast quality can also mean compatible with standard production techniques and facilities.

One-piece camera/recorders have always been available but two-piece camera/recorders allow the user a choice of which recording format to attach to the camera. In the interests of speed and convenience, many organizations need to acquire and edit all production material on the same format coupled with the need for universal technical back-up support for crews working a long way from base. There is continuous market demand for cheaper, broadcast-quality, non-linear editing, especially in news and magazine programme production. This is combined with the development of multi-skilling in acquisition and editing and the pressure to find solutions to edit video material at journalist work stations.

Basic digital acquisition

Digital cameras are either combined camera/recorder or the camera section can be interchanged to work with most formats. For standard broadcast camerawork a camera should be capable of manual exposure, focus, white balance and manual control of audio with standard XLR audio inputs. Timecode is essential for logging and editing. Choosing a format depends on programme type and where the production will be seen.

Because of the expansion of recording formats and the many hundreds of camera models available, it is not possible to provide a specific guide to the many variations of operational controls to be found. In general, whatever make of camera or individual model, most broadcast cameras have similar facilities. There is a core of camera controls that are standard on nearly every broadcast quality camera (see pages 56–109). What may change from camera to camera is the positioning of individual operational controls.

Camera	Lens/lenses + lens cleaning
Camera accessories	Tape, matte box and filters; good pan/tilt head and tripod; batteries and portable chargers; mains adaptor; repeat timecode reader.
Audio	If working in stereo, a sub-mixer and sufficient selection of microphones, radio mics, mic supports, etc. for the subject.
Lighting	At least a 'flight kit' – 2/3 lightweight lamps, filter and diffuser material, reflector board. The more complex the shoot, the more lighting equipment may be needed.
Transport	For everything you need to take to a location. Easy to underestimate how much this will be.

General production overview

During acquisition

- Log all shots.
- Transfer the material from camera to VHS to review.
- Have the digital material transferred at a post-production house to VHS with burnt in timecode for off-line editing.

Off-line editing

Check that the editing software you intend to use to produce an EDL (edit decision list; the off-line edit decisions are recorded on a floppy disk giving the tape source of the shot and its in and out timecode or duration. In order to work across a range of equipment there are some widely adopted standards such as CMX, Sony, SMPTE, and Avid) is compatible with the post-production facility where the material will be conformed.

In drama there is always the need for post-production audio. Make certain that the right quality (and sound quality continuity) has been recorded on location. Sound dubbing is needed to add effects, music and additional looped dialogue if original audio is of poor quality.

Many high-end digital cameras have scene files. These are microchips that are inserted into the camera to configure the image to provide a particular 'look'. Some hire companies have a range of these.

Format and budget

In the mid-1990s, the demarcation between broadcast-quality and consumer cameras was eroded. Some camera formats which had been initially marketed for domestic use were pressed into service for documentary and news production. Not all of these new range of cameras provided for the standard requirements of broadcast camerawork. They often required modification before being suitable for programme production.

Digital technology and de-regulation produced a proliferation of broadcast channels and an escalation in the competition for viewers. The expansion of services created a need to find ways of cutting costs and reducing programme budgets. This also followed the production fashion for less intrusive shooting techniques and the use of small cameras for the coverage of documentary and news. All these changes resulted in the development of digital video recording formats and cameras which were small, cheap (relative to previous broadcast 'quality' cameras) and easy to operate.

Button pressing
In the rush to market the new recording formats, the ability to produce a technically acceptable image from a video camera often became confused with the craft of camerawork. Marketing hype suggested that anyone could be a 'cameraman' once they understood the automatic features of the new compact video camera. But broadcast camerawork is not simply producing technically competent pictures. Communication with images requires the same understanding of visual conventions and visual potentials as the understanding of language, structure and vocabulary is needed when communicating with words. The ability to assess a well-framed picture and the knowledge of the techniques available to achieve this follows on from the ability to manipulate the camera controls.

Economic choice
The development of journalist computer workstations and the trend towards a 'tapeless' newsroom highlighted the problems of back libraries and archive material on a different format to the current operation. There was also the cost to an organization in choosing to have a different format for its news operation than it had for its normal programme acquisition. The economic gain in time saved in acquisition in one format could be outweighed by the cost/time of dubbing across other formats for editing or transmission plus the cost of duplicating a range of post-production equipment able to handle the different formats. But ranged against these considerations were the savings in camera and tape costs and the potential for lap-top editing systems on location when using the smaller digital recording formats. Some recording formats were conceived chiefly as an acquisition option and were not (in the first instance) intended for general use in broadcasting.

Insert track information

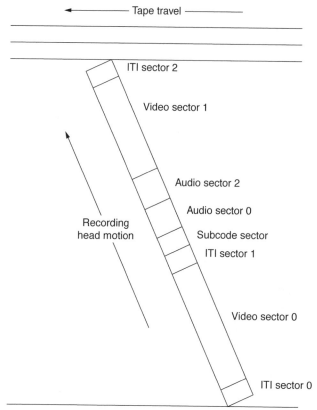

One of 12 tracks that make up one frame of D-9 (625/50 system).

There many different sectors found on each digital recording track (see figure above). There are sectors for video, audio (sometimes as many as 8) and subcode (which contains the digitized timecode). However, the first sector on the tape is usually the ITI sector. The ITI area (or sector) contains useful data needed by the digital recording system, to order the digital blocks of video and audio in their correct position. The ITI track contains an identifier which states if the recording is an SP (Standard Play) or LP (Long Play) type recording. For the moment all recordings made by standard DV format decks are signified as SP, with LP being a future option (but not on professional formats such as DVCPro, DVCam or D-9). When played back by the replay heads, the ITI sector has a number of different sections in it. After a brief pre-amble section, the SSA (Start Sync block Area) section starts. This is a fixed number of bits or 'blocks' of data. These are recognizable by their unique but repetitive coding sequence of 0s and 1s. Once recognized these allow the VTR to start a counter which then counts each 'block' of data as it is read off the tape during replay. Using this method the VTR can predict where each sector (video, audio or subcode) of the track is physically on the tape, so that accurate insert editing can take place without danger of accidentally overwriting the wrong sector on the tape (see also page 35).

Digital recording

Analogue or digital video/audio tape recording requires a moving magnetic tape in contact with a rotating recording/replay head. A rotating recording head allows a higher head-to-tape speed which effectively increases the bandwidth that can be recorded. There are several inherent limitations to perfect reproduction of sound and picture on replay. These include:

- On recording, tape and head rotation may not be continuously stable and some minute variations in speed may occur. This will affect the accuracy of the recording on replay and adjustment of the replay machine is via a time base corrector which ensures constant replay speed.

- Although digital signal processing allows a smaller signal-to-noise ratio when recording, it also requires a much higher bandwidth. Some degree of data compression is required.

- The correct head-to-tape contact is not always maintained due to tape imperfections or a build-up of tape coating or inconsistent tape tension.

Digital recording provides for time compression of the video signal into blocks on recording and an equal and opposite process on replay. This allows track space to be made available for audio. The video and audio signal are recorded in packets of data which are shuffled to assist in error correction. The data is broken up into separate coded blocks and recorded out of sequence to limit the length of missing or corrupted data. On replay, the blocks are decoded and arranged in their correct sequence. The tape is protected in a cassette from dust/dirt contamination to reduce tape/head errors and to allow for easier loading and lacing into a record/replay machine.

Error correction and concealment
Magnetic tape recording suffers from noise and dropouts. A digital signal is composed of binary data and a bit is either correct or wrong. It is a simple matter to correct if an error can be detected. A random error of a single bit on replay can be corrected by either replacing the missing sample with a copy of the preceding sample (although this is only useful for a very few consecutive samples), or replacing it with an average of the preceding and succeeding data.

Dropouts can cause a large number of bits to be missing. Burst error is the loss of a number of consecutive samples when recorded. It is possible to minimize this by arranging the data in a non-sequential order by a controlled code that can be reassembled in its correct temporal order when decoding. This effectively separates the missing data, ensuring that consecutive values are less likely to be lost. Additional correction support is to record duplicate additional data which is redundant if there are no errors but can be used to compare or replace any missing or incorrect data. Error concealment is a process where the value of a missing sample is estimated from those nearby.

Insert track information (continued from page 33)

Because all of the VTR systems are mechanical devices with the usual mechanical accuracies, each sector on the tape has a 'pre-amble' and 'post-amble' section before and after the sector data, which act as a 'landing and take off zone' during insert editing by the flying erase and/or record heads. All digital VTRs use a 'segmented' recording technique, where there is no longer one track per frame, but as many as 24 tracks per frame (see figure on page 33; D-9 uses 12 in 625 line mode). This gives an additional burden to the tape tracking system as it has to find the correct start track for every frame (track 1), so that this can be read out in time to sit on top of the regenerated syncs on the output. Having located and centred the heads up on a track, there is no guarantee that this is the right track to start with. To help with this problem, the ITI area also contains the track number, which the tracking system can then use in its calculations as to how far the tape-to-head phase must be moved to find the right track (usually by Capstan speed adjustment or TSO – tape speed override).

This system of track identification is also important where only certain tracks within the 12-track frame must be overwritten during insert editing. For instance, in 4-channel recording mode, formats like standard DV and DVCam record audio channel sectors for channels 3 and 4 (as a multiplex) into tracks 7 to 12 of the recorded frame. During insert editing, it becomes necessary therefore to ensure that only those audio sectors on tracks 7 to 12 are re-recorded over, or channels 1 and 2 may be wiped out as well. Note that in D-9, 4-channel recordings are different in that every channel is kept in a separate sector and therefore fully independently editable (without the need for stereo pair lay-offs).

Finally, some digital VTRs use a form of digital tracking which is added to the ITI sector data to ensure that the replay heads stay on track during their sweep across the tape. This is done by using a technique known as 24/25 coding which adds in an extra 0 or 1 after every 3 bytes (24 bits) of data before it is layed down on the tape. By carefully controlling the numbers of 0s and 1s added, the DC content of the replay signal can be modified at relatively low frequencies to produce a sine wave or a pilot tone. As these VTRs use slant azimuth recording techniques, different pilot tone frequencies can be recorded on different tracks. The level of these pilot tones relative to each other can then be assessed on replay, indicating how far off-track the replay head is, with corrections to capstan phase to bring the head back on track. The system works only if there are no head clogs. D-9 does use 24/25 modulation, but it does not use this method of tracking as there is a control track added to the tape for more accurate, reliable and faster tracking control. This is combined with a special digital RF sampling system which ensures that the D-9 always stays on track, even in the event of a severe head clog. The ITI area for digital VTRS is very important although not all of them are called ITI.

DV format

In the early 1990s, a consortium of camera manufacturers collaborated on the development of a new, small, digital tape format. The intention was to reach agreement on a single international format. This was achieved with a consumer format which had a compression standard, a mechanism and tape format, a chip set and a standard family of cassettes. Originally intended for the domestic camcorder market, the first generation of DV cameras did not meet the basic ENG requirements of operational features and ruggedness. Later models, intended for the broadcast market, were of much more robust construction, provided XLR audio inputs and operational controls followed the conventional positioning of ENG camera/recorders. They are also equipped with an internal memory system and will not lose timecode settings when the battery is changed. The picture quality is good enough for broadcasters to use the format in productions that required small, inexpensive lightweight kit.

Broadcast operational weaknesses
There are a number of inherent weaknesses if the standard consumer format cameras are used for broadcast production. Apart from the lower specification (see opposite) the cameras are much lighter and extended hand-held work invariably means unsteady camerawork as arms get tired. To overcome unsteady pictures, 'anti-wobble' devices or picture stabilizers are fitted, some of which affect picture quality. Most of the cameras have colour viewfinders and sometimes the viewfinder menu allows the colour option to be deselected to aid focusing. There is also the debatable value of an auto-focusing facility. Exposure can be set by auto-exposure or manually although some camera models have no zebra facility. The biggest weakness for broadcast camerawork applications is the sound provision. Apart from the lack of manual adjustment of sound level on some cameras, there is often only provision for a single audio input usually using a mini-jack microphone socket when the conventional broadcast audio input is via XLR sockets.

DV can be edited by transferring straight onto disk for non-linear editing. The initial transfer to another format adds to the editing time but this is often preferred by picture editors because the DV format records sound on the FM tracks combined with the pictures. There is no longitudinal sound track and therefore editors cannot hear the digital sound as they shuttle through the tape. Often there is no timecode regeneration facility on consumer DV and placing a cassette into the camera resets the timecode to zero. This could possibly result in several shots on the same tape having the same timecode. This can be avoided by either recording 'black and burst' (continuous timecode and black tape) on tapes prior to use or prior to editing, replacing the original timecode with a continuous edit code for the edit machine. Most DV cameras are designed for occasional domestic use by one careful owner and lack the rugged design necessary for hard ENG usage on location. To overcome some of these production limitations, a 'professional' version of the DV format was developed.

DVCPro and DV (consumer) tape formats

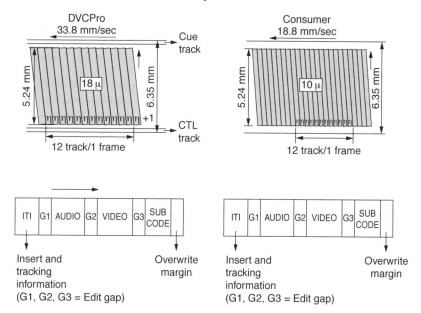

DVCPro
33.8 mm/sec

5.24 mm   18 μ   6.35 mm   +1

Cue track

CTL track

12 track/1 frame

Consumer
18.8 mm/sec

5.24 mm   10 μ   6.35 mm

12 track/1 frame

| ITI | G1 | AUDIO | G2 | VIDEO | G3 | SUB CODE |

Insert and tracking information
(G1, G2, G3 = Edit gap)

Overwrite margin

| ITI | G1 | AUDIO | G2 | VIDEO | G3 | SUB CODE |

Insert and tracking information
(G1, G2, G3 = Edit gap)

Overwrite margin

Outline specification of DV and DVCPro

	DV	DVCPro
Video coding	Component digital 13.5 MHz, 8 bit	Component digital 13.5 MHz, 8 bit
Compression	5:1 intraframe DCT-based standard	5:1 intraframe DCT-based standard
Track layout	12 tracks/frame 10 microns track pitch	12 tracks/frame 18 microns track pitch
Tape speed	18.8 mm/s	33.8 mm/s
Tape	6.35 mm Metal evaporated	6.35 mm Metal particle
Max recording time for cassette	270 minutes	123 minutes
Video data rate	24.948 Mbits/s	24.948 Mbits/s
Audio channels	48 kHz, 16 bits, 2 channel	48 kHz, 16 bits, 2 channel 1 analogue cue channel
Recorded data rate	41.85 Mbits/s	41.85 Mbits/s (also 50 Mbps)

DVCPro format

DVCPro and DVCam are upgrades of the DV format originally designed for news acquisition. The two formats have improved recording specifications and a number of broadcast operational facilities not found on consumer DV cameras.

The camera/recorders are smaller, lighter, cheaper, with less power consumption than previous ENG formats, have smaller cassettes and longer recording times. The lightweight cameras allow easier handling in ENG work and have the ability to provide colour playback. With low power consumption, a two-machine editor can provide rapid, portable editing on location and stories can be put to air more quickly.

DVCPro format

A major difference between DVCam and DV is the increase in track pitch from 10 microns to 18 microns which is wider for frame accurate editing on the 6.35 mm/quarter-inch metal particle tape. The first generation of cameras provided for 5:1 DCT compression with 25 Mbps video data rate, 4:1:1 resolution. The maximum tape length allowed 63 minutes of recording on location increased to 123 minutes on studio machines. DVCPro cameras can be obtained with 1/3-, 1/2- and 2/3-inch CCDs and with switchable 4:3/16:9 aspect ratio.

There are two uncompressed audio channels and two longitudinal audio tracks to give audio access when editing as the digital audio is of limited use in shuttle. This linear audio cue channel is also available as a third, lower quality, audio channel.

4:1:1 systems can exhibit errors on chroma edges when applying special effects (e.g. keying, digital effects) or when recording computer generated graphics but there are DVCPro format camera/recorders with 4:2:2 sampling, 3.3:1 DCT compression, a 50 Mbps video data rate using a larger 123 minute (max) cassette recording at twice the tape speed of the 4:1:1 cameras and with interchangeable lenses.

The DV format has auto-tracking mechanisms that eliminate the need for a control track whereas the DVCPro with a control track provides for a faster lock-up and a shorter pre-roll when editing. DVCPro incorporates both VITC and LTC (see page 92) in the helical scan. This enables the tape size to be kept small and both timecodes to be read at any tape speed. The higher DVCPro specification cameras have 10-bit A/D conversion, 16-bit processing, scene file memory with memory card.

One-frame only (compressed entirely within a single frame) means that the video stream is easily editable, robust and impervious to error propagation. The compression scheme provides a digital structure designed for the special requirements of VTR but it is also suitable for disk-based systems. This allows the interchange of audio and video files between equipment from different manufacturers.

DVCam

DV-based systems use compression in the most cost-effective way to increase tape usage. DVCam has a 4:1:1 compression, 25 Mbps data rate recorded on metal evaporated tape and 4 channels of uncompressed audio to achieve a 40-minute recording on DVCam camera mini-cassette or 184 minutes on a standard cassette. A single DV compression system is used throughout the production process. Non-linear editing is facilitated by high speed transfer at four times the normal speed to a disk recorder.

ClipLink

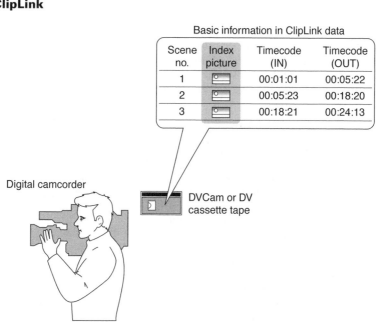

Basic information in ClipLink data

Scene no.	Index picture	Timecode (IN)	Timecode (OUT)
1		00:01:01	00:05:22
2		00:05:23	00:18:20
3		00:18:21	00:24:13

Digital camcorder

DVCam or DV cassette tape

Digital-S format

In the transition from analogue to digital acquisition many camera/recorder manufacturers, when introducing new digital formats, have attempted to provide backward compatibility with existing equipment. In many parts of the world, S-VHS has been used not only for ENG purposes but also for a broad range of local broadcasting productions. Digital-S (D-9 format) uses the same size half-inch tape and cassette as S-VHS and records on metal particle tape. Certain Digital-S studio VTRs can replay standard analogue S-VHS tapes allowing continuing access to previous S-VHS tape libraries. Digital-S uses 4:2:2 processing with a video data rate of 50 Mega bits per second with a 3.3:1 compression. The half-inch width tape allows two linear audio cue tracks for audio access in edit shuttle and four digital audio (16 bit, 48 kHz) tracks and two lines for uncompressed video for closed captioning. Up to 104 minutes of material can be recorded.

Digital processing has allowed opportunities to customize more operational controls compared to analogue camerawork. These include:

- **Iris weighting zones:** Sections of the image can be selected to have more or less effect in calculating auto-exposure.
- **Detail enhancement:** This can be auto adjusted depending on lens angle. A wide-angle shot will have increased detail enhancement.
- **Extended auto-exposure:** Exposure is set automatically by adjustment of iris, gain, shutter and ND filter.
- **Smooth transitions:** Any large adjustment in auto-exposure/auto white balance values can be smoothly carried out avoiding any obvious 'jump' in exposure or colour balance.
- **Black stretch/black compress:** This facility operates in a similar way to knee and highlight compression. The transfer characteristic is altered to allow more/less detail to be seen in the darker tones without affecting highlight exposure.
- **Focusing aid:** It is easier to check focus when operating on a very narrow depth of field (see page 48). When this focusing aid facility is selected, the lens is set at its widest aperture for a few moments and automatically exposed to allow a check on focus.
- **Variable shutter speed:** Shutter speed can be adjusted to the precise rate required (e.g. to avoid flicker when shooting a computer display).
- **Variable detail correction:** This facility allows adjustment of contour correction to user requirement.
- **Timecode:** Digital timecode is written as data and can be read in still mode as well as fast forward/rewind, unlike analogue recording which required two types of timecode (LTC and VITC) to achieve this.

Depending on recording format and camera manufacture, digital processing also allows a reduction of electronic enhancement on selected skin tones (see page 87). a programmed setting of the linear matrix to allow automatic compensation (e.g. when shooting under fluorescent light), and the ability to store camera settings on scene files.

Digital-S (D-9) tape track format

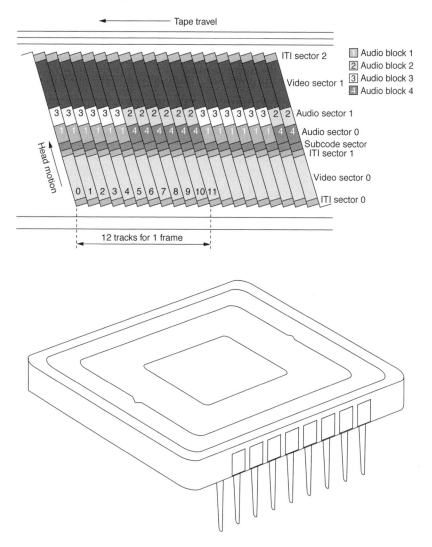

Digital-S interline transfer CCD.

Disk recording

The Camcutter format records direct to disk in the camera/recorder. This allows certain edit functions to be performed in the camera. Whereas the previous digital formats discussed require downloading from tape to disk, the Camcutter's FieldPak (a disk drive in the camera) can be removed and inserted into the desktop FieldPak adaptor and non-linear edited. Each FieldPak can be re-used many thousands of times. The disk recording unit is available in two configurations: as an add-on to a suitable existing Ikegami camera or as an integrated single-piece camera/ recorder unit.

Disk recording allows the following additional production facilities in camera:

- **RetroLoop:** This facility constantly records in a pre-defined loop of time selectable from 15 to 60 seconds. When the record button is pressed, video/audio stored in the RetroLoop is kept as part of the new clip. This stored 15–60 seconds of material is added to the new shot.
- **Intelligent recording:** This facility allows immediate recording without cueing-up blank tracks even during playback. The new data is written onto free tracks avoiding over-recording previous material. There is automatic clip numbering on every separate shot/recording.
- **Time lapse recording:** This function enables intermittent recording at pre-determined intervals for a pre-determined period of time. Disk cameras can be pre-programmed to record one frame at pre-determined intervals.
- **Lip-synching:** Audio can be recorded while video is played back. While video is played, a pre-scripted narration can be recorded.
- **Location control:** Access to any desired point on the disk can be selected by use of camera report or timecode without the need to shuttle. Simple editing can be done with the camera/recorder.
- **Erasing unwanted video:** In camera, previous recordings may be reviewed and unnecessary clips deleted. This function enables only necessary scenes to be left on the disk. About 24–40 minutes (4 Gb) of recording time is normally attainable with a single FieldPak with 6 Gb and 8 Gb units available.

Development with this format has reduced the power consumption and some in-camera editing faculties, although these can still be enabled via a laptop computer.

Random access disk recording: control panel on camera

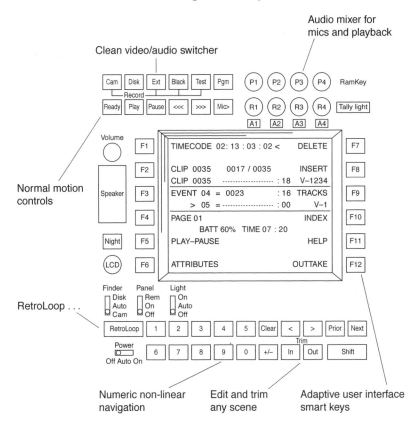

Audio mixer for
mics and playback

Clean video/audio switcher

| Cam | Disk | Ext | Black | Test | Pgm |
| Record |
| Ready | Play | Pause | <<< | >>> | Mic> |

(P1) (P2) (P3) (P4) RamKey

(R1) (R2) (R3) (R4) Tally light

[A1] [A2] [A3] [A4]

Normal motion
controls

Volume

Speaker

Night

LCD

F1	TIMECODE 02: 13 : 03 : 02 < DELETE	F7
F2	CLIP 0035 0017 / 0035 INSERT	F8
	CLIP 0035 ---------------- : 18 V-1234	
F3	EVENT 04 = 0023 : 16 TRACKS	F9
	> 05 = ------------------ : 00 V-1	
F4	PAGE 01 INDEX	F10
	BATT 60% TIME 07 : 20	
F5	PLAY–PAUSE HELP	F11
F6	ATTRIBUTES OUTTAKE	F12

RetroLoop . . .

Finder   Panel   Light
⬜ Disk   ⬜ Rem   ⬜ On
⬛ Auto   ⬛ On   ⬛ Auto
⬛ Cam   ⬛ Off   ⬛ Off

| RetroLoop | 1 | 2 | 3 | 4 | 5 | Clear | < | > | Prior | Next |

Power
Off Auto On

Trim

| 6 | 7 | 8 | 9 | 0 | +/– | In | Out | Shift |

Numeric non-linear
navigation

Edit and trim
any scene

Adaptive user interface
smart keys

43

The zoom lens

The lens as a creative tool

A zoom lens fitted to broadcast camcorders is a complex, sophisticated piece of optical design. Its performance may be described in brochures in impenetrable techno-speak that many, at first glance, may feel has little or nothing to do with the 'real' business of making programmes. To take this view is a mistake, as above all else, the lens characteristics are the most important visual influence on the appearance and impact of an image.

The following pages describe focal length, lens angle, zoom ratio, aperture, depth of field. Altering any one of these zoom settings will have a significant influence on the perspective, the depiction of space and composition when setting up a shot. It is a fallacy to believe that the camera will truthfully record whatever is in shot whenever you put your eye to the viewfinder and press to record. If you are unaware of how the choice of focal length, etc., will affect the chosen image then this important creative decision will be left to chance and accident.

Prime lens or zoom?

Video cameras before the introduction of colour television were usually fitted with four prime lenses (a lens with a fixed focal length), individually mounted on a turret on the front of the camera. A specific focal length lens was chosen for a shot by rotating the turret until the appropriate lens was in front of the pick-up tube. It is still common film practice to select a prime lens to match the needs of the shot. Colour video cameras for technical reasons were almost universally fitted with a zoom lens. A zoom lens allows faster working methods and the option of zooming on shot to capture close-ups without moving the camera. Because of the ease and speed of changing the lens angle of a zoom it is easy to forget exactly what focal length is being used and, as we will discuss later, possibly the space or perspective of the shot will be compromised.

Image size

Because of the different CCD sizes (2/3 inch, 1/2 inch, etc.), the variation in flange-back distance (see page 49), the mechanical connection between lens and camera, and the variation in cable connections with the camera, it is often impossible to interchange lenses between different makes or models of cameras. The image formed by the lens on the face of the CCDs is called the image size of the lens. This must match the size of the camera sensor. Lenses designed for different sized formats (pick-up sensor dimension) may not be interchangeable. The image size produced by the lens may be much smaller than the pick-up sensor (see Image circle and image size opposite) and probably the back focus (flange back) will not have sufficient adjustment. A common lens on a broadcast video camera is a 14 × 8.5 f 1.7 zoom with a minimum object distance of 0.8 m or below. The following pages will identify the implication of this specification and its affects on the practical craft of camerawork.

Image circle and image size

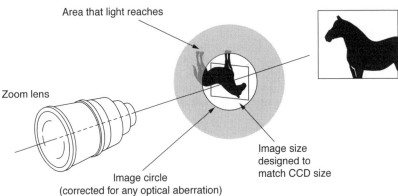

Area that light reaches

Zoom lens

Image circle
(corrected for any optical aberration)

Image size
designed to
match CCD size

Image sizes for 4:3 aspect ratio TV and film (not to scale)

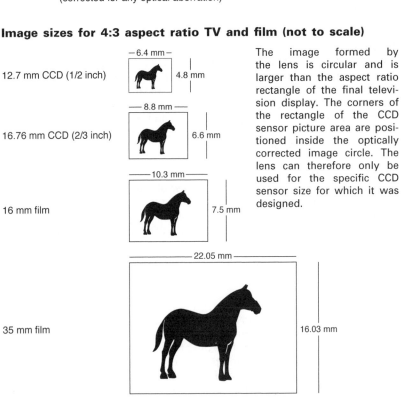

12.7 mm CCD (1/2 inch)

— 6.4 mm —
4.8 mm

16.76 mm CCD (2/3 inch)

— 8.8 mm —
6.6 mm

16 mm film

— 10.3 mm —
7.5 mm

35 mm film

— 22.05 mm —
16.03 mm

The image formed by the lens is circular and is larger than the aspect ratio rectangle of the final television display. The corners of the rectangle of the CCD sensor picture area are positioned inside the optically corrected image circle. The lens can therefore only be used for the specific CCD sensor size for which it was designed.

45

Angle of view

When a camera converts a three-dimensional scene into a TV picture, it leaves an imprint of lens height, camera tilt, distance from subject and lens angle. We can detect these decisions in any image by examining the position of the horizon line and where it cuts similar sized figures. This will reveal camera height and tilt. Lens height and tilt will be revealed by any parallel converging lines in the image such as the edges of buildings or roads. The size relationship between foreground and background objects, particularly the human figure, will give clues to camera distance from objects and lens angle. Camera distance from subject will be revealed by the change in object size when moving towards or away from the lens (see Depiction of space, page 118).

For any specific lens angle and camera position there will be a unique set of the above parameters. The 'perspective' of the picture is created by the camera distance except, of course, where false perspective has been deliberately created.

Focal length
When parallel rays of light pass through a convex lens, they will converge to one point on the optical axis. This point is called the focal point of the lens. The focal length of the lens is indicated by the distance from the centre of the lens or the principal point of a compound lens (e.g. a zoom lens) to the focal point. The longer the focal length of a lens, the smaller its angle of view will be; and the shorter the focal length of a lens, the wider its angle of view.

Angle of view
The approximate horizontal angle of view of a fixed focal length lens can be calculated by using its focal length and the size of the pick-up sensors of the camera.

For a camera fitted with 2/3-inch CCDs the formula would be:

$$\text{Angle of view i.e.} = 2 \tan^{-1} \frac{8.8 \text{ mm (width of CCD)}}{2 \times \text{focal length (mm)}}$$

Zoom
Although there are prime lenses (fixed focal length) available for 2/3-inch cameras, the majority of cameras are fitted with a zoom lens which can alter its focal length and therefore the angle of view over a certain range. This is achieved by moving one part of the lens system (the variator) to change the size of the image and by automatically gearing another part of the lens system (the compensator) to simultaneously move and maintain focus. This alters the image size and therefore the effective focal length of the lens. To zoom into a subject, the lens must first be fully zoomed in on the subject and focused. Then zoom out to the wider angle. The zoom will now stay in focus for the whole range of its travel. If possible, always pre-focus before zooming in.

Focal length of a lens

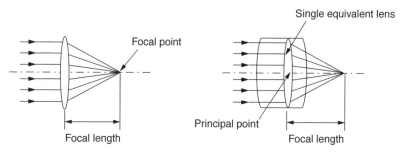

Single equivalent lens

Focal point

Focal length

Focal length of a single lens

Principal point

Focal length

Focal length of a compound lens

Focal length and angle of view for a 2/3" 14:1 zoom (4:3 aspect ratio)

Focal length in mm	8.5	10	20	50	75	100	150	200	300	400
Horizontal angle of view in degrees	54.7	46.5	24.8	10	6.7	5.04	3.3	2.5	1.7	1.2

Minimum object distance

The distance from the front of the lens to the nearest subject that can be kept in focus is called the minimum object distance (MOD). A 14 x 8.5 zoom would have a MOD of between 0.8 m and 0.65 m, whereas a larger zoom ratio lens (33:1) may have an MOD of over 2 m. Many zooms are fitted with a macro mechanism which allows objects closer than the lens MOD to be held in focus. The macro shifts several lens groups inside the lens to allow close focus, but this prevents the lens being used as a constant focus zoom.

Depth of field

The depth of field, how much of scene in shot is in acceptable focus, is a crucial element in shot composition and controlling how the viewer responds to the image. Cinemagraphic fashion has alternated between deep focus shots (Greg Toland's work on *Citizen Kane* (1941)) to the use of long focal lenses with a very limited depth of field only allowing the principal subject in the frame to be sharp. The choice of focal length and *f* number control depth of field.

f number

The *f* number of a lens is a method of indicating how much light can pass through the lens. It is inversely proportional to the focal length of the lens and directly proportional to the diameter of the effective aperture of the lens. For a given focal length, the larger the aperture of the lens the smaller its *f* number and the brighter the image it produces. *f* numbers are arranged in a scale where each increment is multiplied by $\sqrt{2}$ (1.414). Each time the *f* number is increased by one stop (e.g. *f*2.8 to *f*4), the exposure is decreased by half:

*f*1.4   *f*2   *f*2.8   *f*4   *f*5.6   *f*8   *f*11   *f*16   *f*22

The effective aperture of a zoom is not the actual diameter of the diaphragm, but the diameter of the portion of the diaphragm seen from in front of the lens. This is called the entrance pupil of the lens (see diagram opposite). When the lens is zoomed (i.e. the focal length is altered) the diameter of the lens which is proportional to focal length alters and also its entrance pupil. The effective aperture is small at the wide angle end of the zoom and larger at the narrowest angle. This may cause *f* number drop or ramping at the telephoto (longest focal length) end when the entrance pupil diameter equals the diameter of the focusing lens group and cannot become any larger. To eliminate *f* drop (ramping) completely the entrance pupil at the longest focal length of the zoom must be at least equal to the longest focal length divided by the largest *f* number. This increases the size, weight and the cost of the lens and therefore a certain amount of *f* drop is tolerated. The effect only becomes significant when working at low light levels on the narrow end of the zoom.

Depth of field

Changing the *f* number alters the depth of field – the portion of the field of view which appears sharply in focus. This zone extends in front and behind the subject on which the lens is focused and will increase as the *f* number increases (see diagram opposite). The greater the distance of the subject from the camera, the greater the depth of field. The depth of field is greater behind the subject than in front and is dependent on the focal length of the lens. *f* number and therefore depth of field can be adjusted by altering light level or by the use of neutral density filters.

Ramping (f-drop)

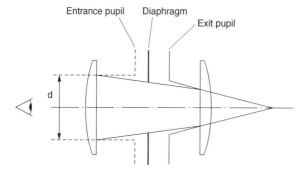

Entrance pupil Diaphragm Exit pupil

d

The entrance pupil of a zoom lens changes in diameter as you zoom in. When the entrance pupil diameter equals the diameter of the lens focusing group it cannot become any larger and f-drop or ramping occurs.

Flange back

Flange back (commonly called back focus) is the distance from the flange surface of the lens mount to the image plane of the pick-up sensor. Each camera type has a specific flange-back distance (e.g. 48 mm in air) and any lens fitted to that camera must be designed with the equivalent flange back. There is usually a flange-back adjustment mechanism of the lens with which the flange back can be adjusted by about ±0.5 mm. It is important when changing lenses on a camera to check the flange-back position is correctly adjusted and to white balance the new lens.

Adjusting the back focus

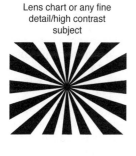

Lens chart or any fine detail/high contrast subject

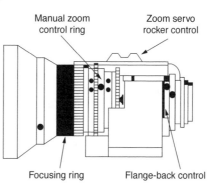

Manual zoom control ring   Zoom servo rocker control

Focusing ring   Flange-back control

1 Open lens to its widest aperture and adjust exposure as necessary by adding ND filters or adjusting shutter speed.
2 Select the widest lens angle.
3 Adjust for optimum focus with the flange-back control on the lens.
4 Zoom the lens in to its narrowest angle on a distant object from the camera and adjust the zoom focus for optimum sharpest.
5 Zoom out and repeat steps 2–4 of the above procedure until maximum sharpness is achieved at both ends of the zoom range.
6 Lock off the flange-back control taking care that its sharpest focus position has not been altered.

Zooming

Variable lens angle

A zoom lens has a continuously variable lens angle and is therefore useful for adjusting the image size without moving the camera position. When operating with a monocular viewfinder on a portable camera, the zoom lens can be controlled manually, or from a rocker switch mounted on the lens, or by a thumb control remoted to the pan bar or on a pistol grip. A good servo zoom should allow a smooth imperceptible take-up of the movement of the zoom which can then be accelerated by the thumb control to match the requirements of the shot. In general, the zoom is used in three ways – to compose the shot, to readjust the composition on shot, to change the shot size in vision.

Readjustment on shot

The zoom lens angle is often used to trim or adjust the shot to improve the composition when the content of the shot changes. Someone joining a person 'in shot' is provided with space in the frame by zooming out. The reverse may happen when they leave shot – the camera zooms in to re-compose the original shot. Trimming the shot 'in vision' may be unavoidable in the coverage of spontaneous or unknown content but it quickly becomes an irritant if repeatedly used. Fidgeting with the framing by altering the zoom angle should be avoided during a take.

Zoom ratio

A zoom lens can vary its focal length. The ratio of the longest focal length it can achieve (the telephoto end) with the shortest focal length obtainable (its wide-angle end) is its zoom ratio. A broadcast zoom lens will state zoom ratio and the wide angle focal length in one figure. A popular zoom ratio is a 14 × 8.5. This describes a zoom with a 14:1 ratio starting at 8.5 mm focal length (angle of view = 54° 44') with the longest focal length of 14 × 8.5 mm = 119 mm (angle of view = 4° 14').

Lenses with ratios in excess of 50:1 can be obtained but the exact choice of ratio and the focal length at the wide end of the zoom will depend very much on what you want to do with the lens. Large zoom ratios are heavy, often require a great deal of power to operate the servo controls and have a reduced f number. A 14:1 8.5 mm zoom lens, for example, will give sufficient length at the narrow end to get good close-ups in sport or at the back of a conference hall, but still provide a reasonable wide angle for close interviewing work in crowds.

Extender

A zoom lens can be fitted with an internal extender lens system which allows the zoom to be used on a different set of focal lengths. A 2× extender on the 14 × 8.5 zoom mentioned above would transform the range from 8.5–119 mm to 17–238 mm but it will lose more than two stops of sensitivity.

Follow focus rig

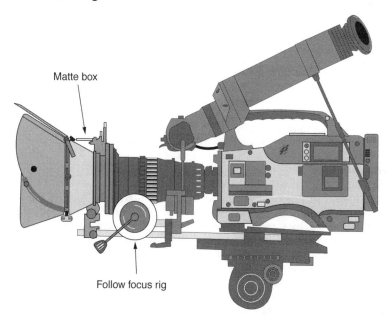

Matte box

Follow focus rig

A follow focus rig is attached to the focus ring on the lens to provide controlled manual movement of focus. It usually consists of support bars which are fastened to the base of the camera and a hand-wheel with marker scale. The hand-wheel on the lens can be replaced by a remote control Bowden cable.

The focus rig may have interchangeable pitch gears (0.5 mm, 0.6 mm and 0.8 mm) to match the lens model. Also the support bars must be designed or be adjustable to the particular combination of lens and camera in use to correctly position the rig to the lens focus ring.

Matte box

A matte box is an adjustable bellows supported on bars attached to the camera and is used in front of the lens as a flexible lens hood to eliminate flares and unwanted light and to hold and position front of lens filters. There is usually one large pivoting ray shield (French flag) and two or more filter holders, one of which is rotatable so that polarizing filters can be positioned.

There are 3 x 3 (3-inch or 75 mm square) or 4 x 4 (4-inch or 100 mm square) filters available for camcorder lenses but the choice will be governed by the focal length range of the lens and whether the filter holder comes into shot on the widest angle. Some lenses have a moving front element when focused. Check for clearance between filter and lens at all points of focus when attaching matte box.

Focus

Focusing is the act of adjusting the lens elements to achieve a sharp image at the focal plane. Objects either side of this focus zone may still look reasonably sharp depending on their distance from the lens, the lens aperture and lens angle. The area covering the objects that are in acceptable focus is called the depth of field.

The depth of field can be considerable if the widest angle of the zoom is selected and, whilst working with a small aperture, a subject is selected for focus at some distance from the lens. When zooming into this subject, the depth of field or zone of acceptable sharpness will decrease.

Follow focus

Television is often a 'talking head' medium and the eyes need to be in sharp focus. Sharpest focus can be checked 'off-shot' by rocking the focus zone behind and then in front of the eyes. As camera or subject moves there will be a loss of focus which needs to be corrected. The art of focusing is to know which way to focus and not to overshoot. Practise following focus as someone walks towards the lens. Adjust the peaking control on the viewfinder which emphasizes edges and is an aid to focusing and does not affect the recorded image.

Zoom lens and focus

A zoom lens is designed to keep the same focal plane throughout the whole of its range (provided the back focus has been correctly adjusted). Always pre-focus whenever possible on the tightest shot of the subject. This is the best way of checking focus because of the small depth of field and it also prepares for a zoom-in if required.

Pulling focus

Within a composition, visual attention is directed to the subject in sharpest focus. Attention can be transferred to another part of the frame by throwing focus onto that subject. Match the speed of the focus pull to the motivating action.

If the focus is on a foreground person facing camera with a defocused background figure and the foreground subject turns away from camera, focus can be instantly thrown back to the background. A slower focus pull would be more appropriate in music coverage, for example, moving off the hands of a foreground musician to a background instrumentalist. Avoid long focus pulls that provide nothing but an extended defocused picture before another subject comes into sharp focus unless this is motivated by the action (e.g. the subjective visual experience of someone recovering consciousness).

Differential focus

Differential focus is deliberately using a narrow depth of field to emphasize the principal subject in the frame in sharp focus which is contrasted with a heavily out of focus background.

Focus problems

- **Back focus:** If, after focusing on a subject in close-up, you zoom out and discover the picture loses definition, it is likely that the back focus of the lens has not been properly set up or has been knocked out of adjustment. See page 52 on adjusting back focus.

- **Lens centring:** If you need to pan or tilt the camera when zooming to a subject in the centre of the frame with the camera horizontal, it is likely that the lens is not optically centred to the CCDs. The optical axis of the lens must line up with the centre of the CCDs to ensure that the centre of the frame is identical when zooming from the widest to the narrowest angle without camera pan/tilt compensation.

- **Resolution:** A television camera converts an image into an electrical signal that will eventually be transmitted. The resolving power required from a TV zoom lens will therefore be related to the maximum frequency of the bandwidth of the signal transmitted plus the specification of the imaging device and line structure. The finesse of detail transmitted will depend on the particular TV standard in use (e.g. 625 PAL; 525 NTSC).

- **Spatial frequency:** Spatial frequency counts the number of black-white pairs of lines contained in 1 mm of the optical image and is a method of quantifying fine detail in a TV picture. Lack of resolution in a recorded image may be due to the limitation of the lens design, CCD design or the choice of recording format.

- **Modulating transfer function:** Modulating transfer function (MTF) measures the range of spatial frequencies transmitted through the lens by focusing on a chart on which black-white lines become progressively more closely spaced until the contrast between black and white can no longer be detected. The modular transfer function is 100 per cent when the transition between white and black is exactly reproduced and zero when the image is uniformly grey and no contrast can be detected. The MTF curve plots reproducibility of contrast against spatial frequency. Different television systems (625, 16:9, 1105 progressive scan, etc.) require a lens design which matches the maximum resolution achievable with the bandwidth of the chosen system.

- **Fluorite and infinity focusing:** Fluorite is used in the manufacture of some zoom lenses to correct chromatic aberrations at the telephoto end. As the refractive index of fluorite changes with temperature more than the refractive index of glass, there is provision when focusing on infinity at low temperatures (e.g. below 0°C) to allow the focus point to go beyond the infinity marking on the lens.

Dual format cameras

The transition between 4:3 aspect ratio television and the conversion to 16:9 has produced an interim generation of dual format cameras. Different techniques are employed to use the same CCD for both formats. If a CCD block design is optimized for the 4:3 shape and is then switched to the 16:9 format, lines are discarded at the top and bottom of the frame in order to convert the image area to a 16:9 shape (see Figure a opposite). As 4:3 working occupies the same area of the CCD as a standard 4:3 camera there is no change in angle of view or resolution. When switched to 16:9, however, there is a reduction in resolution and a decrease in vertical angle of view.

If the CCD block is optimized for 16:9 format working (see Figure b) and is then switched to a 4:3 aspect ratio, the image area now occupies a smaller area than a standard 4:3 CCD image (see Figure a) and therefore has a reduced resolution and a reduction in horizontal lens angle.

Some camera manufacturers claim that it is not possible to satisfy the competing demands of both formats; one of the formats will be compromised in resolution or change in lens angle. Other camera manufacturers claim that they can offer a switchable camera that retains the same number of pixels in both formats.

The horizontal angle of view is related to the focal length of the lens and the width of the CCD image. In a dual format camera, if the CCD is optimized for 16:9 format, the angle of view will be smaller working in the 4:3 format compared to working in 16:9 using the same focal length of the lens. At the shortest focal length the loss is about 20 per cent. When switched to 4:3 working, there will be a 9 mm diameter image (see Figure c) compared to the 11 mm diagonal image when working in 16:9 or the 11 mm diameter image of the conventional 4:3 format camera (see Figure a).

This change in horizontal lens angle when switching formats can be remedied by employing an optical unit in the zoom (similar to an extender but producing negative magnification) which shortens the focal length when working in the 4:3 mode (see Figure d). This 0.8 reduction of focal length produces the same range of angles of view as a conventional 4:3 camera using the equivalent zoom lens.

It is not essential when working in 16:9/4:3 dual aspect ratio camera to fit a lens with a 0.8 convertor, but be aware that the lens angle will be narrower than its equivalent use with a standard 4:3 camera.

Zoom lens aspect ratio conversion

(a)   (b)   (c)   (d)

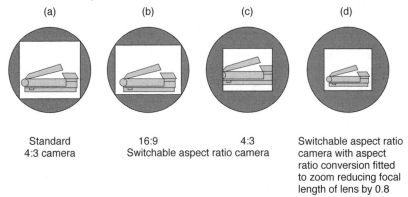

Standard 4:3 camera	16:9 4:3 Switchable aspect ratio camera	Switchable aspect ratio camera with aspect ratio conversion fitted to zoom reducing focal length of lens by 0.8

Power

The cable connecting the lens to camera varies between makes and models of equipment. It is important to match the correct lens cable to the camera it is working with so that the correct drive voltages are connected to avoid lens motors being damaged. Conversion cables are available if lens and camera cable pins do not match.

The servo-driven zoom motor is powered from the battery connected to the camera/VTR. If it is continually operated (i.e. zooming in and out to find the required framing before recording), it can add an unnecessary drain on the battery. To conserve battery power, find the required framing by manual control of the zoom (if fitted) before switching over to servo if you require to zoom on shot.

Essential camera controls

There are a number of mechanical and electronic controls that are found on most broadcast camcorders. The position on the camera of some of these controls will vary between make and model but their function will be similar. The essential operational controls have a significant effect on the recorded image and their function must be understood if the operator is to fully exploit the camcorder's potential. Each switch and function is discussed as a separate topic in the following pages but their effects may interact with other control settings (e.g. white balance and colour temperature filters). The newcomer to digital camerawork should experiment with a range of settings and observe the effect on the recorded image. Camerawork is a craft not a science and a video camera is simply a means to a production end.

Exposure, for example, can be described as a procedure that satisfies certain technical requirements. In those terms it appears to be a mechanical procedure that is objective and unaffected by the person carrying out the operation. But quite often exposure is customized to a specific shot and the engineering quest to produce a perfect electronic reproduction of a subject may be ignored to satisfy more important subjective criteria. Subjective production choices influence whether a face is in semi-silhouette or is fully lit and exposed to see every detail in the shadows.

It is this 'subjective' element that often confuses someone new to camerawork in their search for the 'right way' to record an image. A useful first aim is to achieve fluency in producing television pictures that are sharp, steady, with a colour balance that appears normal to the eye and with a contrast range that falls within the limitation of a television display. The pictures should be free from noise and with a continuity in skin tones between shots of the same face. Similar basic aims are required in recording audio. When this is achieved, the means of customizing an image or audio to serve a specific production purpose can be learnt. Quite often the standard basic picture can be produced with the aid of the auto features on the camera. To progress beyond this point an understanding of how to manipulate the operational controls needs to be gained.

Operational controls

There are a few controls that need adjustment or at least checking on their existing setting before every shot. These include:

- tape remaining and state of battery charge;
- focus, exposure, colour temperature correction filter position, white balance setting;
- gain, shutter speed and timecode;
- adjustment of audio recording level.

The camera set-up controls such as gamma, onset of zebra setting, auto exposure settings, etc., are unlikely to be regularly adjusted unless there is a production need. They can be left at their factory setting until more experience is gained in video recording.

Typical camera control layout

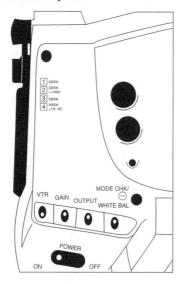

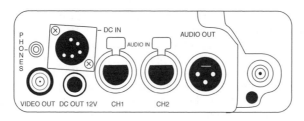

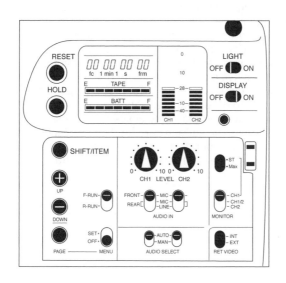

Auto and manual controls

If you have ever used a spell checker on a word processor and found the auto device consistently queries correct words such as your address then you will understand why it is important to intelligently use and monitor the auto features available on a camcorder. A spell checker can be taught new words but the auto features on a camera remain as originally programmed although digital processing now allows much more flexibility in customizing auto facilities. An auto interpretation of what is the main subject in the frame may frequently be at odds with your own requirements. This is why a camcorder used for broadcast production purposes should have manual override on all auto facilities as there are going to be many occasions when the cameraman needs to take control and customize the image the way he/she wants it and not the way the auto feature is programmed to deliver. Auto control is a form of computer control and is stubbornly unintelligent in many situations.

Auto-exposure (see pages 82–3) has advantages and can sometimes accommodate rapid changes in light level faster than any manual correction. But the downside to this is the obvious visual change in the picture. For example, an interviewee may be wearing a white dress in sunlight. Using manual exposure it may be possible to find a compromise aperture setting that provides detail in the dress with acceptable skin tones. If cloud obscures the sun, the light level falls and a reasonable face exposure may need nearly a stop open compared to the bright sunlight condition. If this is done, as soon as the sun appears the dress will burn out and the lens needs to be stopped down. Some cameras provide a 'soft' transition between two auto-exposure conditions (see page 40), so that the sudden, auto-exposure adjustment is not so noticeable. Opening up and stopping down can be done manually to avoid abrupt exposure changes but the cameraman will need to be very attentive to follow a number of rapid light level changes.

Audio auto-gain can be convenient in one-man operations but produces too rapid an attenuation of the main subject sound if a loud background sound occurs. The voice level of a street corner interviewee using audio auto-gain can be pushed down to unintelligibility if a lorry passes close to the live side of the microphone. Obviously manual control is the better option in this situation. But if covering an item where a loud explosion is going to occur (e.g. a twenty-one-gun salute for a VIP), where there is no opportunity to manually check audio levels, auto audio level should accommodate the sudden very loud noise. Deciding between auto and manual control depends on circumstance and either operational technique should not be continually used as a matter of habit.

Manual control

The voice level of the reporter is manually set. The approaching aircraft will eventually force the sound level into the clip level (see page 202) but the reporter's voice level will remain consistent throughout the shot. Television is often a compromise and by staging the item at the end of the runway the appropriate shot is obtained at the expense of far from acceptable sound.

Good auto control

To follow someone from an exterior which has been correctly white balanced with a daylight colour correction filter into a tungsten-lit interior would produce a big change in the appearance of the picture – it would become very yellow. One technique is to work on auto-exposure and switch between two white balance positions A and B which have been set on the same filter in exterior and interior. Many digital cameras have an 'auto white balance correction' and this can achieve a better adjustment when moving between light of different colour temperature. The colour balance is instantly adjusted moving into tungsten light although the adjustment to exposure may still be noticeable.

Lens controls

The three main operational controls on the lens are focus, zoom and the lens aperture (f number).

■ **Focus:** Sharp focus of the image is achieved by looking at the viewfinder image and either manually adjusting the focusing ring on the lens or by connecting a cable to the lens and controlling the focus by servo control mounted on a pan bar. Usually there is a switch on the zoom rocker module marked M (for manual control) and S (for servo control). On some DV format cameras there is the option of auto-focusing. As with other auto facilities, its value is limited and will depend on the shot and if it is sufficiently well designed and set up so that it does not continually hunt to check focus.

As we have discussed on page 52, the zoom must be prefocused on its narrowest angle before recording a zoom into a subject, and the back focus of the lens must be correctly aligned (see page 49) for the sharpest focus to be maintained throughout the zoom.

If the required object in frame is closer to the lens than its minimum object distance (MOD, see page 47), it may be possible to bring the subject into sharp focus by adjusting the macro ring on the back of the lens. The macro device alters several lens groups inside the lens and prevents the zoom operating as a constant focus lens. The macro after use should always be returned to its détente position and locked.

■ **Zoom:** Altering the variable lens angle on the zoom (zooming) can be achieved either by means of the rocker switch servo (or a pistol grip if fitted beneath the lens), or manually by using the zoom lever on the lens. Switching between the two methods of use is by a switch marked S (servo) and M (manual). In a similar way to control of focus, the zoom servo can also be controlled by a hand control attached to a pan bar. Pan bar servo control of zoom and focus is used when a larger viewfinder (possibly 5-inch display) replaces the monocular viewfinder.

■ **Aperture:** Opening up or closing down the lens aperture changes light level reaching the CCDs and therefore is the prime method of controlling exposure. Control of the aperture is via a switch marked M (manual control), A (auto-exposure, which is electronically determined) or R (remote – when the camera's image quality is adjusted remotely from the camera to match the pictures produced by other cameras at the event).

■ **Extender:** If the lens is fitted with an extender, the range of focal lengths from widest to narrowest lens angles can be altered dependent on the extender factor.

Typical zoom lens controls

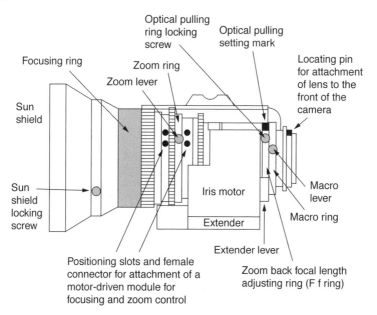

- **Record button/lens electrics:** The cable connecting the lens to camera varies between makes and models of equipment. It is important to match the correct lens cable to the camera it is working with so that the correct drive voltages are connected to avoid lens motors being damaged. Conversion cables are available if lens and camera cable pins do not match.
- **Lens hood:** A ray shield is essential for limiting the effect of degradation from flares. It is designed for the widest lens angle of the zoom but can be augmented on a narrower lens angle by the judicious use of gaffer tape if flare on this angle is a problem. Matte box and effects filters are discussed on page 62.
- **UV filter – skylight filter:** This absorbs short wavelength ultraviolet (UV) rays that the eye cannot see. On a clear day these rays produce a bluish green cast to foliage. A zoom lens has so many lens components that almost all ultraviolet light is absorbed inside the lens. A UV filter is still advisable as a protection filter screwed on to the front of the lens to prevent damage or dirt reaching the front element.

Effects filters

Digital video has an enormous potential for manipulating the appearance of the image in post-production, but there are also the opportunities, when appropriate, to refashion the recorded image at the time of acquisition (see Scene files, page 100). Alongside the need for faithful reproduction, photographers have often attempted to customize the image to suit a particular emotional or aesthetic effect. In their hands the camera was not a 'scientific' instrument faithfully observing reality, but the means of creating a subjective impression. One simple method is in the use of filters usually placed in a filter holder/matte box positioned in the front of the lens. These are used for various reasons such as to control light, contrast or part of the subject brightness, to soften the image or to colour the image. Most camcorders also have one or two filter wheels fitted between lens and prism block carrying colour correction filters and/or neutral density filters.

Altering the appearance of the image

Filters fall into three main groups – colour correction filters (see Colour temperature, page 64), neutral density filters (used as a control in exposure) and effects and polarizing filters. They all alter the quality of light reaching the CCDs, but whereas the first two groups attempt to invisibly make the correction, effects filters are intended to be visually obvious in their impact on the appearance of the image. They are employed to change the standard electronic depiction of a subject. Filters can be chosen to bring about a number of visual changes including reduction in picture sharpness, a reduction in picture contrast, lightening or 'lifting' blacks, to induce highlight effects such as halos or star bursts and to modify the rendition of skin tones. Many of these effects are not reversible in post-production although improvement in picture matching can be attempted.

Factors that affect the filter influence

Many of the effects filters such as black and white dot, frosts, nets, fog, soft and low contrast achieve their results by introducing a varying degree of flare. The potential influence on the picture is identified by grading the effects filter on a scale of 1 to 5 where 1 has the smallest effect and 5 has the largest. Some filters are also available in smaller, more subtle increments and are graded as 1/8th, 1/4 or 1/2. Choosing which grade and which filter to use depends on the shot, lens angle, aperture and the effects of under- or over-exposure. In general, effects filters work more effectively on longer lens and wider apertures (e.g. $f2$ and $f2.8$). To ensure continuity of image over a long sequence of shots it may be necessary to vary the grade of filter depending on lens angle, camera distance and aperture. It is prudent to carry out a series of tests varying the above settings before production commences. Filters mounted on the front of the lens are affected by stray light and flares which can add to the degradation.

Filters that affect the blacks in an image

A strong black makes a picture appear to have more definition and contrast. Diffusion filters reduce the density of blacks by dispersing light into the blacks of an image. This effectively reduces the overall contrast and creates an apparent reduction in sharpness. *White nets* provide a substantial reduction in the black density and whites or any over-exposed areas of the image tend to bloom. If stockings are used stretched across the lens hood, the higher their denier number (mesh size) the stronger the diffusion. A *fog filter* reduces black density, contrast and saturation. The lighter parts of the scene will appear to have a greater fog effect than the shadows creating halos around lights. A double *fog filter* does not double the fog effect and possibly creates less of a fog than the standard fog filter, but does create a glow around highlights. Because of lightening of the blacks, the picture may appear to be over-exposed and the exposure should be adjusted to maximize the intended effect. *Low contrast* filters reduce contrast by lightening blacks and thereby reducing the overall contrast. Strong blacks appear to give the image more definition and low contrast filters may appear soft. They are sometimes employed to modify the effects of strong sunlight. *Soft contrast* filters reduce contrast by pulling down the highlights. Because blacks are less affected, soft contrast filters appear sharper than low contrast filters and do not create halation around lights. As highlights are reduced the picture may appear under-exposed.

Effect on highlights

Some filters cause points of light, highlights or flare to have a diffused glow around the light source. The *black dot filter* limits this diffusion to areas around the highlights and avoids spreading into the blacks. *Super frosts, black frosts, promist, black promists* and *double mists* diffusion work best on strong specular light or white objects against a dark background. The weak grades leave the blacks unaffected providing an apparent sharp image whilst the strong grades cause a haze over the whole image which leaks into the black areas of the picture. *Black, white* and *coloured nets* have a fine mesh pattern causing a softening of the image and a reduction in the purity and intensity of the image's colour. This 'desaturated' look is thought by some to give video images more of a film appearance.

- *Neutral density filters:* These reduce the amount of light reaching the lens and can be used to produce a specific *f* number and therefore depth of field.
- *Graduated filters:* These can help to control bright skies by having a graduated neutral density from the top to clear filter at the bottom. The graduation can be obtained as a hard or a soft transition. There are also filters with a graduated tint to colour skies or the top part of the frame. They are positioned in the matte box for optimum effect but once adjusted the camera can rarely be tilted or panned on shot without disclosing the filter position.
- *Polarizing filters:* These reduce glare reflections, darken blue skies and increase colour saturation. They are useful in eliminating reflections in glass such as shop windows, cars and shooting into water. The filter must be rotated until the maximum reduction of unwanted reflection is achieved. This changes the colour balance (e.g. can affect the 'green' of grass) so a white balance should be carried out when correct filter position has been determined. Moving the camera (panning or titling) once the polarizing filter is aligned may reduce or eliminate the polarizing effect.
- *Star and sunburst filters:* These produce flare lines or 'stars' from highlights. Star filters are cross hatched to produce 2, 4, 6, 8 or 10 points whilst sunburst produces any number of points. They are more effective when placed between lens and prism block and can produce an unwanted degradation of definition when in front of the lens.

Colour temperature

Two sounds cannot be combined to produce a third pure sound but as we have discussed in Light into electricity (page 12), by combing two or more colours a third colour can be created in which there is no trace of its constituents (red + green = yellow). The eye acts differently to the ear. The eye/brain relationship is in many ways far more sophisticated than a video camera and can be misleading when attempting to analyse the 'colour' of the light illuminating a potential shot.

The camera has no brain

In discussing the conversion of a colour image into an electrical system by the three-filter system we overlooked this crucial distinction between how we perceive colour and how a camera converts colour into an electrical signal. Human perception filters sensory information through the brain. The brain makes many additions and adjustments in deciding what we think we see, particularly in observing colour.

A 'white' card will appear 'white' under many different lighting conditions. Without a standard reference 'white', a card can be lit by pink, light blue or pale green light and an observer will adjust and claim that the card is 'white'. The card itself can be of a range of pastel hues and still be seen as white. The brain continually makes adjustments when judging colour. A video camera has no 'brain' and makes no adjustment when the colour of light illuminating a subject varies. It accurately reproduces the scene in the field of view. A person's face lit by a sodium street lamp (orange light) will be adjusted by the brain and very little orange will be seen. The camera will reproduce the prevailing light and when displayed on a screen the face will have an orange hue.

Colour temperature

Because of the fidelity with which the camera reproduces colour, it is important to have a means of measuring colour and changes in colour. This is achieved by using the Kelvin scale – a measure of the colour temperature of light (see opposite). Across a sequence of shots under varying lighting conditions, we must provide continuity in our reference white. Just as the brain makes the necessary adjustment to preserve the continuity of white, we must adjust the camera when the colour temperature of the shot illumination changes (see White balance, page 68).

Colour temperature

Blue skylight	9500–20,000K
Overcast sky	6000–7500K
HMI lamps	5600K
Average summer sunlight	5500K
Fluorescent daylight tubes*	5000K
Early morning/late afternoon	4300K
Fluorescent warm white tubes*	3000K
Studio tungsten lights	3200K
40–60 watt household bulb	2760K
Dawn/dusk	7000K
Sunrise/sunset	2000K
Candle flame	1850–2000K
Match flame	1700K

*All discharge sources are quoted as a correlated colour temperature, i.e. it 'looks like', for example, 5000K.

A piece of iron when heated glows first red and then, as its temperature increases, changes colour through yellow to 'white hot'. The colour of a light source can therefore be conveniently defined by comparing its colour with an identical colour produced by a black body radiator (e.g. an iron bar) and identifying the temperature needed to produce that colour. This temperature is measured using the Kelvin scale** (K) which is equivalent to the Centigrade unit plus 273 (e.g. 0° Centigrade = 273 Kelvin). This is called the colour temperature of the light source although strictly speaking this only applies to incandescent sources (i.e. sources glowing because they are hot). The most common incandescent source is the tungsten filament lamp. The colour temperature of a domestic 40–60 watt tungsten bulb is 2760K, while that of a tungsten halogen source is 3200K. These are not necessarily the operating temperatures of the filaments but the colour temperature of the light emitted. Although we psychologically associate red with heat and warmth and blue with cold, as a black body radiator becomes hotter, its colour temperature increases but the light it emits becomes bluer.

Kelvin scale: The physicist William Thomson, 1st Baron of Kelvin, first proposed an absolute temperature scale defined so that 0K is absolute zero, the coldest theoretical temperature (−273.15°C), at which the energy of motion of molecules is zero. Each absolute Kelvin degree is equivalent to a Celsius degree, so that the freezing point of water (0°C) is 273.15K, and its boiling point (100°C) is 373.15K.

Colour temperature correction filters

Colour camera processing is designed to operate in a tungsten-lit scene. Consequently the output from the red, green and blue CCDs are easily equalized when white balancing a scene lit with tungsten lighting (3200K). When the camera is exposed to daylight, it requires significant changes to the red channel and blue channel gains to achieve a 'white balance'. Many cameras are fitted with two filter wheels which are controlled either mechanically, by turning the filter wheel on the left-hand side at the front of the camera, or by selecting the required filter position from a menu displayed in the viewfinder. The filter wheels contain colour correction and neutral density filters and possibly an effects filter. The position of the various filters varies with camera model.

Variation in colour temperature could be compensated without the use of colour correction filters by adjusting the gains of each channel. With some colour temperatures this would require a large increase in gain in one channel and increase the noise to an unacceptable level (see page 88 for the relationship between gain and noise).

Cameras could be normalized to the colour temperature of tungsten or daylight. Because of the greater light levels of daylight, most cameras are designed to be operated with no colour correction under tungsten. The 3200K filter position is a clear glass filter whereas a 5600K filter (with no ND) is a minus blue filter to cut out the additional blue found in daylight. All colour correction filters decrease the transmission of light and therefore the minus blue filter cuts down the light (by approximately one stop) where most light is available – in daylight. A white balance is required after changing filter position.

In addition to the colour correction filter for daylight, many cameras also provide neutral density filters in the filter wheel. Neutral density filters are used when there is a need to reduce the depth of field or in circumstances of a brightly lit location.

Filter selection
Set the filter to match the colour correction filter appropriate to the light source and light intensity.

- **3200K filter:** When this filter position is selected an optical plain glass filter is placed between the lens and the prism block to maintain back focus. Although the position is marked as 3200K, no colour correction filter is used because the camera is designed to work in a tungsten lit environment with sufficient gain variation of red and blue to cope with 'tungsten' colour temperature.
- **5600K filter:** This position in the filter wheel has the required colour temperature correction filter needed for daylight exposure. The minus blue filter reduces the transmission of blue light but also reduces the exposure by about one stop. This is not usually a problem as daylight light levels are considerably higher than the output of tungsten light.

The colour of the sky

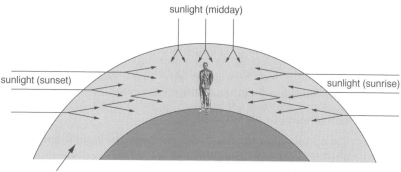

sunlight (midday)

sunlight (sunset)

sunlight (sunrise)

Earth's atmosphere

Sunlight is scattered as it passes through the atmosphere and combined with clouds and the orbit of the earth around the sun, the human perception of the 'colour' of the sky is constantly changing. At midday, visible solar radiation is scattered by air molecules, particularly at the blue end of the spectrum where 30–40 per cent of blue light is dispersed producing a 'blue' sky. The scattering decreases to a negligible amount at the red end. At sunrise/sunset when light from the sun passes through a greater amount of atmosphere, light scattering occurs across the whole of the spectrum and the sky appears redder. The amount of sunlight scattered by the earth's atmosphere depends on wavelength, how far light has to travel through the atmosphere, and atmospheric pollution.

A common combination of colour correction and neutral density filters is:

position (1) 3200K   sunrise/sunset/tungsten/studio
position (2) 5600K + 1/4ND   (neutral density) exterior – clear sky
position (3) 5600K   exterior/cloud/rain
position (4) 5600K + 1/16ND (neutral density) exterior exceptionally bright

NB 1/4ND is a filter with a transmission of 1/4 or 25%, i.e. 0.6 ND *not* 0.25ND!

White balance

Whenever there is a change in the colour temperature of the light illuminating a potential shot it is necessary to adjust the white balance of the camera. Some cameras will compensate for colour temperature variation but often it is necessary to carry out a white balance set-up. The white balance switch may be marked 'auto white balance' but this does not mean the camera will automatically compensate unless the specified white balance procedure is carried out. To successfully white balance a simple routine needs to be followed:

- Select the correct filter for the colour temperature of light being used (e.g. tungsten 3200K or daylight 5600K).
- Select either white balance position A or B. These positions memorize the setting achieved by the white balance. On each filter position there can be two memories (A or B). If *preset* is selected no setting will be memorized. This position always provides the factory default setting of 3200K.
- Fill the frame with a white matte card that is lit by same lighting as the intended shot. Make sure the card does not move during the white balance and that there are no reflections or shading on the card. Avoid any colour cast from surrounding light sources and ensure that you white balance with the main source of shot illumination and that the card is correctly exposed.

A progress report may appear in the viewfinder during white balance, including a number indicating the colour temperature that has been assessed. If this is much higher or lower than your anticipated estimate of the colour temperature then check the white card position and the other requirements of white balance. It could also indicate the camera is either not properly lined-up or malfunctioning. During the white balance procedure, the auto-iris circuit adjusts exposure to make the output of the green signal correct, then the gain of the red and blue channels are adjusted to equal the output of green (see Figure 1 on page 13). This establishes the 'white' of the card held in front of the lens as the reference 'white' and influences all other colour combinations. The fidelity of colour reproduction is therefore dependent on the white balance procedure.

Black balance

Many cameras do not require a manual black balance and this adjustment is carried out automatically when required. Black balance sets the black levels of the R, G and B channels so that black has no colourcast. It is normally only required if the camera has not been in use for some time, or if the camera has been moved between radically different air temperatures or the surrounding air temperature has significantly altered or, on some cameras, when the gain selector values have been changed. If a manual black balance needs to be done, first, white balance to equalize the gains and then black balance; then white balance again.

Light output

In tungsten light sources, light is produced from the heating effect of an electric current flowing through the tungsten filament. The visible spectrum from these sources is continuous and produces a smooth transition of light output between adjacent wavelengths. The intensity of light output will vary if the current is altered (dimming) which also affects the colour temperature although this is usually kept to within acceptable limits (see Continuity of face tones, page 76).

A discharge light source produces light as a byproduct of an electrical discharge through a gas. The colour of the light is dependent on the particular mixture of gas present in the glass envelope or by the phosphor coating of the fluorescent tube. Discharge light sources that are designed for film and television lighting such as HMIs are not as stable as tungsten but have greater efficacy, are compact and produce light that approximates to daylight.

Pulsed light sources

Fluorescent tubes used in the home, office and factory, and neon signs, do not produce a constant light output but give short pulses of light at a frequency depending on the mains supply (see Shutter and pulsed lighting, page 90).

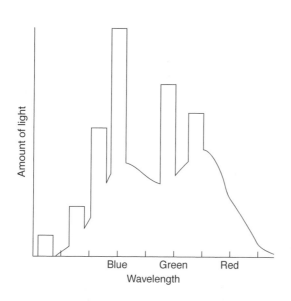

Light output of a typical daylight-type fluorescent tube. Normal eyesight does not register the high intensity blue and green spikes, but they give a bluish green cast to a tungsten-balanced camera.

In recent years the development of improved phosphors has made the fluorescent tube (cold light) acceptable for television and film. Phosphors are available to provide tungsten matching and daylight matching colour temperatures. High frequency operation (>40 kHz) results in a more or less steady light output.

Colour rendition index (Ra)

A method of comparing the colour fidelity and consistency of a light source has been devised using a scale of 0 to 100. The colour rendition index (Ra) can be used as indication of the suitability for use in television production, with an Ra of 70 regarded as the lower limit of acceptability for colour television.

Viewfinder

The monocular viewfinder is the first and often the only method of checking picture quality for the camcorder cameraman. The small black and white image (often colour LCD, liquid crystal display viewfinders on DV format cameras) has to be used to check framing, focusing, exposure, contrast and lighting. It is essential, as the viewfinder is the main guide to what is being recorded, to ensure that it is correctly set up. This means aligning the brightness and contrast of the viewfinder display. Neither control directly affects the camera output signal. Indirectly, however, if the brightness control is incorrectly set, manual adjustment of exposure based on the viewfinder picture can lead to under- or over-exposed pictures. The action of the brightness and contrast controls therefore needs to be clearly understood.

■ **Brightness:** This control is used to set the correct black level of the viewfinder picture and alters the viewfinder tube bias control. Unless it is correctly set up, the viewfinder image cannot be used to judge exposure. The brightness control must be set so that any true black produced by the camera is just not seen in the viewfinder. If, after a lens cap is placed over the lens and the aperture is fully closed, the brightness is turned up, the viewfinder display will appear increasingly grey and then white. This obviously does not represent the black image produced by the camera. If the brightness is now turned down, the image will gradually darken until the line structure of the picture is no longer visible. The correct setting of the brightness control is at the point when the line structure just disappears and there is no visible distinction between the outside edge of the display and the surrounding tube face. If the brightness control is decreased beyond this point, the viewfinder will be unable to display the darker tones just above black and distort the tonal range of the image. There is therefore only one correct setting of the brightness control which, once set, should not be altered.

■ **Contrast:** The contrast control is in effect a gain control. As the contrast is increased the black level of the display remains unchanged (set by the brightness control) whilst the rest of the tones become brighter. This is where confusion over the function of the two viewfinder controls may arise. Increasing the contrast of the image increases the brightness of the image to a point where the electron beam increases in diameter and the resolution of the display is reduced. Unlike the brightness control, there is no one correct setting for the contrast control, other than that an 'over-contrasted' image may lack definition and appear subjectively over-exposed. Contrast is therefore adjusted for an optimum displayed image which will depend on picture content and the amount of ambient light falling on the viewfinder display.

■ **Peaking:** This control adds edge enhancement to the viewfinder picture as an aid in focusing and has no effect on the camera output signal.

Setting up the viewfinder

1 Select aspect ratio if using a switchable format camera. Check that the viewfinder image is in the selected aspect ratio.
2 Switch CAMERA to BARS or place a lens cap on the lens.
3 Check the picture in the viewfinder and then reduce contrast and brightness to minimum.
4 Increase brightness until just before the raster (line structure) appears in the right-hand (black) segment of the bars.
5 Adjust contrast until all divisions of the bars can be seen.
6 Use the bars to check viewfinder focus and adjust the focus of the viewfinder eyepiece to produce the sharpest picture possible.
7 With the camera switched to produce a picture, recheck contrast with correctly exposed picture. Although the contrast control may occasionally need to be adjusted depending on picture content and ambient light change, avoid altering the brightness control.
8 Set peaking control to provide the minimum edge-enhancement that you require to find focus and adjust the eyepiece focus to achieve maximum sharpness of the viewfinder image. Adjust the position of the viewfinder for optimum operating comfort.

Aspect ratios and safety zones

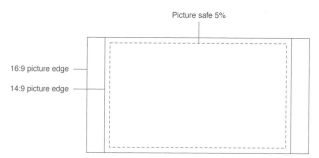

Picture safe 5%

16:9 picture edge

14:9 picture edge

With the introduction of widescreen digital TV and the use of dual format cameras (see Widescreen, page 106), programme productions may be shot in 16:9 aspect ratio but transmitted and viewed on 4:3 television receiver. To ease the transition between the two aspect ratios, many broadcasters use a compromise 14:9 aspect ratio for nominally 4:3 sets, but transmit the whole of the 16:9 frame to widescreen sets.

This requires the cameraman to frame up a 16:9 picture with these competing requirements in mind. Any essential information is included in the 14:9 picture area although the whole of the 16:9 frame may be transmitted in the future. A 14:9 graticule superimposed on the 16:9 viewfinder picture reminds the cameraman of this requirement. For the foreseeable future, actuality events such as sport may be covered for dual transmission – 16:9 and 14:9 – and therefore framing has to accommodate the smaller format if some viewers are not to be deprived of vital action.

Viewfinder indicators

There are usually a number of indicators available to be displayed in the viewfinder in addition to menus which provide information and adjustment to the camera (see Menus, page 98). These include:

● A red cue light or icon when recording. (*continued on page 73*)

Exposure

When viewing a film or television image, it is often easy to accept that the two-dimensional images are a faithful reproduction of the original scene. There are many productions (e.g. news, current affairs, sports coverage, etc.) where the audience's belief that they are watching a truthful representation unmediated by technical manipulation or distortion is essential to the credibility of the programme. But many decisions concerning exposure involve some degree of compromise as to what can be depicted even in 'factual' programmes. In productions that seek to interpret rather than to record an event, manipulating the exposure to control the look of a shot is an important technique.

As we have discussed in Colour temperature (page 64), human perception is more complex and adaptable than a video camera. The eye/brain can detect subtle tonal differences ranging, for example, from the slight variations in a white sheet hanging on a washing line on a sunny day to the detail in the deepest shadow cast by a building. The highlights in the sheet may be a thousand times brighter than the shadow detail. The TV signal is designed to handle (with minimum correction) no more than approximately 40:1 (see Contrast range, page 74).

But there is another fundamental difference between viewing a TV image and our personal experience in observing a subject. Frequently, a TV image is part of a series of images that are telling a story, creating an atmosphere or emotion. The image is designed to manipulate the viewer's response. Our normal perceptual experience is conditioned by psychological factors and we often see what we expect to see; our response is personal and individual. A storytelling TV image is designed to evoke a similar reaction in all its viewers. Exposure plays a key part in this process and is a crucial part of camerawork. Decisions on what ranges of tones are to be recorded and decisions on lighting, staging, stop number, depth of field, etc., all intimately affect how the observer relates to the image and to a sequence of images. The 'look' of an image is a key production tool.

A shot is one shot amongst many and continuity of the exposure will determine how it relates to the proceeding and the succeeding images (see Matching shots, page 156).

Factors which affect decisions on exposure include:

- the contrast range of the recording medium and viewing conditions;
- the choice of peak white and how much detail in the shadows is to be preserved;
- continuity of face tones and the relationship to other picture tones;
- subject priority – what is the principal subject in the frame (e.g. a figure standing on a skyline or the sky behind them?);
- what electronic methods of controlling contrast range are used;
- the lighting technique applied in controlling contrast;
- staging decisions – where someone is placed affects the contrast range.

Exposure overview

- An accurate conversion of a range of tonal contrast from light into an electrical signal and back into light requires an overall system gamma of approximately 1.08 (see Gamma and linear matrix, page 102).
- Often the scene contrast range cannot be accommodated by the five-stop handling ability of the camera and requires either the use of additional lamps or graduated filters or the compression of highlights is necessary.
- The choice of what tones are to be compressed is decided by the cameraman by altering the iris, by a knowledge of the transfer characteristics of the camera or by the use of highlight control.
- Automatic exposure makes no judgement of what is the important subject in the frame. It exposes for average light levels plus some weighting to centre frame. It continuously adjusts to any change of light level in the frame.
- Exposure can be achieved by a combination of f number, shutter speed and gain setting. Increasing gain will increase noise (see page 88). Shutter speed is dependent on subject content (e.g. the need for slow motion replay, shooting computer displays, etc., see page 90). F number controls depth of field and is a subjective choice based on shot content (see below).

Depth of field

Choosing a lens aperture when shooting in daylight usually depends on achieving the required exposure. Depth of field is proportional to f number and if the in-focus zone is a significant consideration in the shot composition (e.g. the need to have an out of focus background on an MCU of a person or alternatively, the need to have all the subject in focus) then the other factors affecting exposure may be adjusted to meet the required stop such as:

- neutral density filters;
- altering gain (including the use of negative gain);
- altering shutter speed;
- adding or removing light sources.

There is often more opportunity to achieve the required aperture when shooting interiors by the choice of lighting treatment (e.g. adjusting the balance between the interior and exterior light sources), although daylight is many times more powerful than portable lighting kits (see Lighting levels, page 176).

Sometimes there may be the need to match the depth of field on similar sized shots that are to be intercut (e.g. interviews). Lens sharpness may decrease as the lens is opened up but the higher lens specification required for digital cameras usually ensures that even when working wide open, the slight loss of resolution is not noticeable. Auto-focus and anti-shake devices usually cause more definition problems, especially when attempting to extend the zoom range with electronic magnification.

(continued from page 71).

- Tape remaining time with a visual warning when tape is close to its end.
- Battery indicator will also warn a few minutes before the battery voltage drops below the minimum level needed to operate the camera/recorder and will remain continually lit when battery voltage is inadequate.
- Gain, shutter, contrast control, selected filter, white balance preset, audio metering, etc. can also be displayed plus error or 'OK' messages when white balancing and fault reports such as tape jammed, humidity, etc.

Contrast range

Every shot recorded by the camera/recorder has a variation of brightness contained within it. This variation of brightness is the contrast range of the scene. The ratio between the brightest part of the subject and the darkest part is the contrast ratio. The average exterior contrast ratio is approximately 150:1 but it can be as high as 1000:1. Whereas the contrast ratios of everyday locations and interiors can range from 20:1 to 1000:1, a video camera can only record a scene range of approximately 32:1. Peak white (100%) to black level (3.125%) is equivalent to five stops. The contrast range can be extended by compressing the highlights using a non-linear transfer characteristic when translating light into the television signal (see Electronic contrast control, page 80).

The result of recording a contrast range greater than the camera can handle is that highlights of the scene will appear a uniform white – details in them will be burnt out – and the darker tones of the scene will be a uniform black. The limiting factor for the reproduction of the acquired image is ultimately the display monitor on which it is viewed. The design, set-up and viewing conditions of the viewer's display monitor and the design of the signal path to the viewer all affect the final contrast range displayed. The darkest black that can be achieved will depend on the amount of light falling on the screen. The viewer also has the ability to increase the contrast on their set which will distort any production preference of image contrast.

The majority of image impairment in discriminating between tones occurs in highlights such as windows, skies, etc., but whether such limitations matter in practice will depend on how important tonal subtlety is in the shot. Loss of detail in a white costume may be noticeable but accepted as a subjective expression of a hot sunny day. A sports arena where a stadium shadow places half the pitch in darkness and half in bright sunlight may cause continuous exposure problems as the play moves in and out of the shadow. Either detail will be lost in the shadows or detail in sunlight will be burnt out.

Often, exposure is adjusted to allow the contrast range of the scene to be accurately reproduced on the recording. The aim is to avoid losing any variation between shades and at the same time to maintain the overall scene brightness relationships. Achieving the correct exposure for this type of shot therefore requires reproducing the detail in the highlights as well as in the shadows of the scene. Additionally, if a face is the subject of the picture then the skin tones need to be set between 70 and 75 per cent of peak white (may be a wider variation depending on country and skin tones; see Exposure continuity, page 76).

Alternatively, many productions require images that create a visual impression. The 'correct' exposure is less a matter of accurately reproducing a contrast range than the technique of setting a mood. Selecting the exposure for this type of shot is dependent on choosing a limited range of tones that creates the desired atmosphere that is appropriate to the subject matter.

The eye

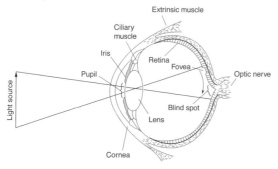

The eye perceives gradations of brightness by comparison. It is the ratio of one apparent brightness to another (and in what context) that determines how different or distinct the two appear to be. The just noticeable difference between the intensity of two light sources is discernible if one is approximately 8 per cent greater/lesser than the other, regardless of them both being of high or low luminous intensity (see Measurement of light, page 173). The amount of light entering the eye is controlled by an iris and it is also equipped with two types of cells; rods, that respond to dim light, and cones, receptor cells that respond to normal lighting levels. For a given iris opening, the average eye can accommodate a contrast range of 100:1, but visual perception is always a combination of eye and brain. The eye adapts fast to changing light levels and the brain interprets the eye's response in such a way that it appears as if we can scan a scene with a very wide contrast range (e.g. 500:1), and see it in a single glance.

The lens

The aperture of a zoom lens is the opening through which light is admitted. The maximum aperture is limited by the design of the lens (see Ramping, page 49). Adjusting the aperture controls the amount of light that reaches the CCDs. Aperture is identified by f number, the ratio of the focal length of the lens to the diameter of the effective aperture and is an indication of the amount of light passing through the lens and therefore an exposure control. An aperture set to $f2$ on a 50 mm lens would have an effective aperture of 25 mm. Increasing the f number (stopping down to $f4$) reduces the amount of light entering the camera. A wider aperture (opening up to $f1.4$) lets in more light (see Depth of field, page 48). Different designs of lenses may have variations in the configuration of lens

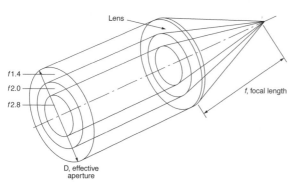

elements and type of glass and may operate with identical f numbers but admit unequal amounts of light. The T number is a formula which takes into account the transmittance of light and therefore lenses with similar T numbers will give the same image brightness.

Exposure continuity

A 'talking head' is probably the most common shot on television. Because the audience is usually more critical in their judgement of correct reproduction of skin tones, video pictures of faces are the most demanding in achieving correct exposure and usually require exposure levels that are high but are free from burn-out in highlight areas. The reflectivity of the human face varies enormously by reason of different skin pigments and make-up. In general, Caucasian face tones will tend to look right when a 'television white' of 60 per cent reflectivity is exposed to give peak white. White nylon shirts, white cartridge paper and chrome plate for example have reflectivity of above 60 per cent which is TV peak white. Without highlight compression (see page 80), these materials would lack detail if the face was exposed correctly. Average Caucasian skin tones reflect about 36 per cent of the light. As a generalization, face tones are approximately one stop down on peak white. If a scene peak white is chosen that has a reflectivity of 100 per cent, the face tones at 36 per cent reflectivity would look rather dark. To 'lift' the face to a more acceptable level in the tonal range of the shot, a scene peak white of 60 per cent reflectivity is preferable. This puts the face tone at approximately half this value or one stop down on the peak white.

Continuity of face tones
An important consideration when shooting the same face in different locations or lighting situations is to achieve some measure of continuity in face tones. There is a small amount of latitude in the colour temperature of light on a face. When white balanced to daylight sources (5500K), a 400K variation can be tolerated without being noticeable. There is a smaller latitude of colour temperature (150K) when white balanced to tungsten sources (3200K). As the viewer is unaware of the 'true' colour of the setting, a greater variation is acceptable in changes in colour temperature in this type of wide shot.

Continuity of face tone can be achieved if it is exposed to same value in different shots. The problem comes with variation in background and a variation in what is chosen as peak white. For example, a person wearing dark clothing positioned beside a white marble fireplace in a panelled room in one shot could have an exposure that set the marble surround at or near peak white so that the face was one stop down on this with the surrounding panelling showing no detail. If a reverse shot was to follow of the same person now seen only against dark panelling, the exposure could be set to show detail in the panelling and 'lift' the picture but this would push the face to a lighter tone than the preceding shot. To maintain continuity of face tone, the same exposure setting for the face would be needed as in the previous shot, with no tone in the frame achieving peak white. It may be necessary to control or adjust the contrast range of the shot to preserve the priority of the face tone at an acceptable level. In the above example, a more acceptable picture would be to light the background panelling to a level that showed some detail and texture whilst maintaining face tone continuity.

The 'film' look

A cinema screen is a highly reflective surface and the audience watch the giant projected images in a darkened auditorium. A television set is a small light box that emits its picture usually into a well-lit room often provided by high intensity daylight. The initial brightness ratio between black and white tones of a subject before a video camera often exceeds the dynamic range of any display monitor. This problem is exacerbated (because of the regulations imposed on the design of the transmission path) by a lower contrast ratio handling ability than is theoretically possible and because television is viewed in less than favourable lighting conditions.

These are simply the differences in viewing conditions between film and video. There are also a number of inherent differences in technology and technique. When film is recorded on 35 mm emulsion it can achieve (if desired) a much higher resolution and contrast range (e.g. some film negative can handle 1000:1) than is possible with standard video broadcasting. Video systems such as 24P 1080 lines (see Widescreen, page 106) are attempting to provide a transparent match between film and video but, to date, HDTV systems are making slow progress with consumers.

Two of the key distinctions between film and video is the use of detail enhancement in video to compensate for lower resolution compared to film and video's handling of highlights and overloads. Digital acquisition and processing allows more selective and subtle control of detail enhancement (see page 87) and CCDs with 600,000 pixels have such good resolution they hardly need contour correction. Digital acquisition allows manipulation of the soft shoulder of the video transfer characteristic to mimic the D log E (density versus the logarithm of exposure) curve of a film negative transfer characteristic. Digital video acquisition also allows the manipulation of gamma and linear matrix to customize the image (see Scene files, page 100). A 'non-video' look is attempted by techniques such as adjusting aperture correction, contour, auto knee, gamma, detail correction, and limited depth of field.

There are many attempts by video to imitate the film look. But which film? The deep focus and wide angle shots of *Citizen Kane* (1940)? The use of a long lens, shooting against the light with out of focus background and misty blobs of foreground colour of *Une Homme et une Femme* (1966)? The amber glow of *Days of Heaven* (1978), where cinematographer Nestor Almendros used the 'magic hour' (actually only 20–25 minutes) after the sun has set each day to produce a sky with light but no sun giving very soft-lit pictures without diffusion?

There are endless variations of style in the history of film making and contemporary fashion often dictates the 'look' at any particular time. Possibly there is a misunderstanding about the so-called 'film look' and the standard video 'look' that ignores the link between production budget and working techniques. Many feature films made for cinema release have a much larger budget than a video programme made for one or two transmissions. Money and customary film-making conventions, for example, allow a production technique that spends time staging action for a prime lens camera position developing a shot that is precisely lit, framed and with camera movement that is perfect or there is a retake. The stereotype multi-camera video production usually has 'compromise' written all over it, basically because television requires 24 hours to be filled day on day across a wide range of channels in the most cost-effective way possible. Zooming to accommodate unrehearsed action, compromise lighting for three/four camera shooting and a recording or transmission schedule that allows little or no time to seek production perfection. Plus a television content that has neither the high audience appeal or high profile performers presented with pace, tension and gloss achieved by editing over an extended post-production process. The 'look' of film may be more about the techniques of acquisition than the technology of acquisition.

77

Contrast control

The control of the contrast range can be achieved by several methods:

- The simplest is by avoiding high contrast situations. This involves selecting a framing that does not exceed the 32:1 contrast range the camera can handle. This obviously places severe restrictions on what can be recorded and is frequently not practical.
- A popular technique is to stage the participants of a shot against a background avoiding high contrast. In interiors, this may mean avoiding daylight, windows or closing curtains or blinds, or, in exteriors, avoiding shooting people in shadow (e.g. under a tree) with brightly lit backgrounds or against the skyline.
- If luminaries or reflectors of sufficient power and numbers are available they can be used to lighten shadows, modify the light on faces (see Lighting a face, page 180), etc. Even a lamp mounted on a camera can be a useful contrast modifier at dusk on an exterior or in some interior situations.

Staging

The rule of thumb that claims you should expose for the highlights and let the shadows look after themselves may give bright colourful landscapes but becomes very limited advice when shooting a face lit by sunlight under a cloudless summer sky. There may be more than three to four stops difference between the lit and the unlit side of the face. Ways of controlling the contrast in a shot need to be found if there is to be no loss of detail in highlights or shadows. A simple but effective method is to frame the shot to avoid areas of high contrast. Stage people against buildings or trees rather than the sky if there are bright sunlight conditions. Avoid direct sunlight on faces unless you can lighten shadows. With interiors, use curtains or blinds to reduce the amount of light entering windows and position people to avoid a high-contrast situation.

The problem of a bright sky can be controlled by a ND graduated filter if the horizon allows and other important elements of the shot are not in the top of frame. Low contrast filters and soft contrast filters may also help (see Effects filters, page 62).

Avoid staging people, if possible, against an even white cloud base. Either the overcast sky is burnt out or the face is in semi-silhouette if exposure for detail in the clouds is attempted.

Methods of altering contrast range by additional lamps or reflector boards are discussed in Lighting a face, page 180.

Portable waveform monitor

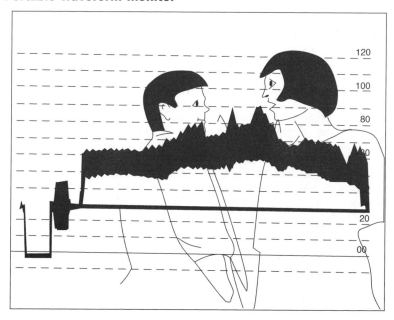

Diagrammatic representation of waveform supered on picture.

A portable waveform test measurement device will allow a waveform signal to be superimposed on a monitor screen. For example, a particular face tone signal level can be marked by a cursor. When the same signal level is required for another shot with the same face, the exposure, lighting, etc., can be adjusted so that the signal level signifying the face tone matches up to the memory cursor.

Electronic contrast control

As we discussed in Charge-coupled devices (page 18), the CCDs in the camera respond to light and convert the variations of brightness into variations in the electrical signal output. There is a minimum light level required to produce any signal (see Gain, noise and sensitivity, page 88). Below this level the camera processing circuits produce a uniform black. This is called black clip (see figure opposite). As the intensity of light increases, the signal increases proportionally until a point is reached when the signal is limited and no further increase is possible even if the light intensity continues to increase. This point is called the white clip level and identifies the maximum allowable video level. Any range of highlight tones above this level will be reproduced as the peak white tone where the signal is set to be clipped. Variation in the brightness of objects will only be transferred into a video signal if they are exposed to fall between the black clip level and white clip level.

This straight line response to light is modified to allow a greater range of brightness to be accommodated by reducing the slope of the transfer characteristic at the top end of the CCD's response to highlights (see figure opposite). This is called the knee of the response curve and the point at which the knee begins and the shape of the response above the knee alters the way the video camera handles highlights. By reducing the slope of the transfer characteristic a greater range of highlights can be compressed so that separation remains and they do not go into 'overload' above the white clip level and become one featureless tone. If the shape of this portion of the graph is more of a curve, the compression of highlights is non-linear and the transition to overload is more gradual.

Modifying this transfer slope provides the opportunity to alter the gamma of the camera (see Gamma and linear matrix, page 102) and a method of handling contrast scenes which exceed the 32:1 contrast range of the standard video camera response.

Exposing for highlights

A highlight part of the shot (e.g. white sheets on a washing line in bright sun) which may produce a signal five times peak white level can be compressed into the normal video dynamic range. With the above example this means that the darker areas of the picture can be correctly exposed whilst at the same time maintaining some detail in the sheets.

If someone was standing in a room against a window and it was necessary to expose for exterior detail and the face, without additional lighting or filtering the windows, it would not be possible to reproduce detail in both face and exterior. Using highlight compression, the highlights outside the window would be squashed and although their relative brightness to each other would not be faithfully reproduced, the compression would allow the reproduction of detail across a greater range to be recorded.

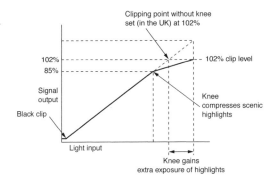

Clipping point without knee
set (in the UK) at 102%

102%
85%

102% clip level

Signal
output

Knee
compresses scenic
highlights

Black clip

Light input

Knee gains
extra exposure of highlights

The 'knee' which is introduced in the camera head amplifiers progressively compresses highlights which otherwise would be lost in the peak white clipper. It extends the camera's response to a high contrast range but with some loss of linearity. Many cameras also provide a black stretch facility which helps to reveal detail in the black areas, but will also introduce some extra noise.

Variable slope highlight control

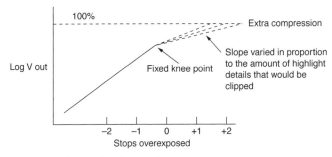

100%

Log V out

Extra compression

Fixed knee point

Slope varied in proportion
to the amount of highlight
details that would be
clipped

−2   −1   0   +1   +2
Stops overexposed

Variable knee point highlight control

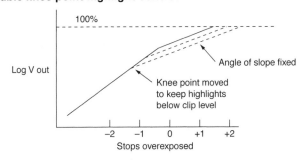

100%

Log V out

Angle of slope fixed

Knee point moved
to keep highlights
below clip level

−2   −1   0   +1   +2
Stops overexposed

Transient highlights

One type of contrast control uses average feedback and avoids unnecessary compression by not responding to transient high intensity light such as car head-lamps. If highlight compression is used with a normal contrast range scene (below 40:1) there is the risk that highlights will be distorted and the compression may result in a lower contrast reproduction than the original. Low contrast pictures have little impact and are visually less dynamic.

Adjusting exposure

There are various ways of deciding the correct exposure:

■ using the zebra exposure indicator in the viewfinder (see page 84);
■ manually adjusting the iris setting whilst looking at the viewfinder picture;
■ using the auto iris-exposure circuit built into the camera.

Many cameramen use a combination of all three and some cameramen use a light meter.

Manual adjustment

The simplest method is to look at the viewfinder picture (make certain that it is correctly set up – see page 70) and turn the iris ring on the lens to a larger f number (this reduces the amount of light reaching the CCDs) if the brightest parts of the scene have no detail in them, or to a smaller f number (increasing the amount of light reaching the CCDs) if there is no detail in important parts of the subject. In some situations there may be insufficient light even with the iris wide open to expose the shot. Check that no ND filter is being used and then either switch in additional gain (see page 88), change the shutter if it is set to a faster speed than 1/50th or 1/60th (depending on country) or add additional light (see Lighting topics, pages 172–85).

If you are uncertain about your ability to judge exposure with this method (and it takes time to become experienced in all situations) then confirm your exposure setting by depressing the instant auto-exposure button which gives the camera's auto-exposure estimation of the correct f number. When the button is released you can either stay at the camera setting or return to your manual estimation.

The camera as light meter

A television camera has been called the most expensive light meter produced. If auto-exposure is selected, the feedback to the iris can be instantaneous and the auto circuit will immediately stop down the lens if any significant increase of scene brightness is detected. Auto-exposure works by averaging the picture brightness (see figures opposite) and therefore needs to be used intelligently. In some cameras, different portions of the frame can be monitored and the response rate to the change of exposure can be selected. In general, expose for the main subject of the shot and check that the auto-iris is not compensating for large areas of peak brightness (e.g. overcast sky) in the scene.

The lens iris is controlled by the highest reading from the red, green or blue channel and therefore the auto circuit reacts whenever any colour combination approaches peak signal. This auto decision making about exposure may have disadvantages as well as advantages. The rate of response of the auto-iris system needs to be fast enough to keep up with a camera panning from a bright to a dark scene, but not so responsive that it instantly over- or under-exposes the picture for a momentary high-light brightness (e.g. a sudden background reflection).

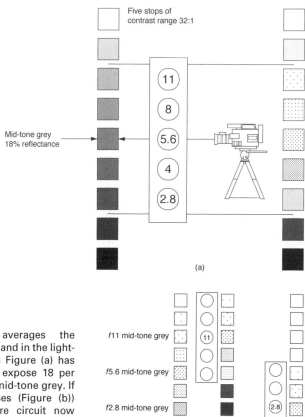

Five stops of contrast range 32:1

Mid-tone grey 18% reflectance

(a)

Auto-exposure averages the scene brightness and in the lighting conditions in Figure (a) has selected *f*5.6 to expose 18 per cent reflectance mid-tone grey. If the light increases (Figure (b)) the auto-exposure circuit now selects *f*11 to expose for a mid-tone grey. If the light decreases (Figure (c)), *f*2.8 is chosen to expose for a mid-tone grey.

*f*11 mid-tone grey

*f*5.6 mid-tone grey

*f*2.8 mid-tone grey

(b)

(c)

Auto-exposure problems

A common problem with auto-exposure occurs when an interview is being recorded and auto-exposure has been selected and left on. The interviewee may be correctly exposed at the start of the interview but if any highly reflective object enters the background of the frame then the auto-exposure circuit may be triggered and will stop down the iris to expose for detail. The interviewee's face will be underexposed. Additionally, there may be a problem with changing light conditions such as intermittent sunlight requiring significant and rapid changes in face exposure which may be intrusive and visible if controlled by an auto-exposure rapid exposure. If using auto-exposure, check that the rate of pan is in step with the ability of the auto-iris to change exposure. Some cameras have switchable auto-iris response rates to suit the changing requirements of camera movement. If working with a camera for the first time check that the auto-iris is correctly aligned.

Zebra exposure indicators

The zebra pattern is a visual indicator in the viewfinder when areas of the picture have reached a certain signal level. If the zebra exposure indicator is switched on, those elements of the image that are above this pre-set level are replaced by diagonal stripes in the picture. The cameraman can respond by closing the iris to adjust the exposure until part or all of the zebra diagonals have been removed.

Onset of zebra level

The level at which the zebra indicator is triggered is obviously a critical factor in this method of assessing exposure and can be adjusted to suit particular operational preferences. Some camera designs have their zebra stripe indicator driven by the luminance signal. The zebra stripe warning is then only valid for nearly white subjects and exposure of strongly coloured areas may go into over-exposure without warning. Other systems use any of the red, green or blue outputs which exceed the selected signal level to trigger the zebra indicator.

Selecting zebra level

The exposure point at which the zebra indicator is triggered can be a personal operational preference but criteria to consider when setting that point are:

■ If there is a 'pool' of cameras in use then that point should be standard on all cameras.

■ The onset point should be close to full exposure but should warn before full burn-out occurs.

■ The zebra stripe indicator should not obscure important picture information such as the face but it should indicate when flesh tones are in danger of going into over-exposure.

Some UK zebra onset levels are 90–95 per cent for RGB-driven systems and 68–70 per cent for luminance systems, but the final limiting factor on exposure level is loss of detail, either to noise in the blacks or burn-out in the peak white clipper. Both losses are irrecoverable.

Adjusting f number

Controlling the light through the lens can be by aperture or ND filter. The f number is defined as a ratio between focal length and the effective diameter of the lens aperture (see Depth of field, page 48).

The f number is not an accurate indication of the speed of the lens because the f number formula is based on the assumption that the lens transmits 100 per cent of the incident light. Because of the variation in the number of elements in the lens and the variation in lens design, different lenses may have different transmittance. Two lenses with the same f number may transmit different amounts of light to the prism block.

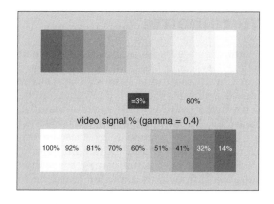

video signal % (gamma = 0.4)

=3%   60%

100%   92%   81%   70%   60%   51%   41%   32%   14%

A nine-step wedge chart + a 'super black' in the centre. The peak white wedge has 60% reflectance. The wedge tones are graded as a % of peak white of the video signal and form equal changes in signal output when displayed on a waveform monitor. The background tone is 60% of peak white representing a tone with 18% reflectivity. The wedges are displayed with a gamma correction of 0.4.

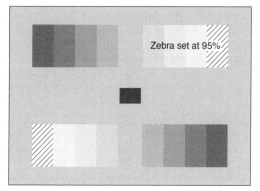

Zebra set at 95%

With a zebra setting triggered by any part of the signal going above 95%, only nearly peak white picture areas such as the 100% wedge on the grey scale will display the diagonal pattern.

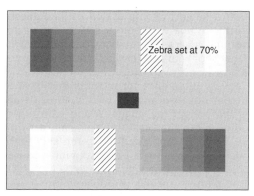

Zebra set at 70%

With a zebra setting triggered by any part of the signal falling between 70% (approximate reflectivity of the average Caucasian face tone) and 80%, the appropriate step wedge will display the diagonal pattern.

Using a properly lined-up and exposed camera on a grey scale will give a rough indication of how the zebra setting has been set up. The signal displayed on a waveform will allow more accurate measurement. On most cameras, the zebra setting can be adjusted to suit individual requirements.

If a grey scale with a 32:1 contrast is correctly exposed, a reduction in exposure by five stops will reduce the signal to almost zero, confirming the five-stop dynamic range of a camera with no electronic contrast control.

Production requirements

It is easy to chase after the 'correct' exposure for a shot and lose sight of the purpose of the production. News and factual programmes have the fairly simple visual requirement of 'see it and hear it'. This usually requires a technique that produces a neutral record of the event with the least discernible influence of the cameraman's attitude to the material. The choice of exposure is based on the aim of providing the clearest possible image of the action. The 'correct' exposure in these circumstances is the one that produces clarity of image. Other programme genres have more diverse production aims. It is not simply a question of finding the 'correct' exposure but of finding an exposure that reflects a mood, emotion or feeling.

The appearance of the image has an important influence on how the audience reacts to the visual message. The choice of lens, camera position and framing play a crucial part in guiding that response. The choice of exposure and the resultant contrast of tones is another powerful way to guide the viewer's eye to the important parts of the frame.

The cameraman can manipulate contrast by the choice of exposure and gamma setting (see page 100), to produce a range of different images such as:

- stark contrasty pictures suggesting a brutal realism;
- pictures with no highlights or blacks – simply a range of greys;
- low key pictures with a predominance of dark tones and heavy contrast;
- high key pictures with a predominance of light tones, little depth and contrast.

If the production is aiming at a subjective impression of its subject, then the choice of the style of the image will require a high degree of continuity. The viewer will become aware if one shot does not match and may invest the content of that shot with special significance as apparently attention has been drawn to it.

A television engineer may have a preference for pictures that have a peak white with no highlight crushing, a good black with shadow detail and an even spread of tones throughout the image. Along with other correct engineering specifications, this is often called a technically acceptable picture. Using a low contrast filter, flares and filling the shot with smoke may lift the blacks to dark grey, eliminate any peak white, cause highlights to bloom and definition to be reduced. It may also be the exact requirement for the shot at that particular production moment. Remember that the term broadcast quality comes from the engineering requirements for the video signal, not the way the picture looks. There are no hard-and-fast rules to be followed in the creative use of exposure. Although resultant images may lack sparkle because of low contrast and fail to use the full contrast range that television is capable of providing, if the pictures create the required mood, then the aims of the production have been satisfied.

Image enhancement and contour correction

As we have discussed, the resolution of the video image is partly limited by the CCD design (although this is continuously improving), and partly by the constraints of the video signal system. In most camera/recorder formats, image enhancement is used to improve picture quality. One technique is to raise the contrast at the dark-to-light and light-to-dark transitions, to make the edges of objects appear sharper, both horizontally and vertically. This is done electronically by overshooting the signal at the transition between different tones to improve the rendering of detail. This edge enhancement is often applied to high-frequency transitions and can be controlled by adjusting various processing circuits such as aperture correction, contour, detail correction, etc.

It is important to remember that the degree of artificial enhancement is controllable with, for example, separate controls for vertical and horizontal enhancement. When overdone, artificial enhancement of picture resolution is often the main distinguishing characteristic between a video and a film image. Because an audience may connect this type of image quality with multi-camera coverage of sport or actuality events, an electronic image is often paradoxically considered more realistic and credible.The amount of enhancement is a subjective value and will vary with production genre and production taste. It is difficult to remove image enhancement in post-production although it may be added.

Detail enhancement and skin tone detail

The degree of electronic manipulation of edge detail is variable, but one limiting factor in the amount of enhancement that can be used is the adverse effect on faces. When pictures are 'over-contoured' skin detail can appear intrusive and unnatural; every imperfection is enhanced and becomes noticeable.

To overcome this problem, some cameras provide for selective reduction in skin detail to soften the appearance of faces. While variable electronic 'sharpening' or image enhancement may be applied to the overall shot, skin tone detail control allows for the separate handling of the specific degree of enhancement on any selected facial tones within that scene.

This is achieved by a circuit that separates facial skin colour from all other colours in a given shot, and its electronic detail level can be reduced without affecting other areas of the picture. The specific skin colour to be treated in this way is selectable and can be memorized to follow movement or recalled for subsequent shots. Some cameras have as many as three independent skin tone detail circuits.

Gain, noise and sensitivity

Camera sensitivity is usually quoted by camera manufacturers with reference to four interlinking elements:

1. A subject with peak white reflectivity.
2. Scene illumination.
3. f number.
4. Signal-to-noise ratio for a stated signal.

It is usually expressed as being the resulting f number when exposed to a peak white subject with 89.9 per cent reflectance lit by 2000 lux quoting the signal/noise ratio. For most current digital cameras this is at least f8 or better with a signal/noise ratio of 60 dB. This standard rating is provided to allow different camera sensitivity to be compared and is not an indication of how much light or at what stop the camera should be used (see page 176).

Noise

The sensitivity of the camera could be increased by simply greater amplification of weak signals but this degrades the picture by adding 'noise' generated by the camera circuits. The signal/noise ratio is usually measured without contour or gamma correction. As manufacturers vary in the way they state camera sensitivity, comparison between different models often require a conversion of the specification figures. In general, with the same f number, the higher the signal/noise ratio and the lower the scene illuminance (lux), the more sensitive the camera.

Gain

The gain of the head amplifiers can be increased if insufficient light is available to adequately expose the picture. The amount of additional gain is calibrated in dBs. For example, switching in +6 dB of gain is the equivalent of opening up the lens by one f stop, which would double the amount of light available to the sensors. The precise amount of switched gain available differs from camera to camera. A camera may have a +9 dB and +18 dB switch with an additional +24 dB available from a pre-set inside the camera. Other camera designs allow a user pre-set to programme the value of each step of switchable gain. Some cameras allow a specific f number (aperture priority) to be selected and then automatically increase gain if the light level decreases. This may increase noise to an unacceptable level without the cameraman being aware of how much gain is switched in. Cameras may have a negative gain setting (i.e. a reduction in gain). This reduces noise and is a way of controlling depth of field without the use of filters. For example, an exposure is set for an aperture setting of f2.8 with 0 dB gain. If 6 dB of negative gain is switched in, the aperture will need to be opened to f2 to maintain correct exposure and therefore depth of field will be reduced.

Gain and stop comparison

+3 dB is equivalent to opening up 0.5 stop.
+6 dB is equivalent to opening up 1 stop.
+9 dB is equivalent to opening up 1.5 stops.
+12 dB is equivalent to opening up 2 stops.
+18 dB is equivalent to opening up 3 stops.
+24 dB is equivalent to opening up 4 stops.

The extra gain in amplification is a corresponding decrease in the signal-to-noise ratio and results in an increase in noise in the picture. For an important news story shot with insufficient light, this may be an acceptable trade-off.

Calculating the ASA equivalent for a video camera

A video broadcast camera/corder with a good auto-exposure system is in effect a very reliable light meter. Most cameramen use a combination of manual exposure, instant auto-exposure and/or the zebra exposure indicator (see pages 84–5), but some cameramen with a film background often feel more comfortable using a light meter to check exposure level. In order to achieve this, the sensitivity of the camera requires an equivalent ASA rating which is logarithmic, e.g. doubling ASA numbers allows a decrease of one stop. There are several methods to determine the rating, including the following formula:

- The sensitivity of the video camera is quoted using a stated light level, signal-to-noise level, a surface with a known reflectance value and with the shutter set at 1/50 (PAL working).
- Japanese camera manufacturers use a standard reflectance of 89.9% as peak white while UK television practice is to use a 60% reflectance value as peak white therefore an illuminance level of 3000 lux must be used when transposing a rating of 2000 lux with 89.9% reflectance to 60% peak white working.

The formula below is for 60% reflectance, 1/50th shutter speed.

$$ASA = \frac{(f\ number)^2 \times 1250\ (a\ mathematical\ constant)}{illuminance\ in\ ft\ candles*}$$

*(10.76 lux = 1 foot candle, e.g. 3000 lux/10.76 = 278.81 ft candles)

Year-on-year video camera sensitivity has increased. In the last few years, a negative gain setting has begun to appear on cameras. Why not have the negative figure as 0 dB gain? One reason may be that manufacturers like to advertise their cameras as more sensitive than their competitors and a higher notional '0 dB' allows a smaller stop. Another suggestion is that on a multi-camera shoot, lights can be set for a 0 dB exposure and thereafter, if a lower depth of field is required, negative gain can be switched in and the iris opened without resorting to the use of an ND filter.

Image intensifiers

When shooting in very low light levels (e.g. moonlight) image intensifiers can be fitted between camera and lens to boost sensitivity. The resultant pictures lack contrast and colour but produce recognizable images for news or factual programmes.

Electronic shutters

One complete frame of the standard PAL television signal is made up of two interlaced fields with a repetition rate of 50 fields per second (25 complete frames per second). The CCD scans the image 50 times a second which is the 'normal' shutter speed of a PAL video camera. CCDs can be adjusted to reduce the time taken to collect light from a field (see figure opposite), and reducing the length of the read-out pulse is equivalent to increasing the shutter speed. This electronic shutter reduces the time the CCDs are exposed to the image by switched steps, improving reproduction of motion but reducing sensitivity.

Movement blur

The standard shutter speed (PAL) is set to 1/50th second. A fast-moving subject in front of the camera at this shutter speed will result in a blurred image due to the movement of the subject during the 1/50th of a second exposure. Reducing the time interval of exposure by increasing the electronic shutter speed improves the image definition of moving subjects and is therefore particularly useful when slow motion replay of sporting events is required. But reducing the time interval also reduces the amount of light captured by the CCD and therefore increasing shutter speed requires the aperture to be opened to compensate for the reduction in light.

Shutter speeds

The shutter speed can be altered in discrete steps such as 1/60, 1/125, 1/500, 1/1000 or 1/2000 of a second or, on some cameras, continuously varied in 0.5 Hz steps. Often, when shooting computer displays, black or white horizontal bands appear across the computer display. This is because the scanning frequencies of most computer displays differ from the (50 Hz) frequency of the TV system (PAL). Altering the shutter speed in discrete steps allows the camera exposure interval to precisely match the computer refresh scanning frequency and reduce or even eliminate the horizontal streaking.

Pulsed light sources and shutter speed

Fluorescent tubes, HMI discharge lamps and neon signs do not produce a constant light output but give short pulses of light at a frequency dependent on the mains supply (see figure, page 69). Using a 625 PAL camera lit by 60 Hz mains fluorescent (e.g. when working away from the country of origin mains standard) will produce severe flicker. Some cameras are fitted with 1/60th shutter so that the exposure time is one full period of the lighting.

If a high shutter speed is used with HMI/MSR light sources, the duration of the pulsed light may not coincide with the 'shutter' open and a colour drift will be observed to cycle, usually between blue and yellow. It can be eliminated by switching the shutter off. FT sensors have a mechanical shutter which cannot be switched off and therefore the problem will remain.

Shutter pulse

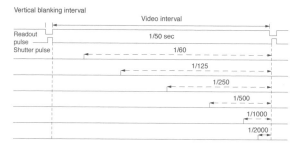

shutter I/f-number

Shutter	f-number	Shutter	f-number
1/50		1/500	approx. 3 stops
1/125	approx. 1 stop	1/1000	approx. 4 stops
1/250	approx. 2 stops	1/2000	approx. 5 stops

Time-lapse controls

Time lapse is a technique where at specified intervals the camera is programmed to make a brief exposure. Depending on the type of movement in the shot, the time interval and the time the camera is recording, movement which we may not be aware of in normal perceptual time is captured. The classic examples are a flower coming into bloom with petals unfolding, clouds racing across the sky or car headlights along city streets at night shot from above, comet tailing in complex stop/start patterns. Time lapse can also be used as an animation technique where objects are repositioned between each brief recording. When the recording is played at normal speed, the objects appear to be in motion. The movement will be smooth if sufficient number of exposures and the amount of movement between each shot has been carefully planned.

The crucial decisions when planning a time-lapse sequence is to estimate how long the sequence will run at normal speed, how long the real-time event takes to complete the cycle that will be speeded up and the duration of each discrete 'shot'. For example, do you shoot every minute, every hour, or once a day? These decisions will be influenced by the flexibility of the time-lapse facility on the camera in use. Some models will allow you to compile time-lapse sequences with shots lasting just an eighth of a second; others will only allow you to fit in three shots on each second of tape.

For example, a speeded-up sequence is required of an open air market being set up, then filled with shoppers and finally the market traders packing away to end on a deserted street. If you plan to have a normal running time of 5 seconds to set up, 5 seconds of shopping during the day and 5 seconds of clearing away you need to time how long the market traders take to open and close their stalls. If this takes 30 minutes in the morning and the same in the evening, and your camera will record 0.25 second frames, the total number of shots will be 15 seconds divided by 0.25 = 60 separate shots. The time lapse will be shot in three separate sequences. Sequence 1 (opening) will require 30 minutes divided by 20 shots equals a shot every minute and a half. Sequence 2 can be shot any time during the day when the market is crowded and will be the same ratio of 1 shot every 1.5 minutes for 30 minutes. The end sequence will be a repeat of sequence 1 taken at the end of the day. The light level may well change within and between sequences and can be compensated by using auto-iris or, if the change in light is wanted, setting a compromise exposure to reveal the changing light levels.

91

Timecode

Timecode enables every recorded frame of video to be numbered. A number representing hours, minutes, seconds and frame (television signal) is recorded. There are 25 frames per second in the PAL TV signal and so the frame (PAL television signal) number will run from 1 to 25 and reset at the end of every second. In a continuous recording, for example, one frame may be numbered 01:12:45:22, with the following frame numbered 01:12:45:23. This allows precise identification of each frame when editing. The camera operator arranges, at the start of a shoot, the method of frame numbering by adjusting the timecode controls which are usually situated on the side of the camera on the video recorder part of the unit (see figure opposite).

The choice is between numbering each frame with a consecutive number each time the camera records. This is called 'record run' timecode. Alternatively, the camera's internal clock can be adjusted to coincide with the actual time of day and whenever a recording takes place, the time at that instant will be re-coded against the frame. This is usually called 'time of day' or 'free run' recording. The decision on which type of timecode to record will depend on editing and production requirements (see Timecode and production, page 94).

Historically there have been two methods of recording this identification number:

■ **Longitudinal timecode:** Longitudinal timecode (LTC) is recorded with a fixed head on a track reserved for timecode. It can be decoded at normal playback speed and at fast forward or rewind but it cannot be read unless the tape is moving as there is no replayed signal to be decoded.

■ **Vertical interval timecode:** Vertical interval timecode (VITC) numbers are time-compressed to fit the duration of one TV line and recorded as a pseudo video signal on one of the unused lines between frames. It is recorded as a variation in signal amplitude once per frame as binary digits. 0 equals black and 1 equals peak white. Although they are factory set, if needed, some cameras can be adjusted to insert VITC on two non-consecutive lines. Unlike longitudinal timecode, VITC timecode is recorded as a pseudo TV signal and can be read in still mode which is often required when editing. Longitudinal timecode is useful when previewing the tape at speed. For editing purposes, the two timecode recording methods have complemented each other.

Digital timecode

Digital signal processing has allowed timecode to be stored as digital data in the sub code track of DVCPro and Digital-S tape formats. Because this is written as data it can be read in still mode as well as fast forward/rewind. During editing, timecode can be read when shuttling through the tape to find a shot but can still be read in still mode.

Timecode track (DVCPro)

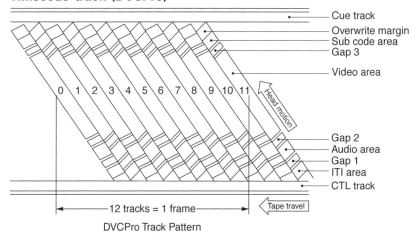

DVCPro Track Pattern

The sub-code area of the DVCPro track is used to record timecode and user-bit data. It can be read in still mode and during high-speed fast-forward and rewind of the tape.

CTL: control track

This is a linear track recorded on the edge of the tape at frame frequency as a reference pulse for the running speed of the replay VTR. It provides data for a frame counter and can be displayed on the camera's LCD (liquid crystal display). It is important for editing purposes that the recorded cassette has a continuous control track and it is customary to reset to zero at the start of each tape.

When CTL is selected to be displayed, the numbers signifying hours, minutes, seconds and frames are a translation of the reference pulse into a convenient method of displaying tape-elapsed time. Although equivalent, this time is not a read-out of the recorded timecode and if CTL is reset to zero in mid-cassette and the tape rewound, the displayed numbers would count backwards with a minus sign. One of the main purposes of striping a tape for editing purposes is to record a continuous control track (see Editing technology, page 146). To ensure a continuous control track on acquisition, see page 97 for procedure when changing a battery or using a partially recorded cassette. Also be aware that if CTL is selected in mid-cassette and the Reset button is depressed, the control track will reset to zero and will no longer indicate tape-elapsed time.

Timecode and production

Timecode is an essential tool for editing a programme (see Camerawork and editing, page 144). If a shot log has been compiled on acquisition or in post-production review, the timecode identifies which shots are preselected and structures off-line editing. There are two types of timecode available to accommodate the great diversity in programme content and production methods. The cameraman should establish at the start of the shoot which method is required.

■ **Record run:** Record run only records a frame identification when the camera is recording. The timecode is set to zero at the start of the day's operation and a continuous record is produced on each tape covering all takes. It is customary practice to record the tape number in place of the hour section on the timecode. For example, the first cassette of the day would start 01.00.00.00 and the second cassette would start 02.00.00.00. Record run is the preferred method of recording timecode on most productions.

■ **Free run:** In free run, the timecode is set to the actual time of day and when synchronized is set to run continuously. Whether the camera is recording or not, the internal clock will continue to operate. When the camera is recording, the actual time of day will be recorded on each frame. This mode of operation is useful in editing when covering day-long events such as conferences or sport. Any significant action can be logged by time as it occurs and can subsequently be quickly found by reference to the time of day code on the recording. In free run (time of day), a change in shot will produce a gap in timecode proportional to the amount of time that elapsed between actual recordings. Missing timecode numbers can cause problems with an edit controller when it rolls back from intended edit point and is unable to find the timecode number it expects there (i.e. the timecode of the frame to cut on, minus the pre-roll time).

Shot logging

An accurate log of each shot (also known as a dope sheet) with details of content and start and finish timecode is invaluable at the editing stage and pre-editing stage. It requires whoever is keeping the record (usually a PA, production assistant) to have visual access to the LCD display on the rear of the camera. As the timecode readout is often situated behind the cameraman's head, it is often difficult for the PA to read although the Hold button will freeze the LCD readout without stopping the timecode. There are a number of repeat timecode readers which are either attached to the camera in a more accessible position, or fed by a cable from the timecode output socket away from the camera or fed by a radio transmitter which eliminates trailing cables. A less precise technique is sometimes practised when using time of day timecode. This requires the camera and the PA's stopwatch to be synchronized to precisely the same time of day at the beginning of the shoot. The PA can then refer to her stopwatch to record timecode shot details. It is not frame accurate and requires occasional synchronizing checks between camera and watch, with the watch being adjusted if there has been drift.

94

Setting timecode

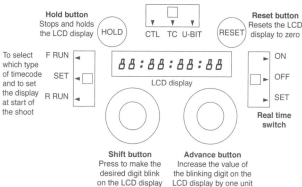

Display switch
This controls what is displayed on the LCD

Hold button
Stops and holds
the LCD display

HOLD

CTL TC U-BIT

Reset button
Resets the LCD
display to zero

RESET

To select
which type
of timecode
and to set
the display
at start of
the shoot

F RUN
SET
R RUN

$88:88:88:88$

LCD display

ON
OFF
SET

**Real time
switch**

Shift button
Press to make the
desired digit blink
on the LCD display

Advance button
Increase the value of
the blinking digit on the
LCD display by one unit

To set record run timecode

1 Set DISPLAY switch to TC.
2 Set REAL TIME switch to OFF.
3 Set F-RUN/R-RUN to SET position. The display will stop at its existing value, and the first numeral (representing hours) will start to flash.
4 Press RESET to zero counter if required.
5 Switch F-RUN/SET/R-RUN to R-RUN position.
6 The timecode will increase each time the camera records.
  If you wish to use the hour digit to identify each tape (e.g. 1 hour equals first tape, 2 hours equals second tape, etc.), set the hour timecode with the SHIFT and ADVANCE button.
    SHIFT: Press to make the hour digit blink.
    ADVANCE: Press to increase the value of the blinking digit by one unit to equal the cassette tape in use.
  If the F-RUN/R-RUN switch should be accidentally knocked to the SET position, the timecode will not increase during a recording and only the static number will be recorded. Also, if display is switched to CTL and SET is selected, time-code will be displayed and ADVANCE and SHIFT will alter its value but leave the CTL value unaffected. CTL can only be zeroed, otherwise it will continue to increase irrespective of tape changes.

Real time

1 Set DISPLAY switch to TC.
2 Set REAL TIME switch to OFF.
3 Set F-RUN/R-RUN to SET.
4 Press RESET to zero counter.
5 Set the time of day with the SHIFT and ADVANCE buttons until the timecode reads a minute or so ahead of actual time. The numeral that is selected to be altered by the SHIFT button will blink in the SET position:
    SHIFT: Press to make the desired digit blink.
    ADVANCE: Press to increase the value of the blinking digit by one unit.
6 When real time equals 'timecode time', switch to F-RUN and check that time-code counter is increasing in sync with 'real' time. If you switch back to SET the display stops, and does not continue until you return to F-RUN (i.e. the clock has been stopped and is no longer in step with the time of day it was set to).
User-bit: If any USER-BIT information is required, then always set up user-bit information first. Wait approximately 20 seconds after camera is turned on.

Timecode lock

So far we have discussed setting the timecode in one camera but there are many occasions when two or more camcorders are on the same shoot. If each camera simply recorded its own timecode there would be problems in editing when identifying and synchronizing shots to intercut. The basic way of ensuring the timecode is synchronized in all cameras in use is by cables connected between the TC OUT socket on the 'master' camera to the TC IN socket on the 'slave' camera. Another cable is then connected to the TC OUT of the first 'slave' camera and then connected to the TC IN of the second 'slave' camera and so on although in a multi-camera shoot, it is preferable to genlock all the cameras to a central master sync pulse generator. This is essential if, as well as each camera recording its own output, a mixed output selected from all cameras is also recorded.

The TC OUT socket provides a feed of the timecode generated by the camera regardless of what is displayed on the LCD window. A number of cameras can be linked in this way but with the limitation of always maintaining the 'umbilical' cord of the interconnecting cables. They must all share the same method of timecode (i.e. free run or record run) with one camera generating the 'master' timecode and the other cameras locked to this. The procedure is:

- Cable between cameras as above.
- Switch on the cameras and select F-Run (free run) on the 'slave' cameras.
- Select SET on the 'master' camera and enter the required timecode information (e.g. zero the display if that is the production requirement). Then switch to record-run and begin recording.
- In turn start recording on the first 'slave' camera, and then the second and so on. Although recording can start in any order on the 'slave' cameras, the above sequence routine can identify any faulty (or misconnected!) cables.
- All the cameras should now display the same timecode. Check by audibly counting down the seconds on the 'master' whilst the other cameramen check their individual timecode read-out.
- During any stop/start recordings, the 'master' camera must always run to record before the 'slave' cameras. If there are a number of recording sessions, the synchronization of the timecode should periodically be confirmed.

Often it is not practical and severely restricting to remain cable connected and the cameras will need to select free run after the above synchronization. Some cameras will drift over time but at least this gives some indication of the time of recording without providing 'frame' accurate timecode. Alternatively, a method known as 'jam sync' provides for a 'rough' synchronization over time without cables (see opposite).

Jam sync

The set-up procedure is:

- From the 'master' TC OUT socket connect a cable with a BNC connector to the 'slave' TC IN.
- Power up the cameras and select free run on the 'slave' camera.
- On the 'master' camera select SET and enter 'time of day' some seconds ahead of the actual time of day.
- When actual time coincides with LCD display switch to free run.
- If both cameras display the same timecode, disconnect the cable.
- Because of camera drift, the above synchronization procedure will need to be repeated whenever practical to ensure continuity of timecode accuracy.

Pseudo jam sync

Pseudo jam sync is the least accurate timecode lock, but often pressed into service as a last resort if a BNC connector cable is damaged and will not work. The same time of day in advance of actual time of day is entered into all cameras (with no cable connections), and with one person counting down from their watch, when actual time of the day is reached, all cameras are simultaneously (hopefully) switched to F-RUN. This is obviously not frame accurate and the timecode error between cameras is liable to increase during the shoot.

Reviewing footage

Broadcast camcorders are equipped with a memory, powered by a small internal battery similar to the computer EPROM battery. It will retain some operational values for several days or more. There should be no loss of timecode when changing the external battery but precautions need to be taken if the cassette is rewound to review recorded footage or the cassette is removed from the camera and then reinserted.

After reviewing earlier shots, the tape must be accurately reset to the point immediately after the last required recorded material. On many cameras, time-code will be set by referring to the last recorded timecode. Reset to the first section of blank tape after the last recorded material, and then use the return or edit search button on the lens or zoom control so that the camera can roll back and then roll forward to park precisely at the end of the last recorded shot. This is an edit in-camera facility. CTL will not be continuous unless you record from this point. There will be a gap in record-run timecode if you over-record material as the timecode continues from the last recorded timecode (even if this is now erased), unless you reset timecode. CTL cannot be reset to follow on continuously but can only be zeroed. Allow 10 seconds after the start of the first recording to ensure CTL stability in post-production.

Recording on a partly recorded cassette

Insert the cassette and replay to the point at which the new recording is to start. Note the timecode at this point before you stop the replay, otherwise, with the tape stopped, the timecode will read the last timecode figure from the previous tape/shot. Select SET and enter a timecode that is a few seconds in advance of the noted timecode so it will be obvious in editing that timecode has been restarted. CTL cannot be adjusted other than zeroed. To ensure edit stability, post-production requires a 10-second run-up on the next recorded shot before essential action. (See also page 99.)

Menus

Digital signal processing allows data to be easily manipulated and settings memorized. In nearly all digital camera/recorder formats, all the electronic variables on the camera can be stored as digital values in a memory and can be controlled via menu screens displayed in the viewfinder. These values can be recalled as required or saved on a removable storage file. This provides for greater operational flexibility in customizing images compared to analogue work. Menus therefore provide for a greater range of control with the means to memorize a specific range of setting. There are, however, some disadvantages compared to mechanical control in day-to-day camerawork. Selecting a filter wheel position is a simple mechanical operation on many cameras. If the selection is only achievable through a menu (because the filter wheel position needs to be memorized for a set-up card), time is taken finding the required page and then changing the filter wheel setting.

Adjustment

Access to the current settings of the electronic values is by way of menus which are displayed, when required, on the viewfinder screen. These menus are accessed by using the menu switch on the camera. Movement around the menus is by button or toggle switch that identifies which camera variable is currently selected. When the menu system is first accessed, the operation menu pages are usually displayed. A special combination of the menu controls allows access to the user menu which, in turn, provides access to the other menus depending on whether or not they have been unlocked for adjustment. Normally only those variables associated with routine recording (e.g. gain, shutter, etc.) are instantly available. Seldom used items can be deleted from the user menu to leave only those menu pages essential to the required set-up procedure. Menu pages are also available on the video outputs. The values that can be adjusted are grouped under appropriate headings listed in a master menu.

Default setting

With the opportunity to make adjustments that crucially affect the appearance of the image (e.g. gamma, matrix, etc.), it is obviously necessary that the only controls that are adjusted are ones the cameraman is familiar with. As the cliché goes, if it ain't broke, don't fix it. If you have the time and are not under recording pressure, each control can be tweaked in turn and its effect on the picture monitored. This may be a valuable learning experience which will help you customize an image should a special requirement occur. There is obviously the need to get the camera back to square one after experimenting. Fortunately there is a safety net of a factory setting or default set of values so that if inadvertently (or not) a parameter is misaligned and the image becomes unusable, the default setting can be selected and the camera is returned to a standard mode of operation.

A typical set of sub-menus would provide adjustment to:

- **Operational values:** The items in this set of menus are used to change the camera settings to suit differing shooting conditions under normal camera operations. They would normally include menu pages which can alter viewfinder display, viewfinder marker aids such as safety zone and centre mark, etc., gain, shutter selection, iris, format switching, monitor out, auto-iris, auto-knee, auto set-up, diagnosis.
- **Scene file:** These can be programmed to memorize a set of operational values customized for a specific camera set-up and read to a removable file.
- **Video signal processing:** This menu contains items for defining adjustments to the image (e.g. gamma, master black level, contour correction, etc.) and requires the aid of a waveform monitor or other output device to monitor the change in settings.
- **Engineering:** The engineering menu provides access to all of the camera set-up parameters, with only selected parameters available in the master menu to avoid accidental changes to the settings.
- **Maintenance:** This menu is mainly for initial set-up and periodic maintenance, and normally not available via the master menu.
- **Reference file (or system configuration):** This file contains factory settings or initial customization of reference settings to meet the requirements of different users. It is the status quo setting for a standard operational condition. This menu is not usually accessible via the master menu and should never be adjusted on location except by qualified service personnel. Never try to adjust camera controls if you are unsure of their effect and if you have no way of returning the camera set-up to a standard operational condition.

(continued from page 97)

Battery changes when timecode locked

A battery change on the 'master' camera requires all cameras to stop recording if synchronous timecode is an essential production requirement. A battery change on a 'slave' camera may affect any camera that is being supplied by its timecode feed. If synchronous timecode is critical, either all cameras use mains adaptors if possible, or arrange that a battery change occurs on a recording break at the same time on all cameras. Check timecode after re-powering up.

Mini DV cameras

DV timecode circuitry is less sophisticated than many broadcast formats and if a cassette is parked on blank tape in mid-reel, the camera assumes that it is a new reel and resets the timecode to 00:00:00. There may not be an edit search/return facility and so after reviewing footage, park the tape on picture of the last recorded material and leave an overlap for the timecode to pick up and ensure continuous timecode. In all formats after rewinding and reviewing shots, inserting a partially used cassette, changing batteries or switching power off, use the edit search/return facility to check at what point the tape is parked. Reset timecode and zero CTL as required.

Scene files

A scene file is a method of recording the operational settings on a digital camera. In use it is like a floppy disk on a computer and can be removed from the camera with the stored values and then, when required, loaded back into the camera to provide the memorized values. The operational variables on a camera such as filter position, white balance, gain, speed of response of auto-exposure, shutter speed, electronic contrast control, the slope of the transfer characteristic (gamma), and its shape at the lower end (black stretch) or the upper end (highlight handling and compression), and the matrix, all affect the appearance of the image. The same shot can change radically when different settings of several or many of the above variables are reconfigured. If for production reasons these variables have been adjusted differently from their standard settings (e.g. a white balance arranged to deliberately warm up the colour response), it may be necessary, for picture continuity, to replicate the customized appearance over a number of shots recorded at different locations, or on different days. The scene file allows an accurate record to be kept of a specific set of operational instructions.

An additional useful feature of a removable record of a camera set-up occurs when a number of cameras (of the same model) are individually recording the same event and their shots will be edited together (see also Timecode, page 92). Normal multi-camera coverage provides for each camera's output to be monitored, matched and adjusted before recording or transmission. Individual camcorders, if they not aligned, could produce very noticeable mismatched pictures when intercut. To avoid this, all cameras can be configured to the same set-up values by transferring a file card and adjusting each camera with the same stored values. A file card can be compiled, for example, that allows an instant set-up when moving between location and a tungsten-lit studio.

Programming the camera

The flexibility of memorized values has led to the creation of a range of software cards for specific makes of cameras which provide a set 'look' instantly. Among the choices available, for example, are sepia, night scenes or the soft image of film. Other cards produce a warm ambience or a colder-feeling atmosphere. Scene files that duplicate the appearance of front-of-lens filters are also available and these electronic 'gels' provide a quick way of adding an effect. There are also pre-programmed scene files that help to 'normalize' difficult lighting conditions such as shooting under fluorescent lighting or scenes with extreme contrast. Low-contrast images can also be produced with the option to selectively control contours in areas of skin, offering more flattering rendition of close-ups. Fundamentally altering the look of an image at the time of acquisition is often irreversible and unless there is the opportunity to monitor the pictures on a high-grade monitor in good viewing conditions, it may be prudent to leave the more radical visual effects to post-production.

Image stability

Many DV format cameras have an electronic image stabilization facility. This is intended to smooth out unintended camera shake and jitter when the camera is operated hand-held. Usually these devices reduce resolution. Another method of achieving image stability, particularly when camera shake is the result of consistent vibration, is by way of optical image stabilization.

The optical image stabilizer on the CanonXL1 is effected by a vari-angle prism formed from two glass plates separated by a high-refracted-index liquid. A gyro sensor in the camera detects vibration and feeds data to the prism, which reacts by changing shape. This bends the rays of light to keep the image stable when it reaches the CCDs. The CCD image is examined to check for any low-frequency variations that have not been compensated for by the gyro. This data is fed back to the prism to further reduce vibration. Other devices can be 'tuned' to a consistent vibration such as produced when mounting a camera in a helicopter. Some forms of image stabilization add a slight lag to intended camera movement giving an unwanted floating effect.

Other equipment uses a variety of techniques to track a moving target such as off-shore power boat racing from a moving camera to keep the main subject in the centre of frame. The camera can be locked-on to a fast-moving subject like a bobsleigh and hold it automatically framed over a designated distance.

A schematic showing the principles of image stabilization

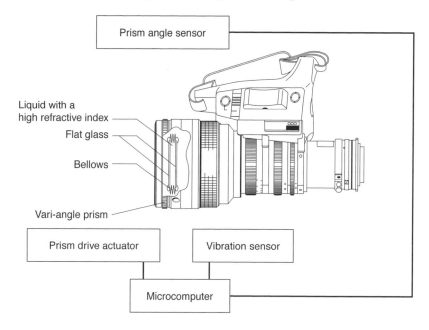

Prism angle sensor

Liquid with a high refractive index

Flat glass

Bellows

Vari-angle prism

Prism drive actuator

Vibration sensor

Microcomputer

Gamma and linear matrix

After the image manipulation discussed on the previous pages, the picture the viewer will finally see depends on the characteristics of their TV set. The cathode ray display tube, however, has certain limitations. The television image is created by a stream of electrons bombarding a phosphor coating on the inside face of the display tube. The rate of change of this beam and therefore the change in picture brightness does not rise linearly, in step with changes in the signal level corresponding to the changes in the original image brightness variations.

As shown in graph (a) opposite, the beam current, when plotted against the input voltage, rises in an exponential curve. This means that dark parts of the signal will appear on the tube face much darker than they actually are, and bright parts of the signal will appear much brighter than they should be. The overall aim of the television system is to reproduce accurately the original image and therefore some type of correction needs to be introduced to compensate for the non-linear effect of the cathode ray tube beam. The relationship between the input brightness ratios and the output brightness ratios is termed the gamma of the overall system. To achieve a gamma of 1 (i.e. a linear relationship between the original and the displayed image – a straight line in graph (b)), a correcting signal in the camera must be applied to compensate for the distortion created at the display tube. Uncorrected, the gamma exponent of the TV system caused by the display tube characteristics is about 2.4. Thus the camera's gamma to compensate for the non-linearity of the TV system is about 0.44/0.45. This brings an overall gamma of approximately 1.1 (2.4 x 0.45) slightly above a linear relationship to compensate for the effect of the ambient light falling on the viewer's display tube. There is the facility to alter the amount of gamma correction in the camera for production purposes. The application of gamma correction to the signal in the camera also helps to reduce noise in the blacks. Some cameras have a multi matrix facility which allows a user to select a small part of the colour spectrum and adjust its hue and saturation without affecting the rest of the picture.

Linear matrix
As detailed on page 12, all hues in the visible spectrum can be matched by the mixture of the three colours, red, green, and blue. In the ideal spectrum characteristics of these colours, blue contains a small proportion of red and a small negative proportion of green. Green contains a spectral response of negative proportions of both blue and red. It is not optically possible to produce negative light in the camera but these negative light values cannot be ignored if faithful colour reproduction is to be achieved. The linear matrix circuit in the camera compensates for these values by electronically generating and adding signals corresponding to the negative spectral response to the R, G and B video signals. This circuit is placed before the gamma correction so that compensation does not vary due to the amount of gamma correction, i.e. at the point where the signals are 'linear' – a gamma of 1.

Gamma correction

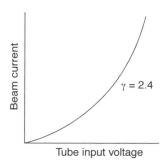

(a) Gamma due to tube characteristic

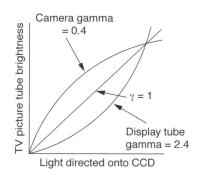

(b) Gamma correction

Matrix

	EBU			Skin		
	Red	Green	Blue	Red	Green	Blue
Red	1.22	−0.18	−0.04	1.1	−0.07	−0.03
Green	−0.05	1.11	−0.06	−0.04	1.15	−0.11
Blue	0	−0.33	1.33	0	−0.2	1.2

	BBC			RAI		
Red	0.89	0.04	−0.15	1.22	−0.18	−0.04
Green	−0.1	0.99	0.11	−0.05	1.14	−0.09
Blue	−0.01	−0.21	1.22	0	−0.18	1

Aspect ratios

At the same moment that we perceive the identity of an object within a frame, we are also aware of the spatial relationship between the object and the frame. These frame 'field of forces' exert pressure on the objects contained within the frame and all adjustment to the composition of a group of visual elements will be arranged with reference to these pressures. Different placement of the subject within the frame's 'field of forces' can therefore induce a perceptual feeling of equilibrium, of motion or of ambiguity (see figure opposite).

The *closed frame* compositional technique is structured to keep the attention only on the information that is contained in the shot. The *open frame* convention allows action to move in and out of the frame and does not disguise the fact that the shot is only a partial viewpoint of a much larger environment.

Frames within frames
The ratio of the longest side of a rectangle to the shortest side is called the aspect ratio of the image. The aspect ratio of the frame and the relationship of the subject to the edge of frame has a considerable impact on the composition of a shot. Historically, film progressed from the Academy aspect ratio of 1.33:1 (a 4 × 3 rectangle) to a mixture of Cinemascope and widescreen ratios. TV inherited the 4:3 screen size and then, with the advent of digital production and reception, took the opportunity to convert to a TV widescreen ratio of 1.78:1 (a 16 × 9 rectangle).

Film and television programmes usually stay with one aspect ratio for the whole production but often break up the repetition of the same projected shape by creating compositions that involve frames within frames. The simplest device is to frame a shot through a doorway or arch which emphasizes the enclosed view, or by using foreground masking an irregular 'new' frame can be created which gives variety to the constant repetition of the screen shape. The familiar over-the-shoulder two shot is in effect a frame within a frame image as the back of the foreground head is redundant information and is there to allow greater attention on the speaker and the curve of the head into the shoulder gives a more visually attractive shape to the side of the frame.

There are compositional advantages and disadvantages in using either aspect ratio. Widescreen is good at showing relationships between people and location. Sports coverage benefits from the extra width in following live events. Composing closer shots of faces is usually easier in the 4:3 aspect ratio, but as in film during the transition to widescreen framing during the 1950s, new framing conventions are being developed and old 4:3 compositional conventions that do not work are abandoned. The shared priority in working in any aspect ratio is knowing under what conditions the audience will view the image.

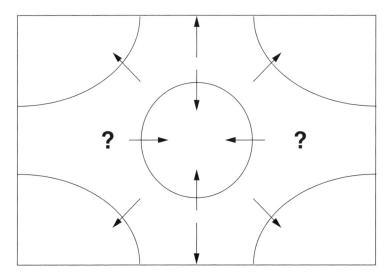

A field of forces can be plotted, which plots the position of rest or balance (centre and midpoint on the diagonal between corner and centre) and positions of ambiguity (?) where the observer cannot predict the potential motion of the object and therefore an element of perceptual unease is created. Whether the object is passively attracted by centre or edge or whether the object actively moved on its own volition depends on content.

The awareness of motion of a static visual element with relation to the frame is an intrinsic part of perception. It is not an intellectual judgement tacked on to the content of an image based on previous experience, but an integral part of perception.

Widescreen

The world-wide change-over period from mass viewing on a 4:3 analogue set to mass viewing on a 16:9 digital monitor, and therefore mass programme production for 16:9 television, will take many years. The transition period will require a compromise composition (see opposite) and many broadcasters are adopting an interim format of 14:9 to smooth the transition from 4:3 to full 16:9. But the compositional problems do not end there. The back-library of 4:3 programmes and films is enormous and valuable and will be continued to be transmitted across a wide range of channels in the future. The complete image can be viewed on a 16:9 screen if black bars are displayed either side of the frame (see (a) opposite). They can be viewed by filling the full width of the 16:9 display at the cost of cutting part of the top and bottom of the frame (see (c) opposite) or, at the viewer's discretion, they can be viewed by a non-linear expansion of picture width, progressively distorting the edges of the frame to fill the screen (see (b) opposite).

Viewfinder set-up

As many broadcast organizations have adopted the 14:9 aspect ratio as an interim standard, cameramen shooting in 16:9 follow a 'shoot and protect' framing policy. The viewfinder is set to display the full 16:9 picture with a graticule superimposed showing the border of a 14:9 frame and a 4:3 frame. Significant subject matter is kept within the 14:9 border or, if there is a likelihood of the production being transmitted in 4:3, within the smaller 4:3 frame. The area between 16:9 and 14:9 must be still usable for future full digital transmissions and therefore must be kept clear of unwanted subject matter. Feature film productions that were shot in 4:3 but were intended to be projected in the cinema with a hard matte in widescreen can sometimes be seen in a TV transmission with booms, etc., in the top of the frame that would not have been seen in the cinema. 'Shoot and protect' attempts to avoid the hazards of multi-aspect viewing by centring most of the essential information. This does of course negate the claimed advantages of the widescreen shape because for the transitional period the full widescreen potential cannot be used. For editing purposes, it is useful to identify within the colour bars the aspect ratio in use. Some cameramen in the early days of widescreen video shooting would frame up a circular object such as a wheel or lens cap to establish in post-production if the correct aspect ratio was selected.

The same size camera viewfinders used for 4:3 aspect ratio are often switched to a 16:9 display. This in effect gives a smaller picture area if the 14:9 'shoot and protect' centre of frame framing is used and makes focus and following distant action more difficult. Also, video cameramen are probably the only monochrome viewers still watching colour TV pictures. Colour is not only essential to pick up individuals in sports events such as football where opposing team shirts may look identical in monochrome, but in all forms of programme production, colour plays a dominant role in composition.

Protect and save

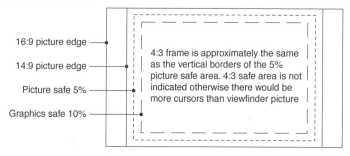

16:9 picture edge

14:9 picture edge

Picture safe 5%

Graphics safe 10%

4:3 frame is approximately the same as the vertical borders of the 5% picture safe area. 4:3 safe area is not indicated otherwise there would be more cursors than viewfinder picture

Composition problems will continue while 16:9 and 4:3 simultaneous productions are being shot during the analogue/digital changeover. They neither take full advantage of the width of 16:9 nor do they fit comfortably with the old 4:3 shape. After many years of dual format compromise composition, the resultant productions will continue to be transmitted even though 16:9 widescreen will be the universal format. The only safe solution is the 'protect and save' advice of putting essential information in the centre of frame but that is a sad limitation on the compositional potential of the widescreen shape.

Viewing 4:3 pictures on a 16:9 display

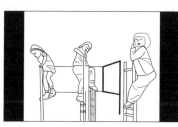

(a)

4:3 aspect ratio picture displayed on 16:9 set with black borders.

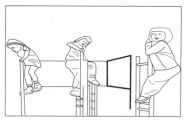

(b)

Complete 4:3 aspect ratio picture displayed on 16:9 set with progressive rate of expansion towards the vertical edges of the screen. With this system people change shape as they walk across the frame.

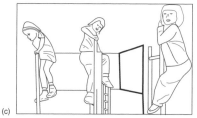

(c)

4:3 aspect ratio picture displayed on 16:9 set. The 4:3 aspect ratio picture has been 'zoomed' in to fill the frame cropping the top and bottom of the frame.

107

Widescreen composition

The growth of the cinema widescreen format in the 1950s provoked discussion on what changes were required in the standard 4:3 visual framing conventions that had developed in cinema since its beginnings. The initial concern was that the decrease in frame height meant that shots had to be looser and therefore had less dramatic tension. Another problem was that if artistes were staged at either side of the screen, the intervening setting became more prominent. Compositional solutions were found but the same learning curve is being experienced in television as the move is made to widescreen images. If anything, television is more of a 'talking heads' medium than cinema but the advent of a large, wider aspect screen has tended to emphasize the improvement in depicting place and setting.

One of the main compositional conventions with 4:3 television framing is the search for ways of tightening up the overall composition. If people are split at either end of the frame, either they are restaged or the camera is repositioned to 'lose' the space between them. Cinema widescreen compositions relied less on the previous fashion for tight, diagonal, dynamic groupings in favour of seeing the participants in a setting. Initially, directors lined the actors up across the frame but this was quickly abandoned in favour of masking off portions of the frame with unimportant bland areas in order to emphasize the main subject. Others simply grouped the participants in the centre of the frame and allowed the edges to look after themselves – in effect 'protect and save'. There were other directors who balanced an off-centre artiste with a small area of colour or highlight on the opposite side of the frame. This type of widescreen composition is destroyed if the whole frame is not seen.

Many directors exploited the compositional potential of the new shape. They made big bold compositional widescreen designs knowing that they would be seen in the cinema as they were framed. Their adventurous widescreen compositions were later massacred on TV with pan and scan or simply being shown in 4:3 with the sides chopped off. The problem with the video compositional transition to widescreen is the inhibition to use the full potential of 16:9 shape because the composition has to be all things to all viewers. It must fit the 14:9 shape but also satisfy the 4:3 viewer. It is difficult to know when the full potential of the widescreen shape can be utilized because even if the majority of countries switch off analogue transmissions at some time in the first decade of the century, there will probably be billions of TV sets world-wide that will still be analogue.

A conventional TV single can cause problems in staging and bits of people tend to intrude into the edge of frame. Headroom has tended to be smaller than 4:3 framing and there are some problems in editing certain types of GVs (general views). Wide shots need to be sufficiently different in their distribution of similar objects to avoid jump cuts in editing. A good cut needs a change in shot size to be invisible.

Viewing distance

There is a further consideration in the format/composition debate which concerns the size of the screen. Someone sitting in a front row cinema seat may have as much as 58° of their field of view taken up by the screen image. This can be reduced to as little as 9.5° if he/she views the screen from the back row. The average television viewer typically sees a picture no wider than 9.2°. Dr Takashi Fujio at the NHK research laboratories carried out research on viewers' preference for screen size and aspect ratio and his findings largely formed the justification for the NHK HDTV parameters. His conclusion was that maximum involvement by the viewer was achieved with a 5:3 aspect ratio viewed at 3 to 4 picture height distance. Normal viewing distance (in Japan) was 2 to 2.5 metres which suggested an ideal screen size of between 1 m × 60 cm and 1.5 m × 90 cm. With bigger room dimensions in the USA and Europe, even larger screen sizes may be desirable. Sitting closer to a smaller screen did not involve the viewer in the action in the same way.

Estimating the compositional effect of space and balance in a widescreen frame is complicated by the concept that framing for cinema widescreen and television widescreen compositions is different because of the screen size. The accepted thinking is that what works on a large cinema screen may be unacceptable with TV. Cinema screens are very large compared to television sets but for someone sitting at the back of a cinema the size of the screen in their field of view (e.g. 9.2°) may be the same as someone watching a 36-inch TV screen at normal domestic viewing distance. It is a mistake to confuse screen size with actual perpetual size which is determined by viewing distance.

Transfer between film and television

Many television productions are shot on film and there is a continuous search for a world-wide video standard to allow a transparent transfer of film to video and video to film. There have also been many proposals for a high-definition television format. Since the early 1970s, when NHK (the Japan Broadcasting Corporation) first began research into a high definition television system, there has been international pressure for agreement on a standard HDTV system. One solution suggested is to have a HDTV acquisition format of 24 frame, 1080 line, progressive scanning video system that would allow high-definition video productions suitable for transfer to film for cinema presentation. It would be the video equivalent of 35 mm film and allow a seamless translation to all other standard definition (SD) video formats.

Camera technique

The basic principles of camerawork
There are a number of basic visual conventions used by the majority of cameramen operating broadcast camera/recorders. Many of these standard camera techniques were developed in the early part of the twentieth century when the first film makers had to experiment and invent the grammar of editing, shot size and the variety of camera movements that are now standard. The ability to find ways of shooting subjects and then editing the shots together without distracting the audience was learnt by the commercial cinema over a number of years. The guiding concept was the need to persuade the audience that they were watching continuous action in 'real' time. This required the mechanics of film making to be hidden from the audience; that is to be invisible. Invisible technique places the emphasis on the content of the shot rather than production technique in order to achieve a seamless flow of images directing the viewers' attention to the narrative. It allows shot change to be unobtrusive and directs attention to what is contained within the frame and to smoothly move the camera to a new viewpoint without distracting the audience.

Alternative technique
There are alternative conventions of presentation which intentionally draw attention to the means of production. The production methods and camera movements are emphasized in order to simulate the realism of the unrehearsed shot or to remind the audience that they are watching a piece of fiction. Similar to news coverage, it appears as if the camerawork is surprised by the action (see Standard camerawork, page 128). In general, television production has adopted the 'Hollywood' model of invisible technique.

A coherent technique
The point of this brief history of camerawork is rather than simply committing to memory a list of do's and don'ts about TV camerawork it is better for you to understand *why* these visual conventions exist. There is a coherent technique behind most TV camerawork. The way a shot is framed up, the way a zoom is carried out, the amount of headroom you give to a certain size of shot is not simply a matter of personal taste, although that often affects shot composition, it is also a product of 90 odd years of telling a story in pictures. The development of invisible technique created the majority of these visual conventions. Knowing why a camerawork convention exists is preferable to simply committing to memory a string of instructions. You can then apply the principles of invisible technique whenever you meet up with a new production requirement.

The basic aims of television camerawork can be summarized as:

- to produce a technically acceptable picture (e.g. correct exposure, white balance, in focus, etc.);
- to provide a shot that is relevant to the story or event in a style that is suitable for the genre;
- to provide a shot that will hold the audience's attention (e.g. by the appropriate use of framing, camera movement, composition, lighting, etc.);
- to provide shots that can be cut together (see Editing topics, pages 144–71).

The aim of invisible technique is to convince the audience that they are watching a continuous event in 'real' time:

- Shots are structured to allow the audience to understand the space, time and logic of the action.
- Each shot follows the line of action to maintain consistent screen direction so that the geography of the action is completely intelligible (e.g. camera positions on a football match).
- Unobtrusive camera movement and shot change directs the audience to the content of the production rather than the mechanics of film/television production.
- Invisible technique creates the illusion that distinct, separate shots (possibly recorded out of sequence and at different times) form part of a continuous event being witnessed by the audience.

This is achieved by:

- unobtrusive intercutting (see Editing topics, pages 144–71);
- camera movement motivated by action or dialogue (see Camera movement, page 120);
- camera movement synchronized with action;
- continuity of performance, lighting, atmosphere and action.

Shot structure

As demonstrated in most holiday and wedding home movies, many people new to camerawork assume that a video of an event is simply shooting a collection of 'pretty' or informative images. It is only later when they view the unedited material that they may begin to understand that their collection of individual shots do not flow together and communicate the points they were hoping to make. Watching a sequence of random and erratic images soon becomes tedious and visually distracting if the elementary principle, i.e. that when viewed each shot is connected with the preceding and succeeding shot, is forgotten or ignored. Good camerawork, as well as providing visually and technically acceptable pictures, is constantly thinking in shot structures. In broadcasting, each shot must help to advance the points being communicated. The collection of shots produced on location will be edited together and paired down to essentials. The editor can only do so much (see What the editor requires, page 164) with the material the cameraman provides. Essentially the cameraman (or, if present, the director) must impose an elementary structure to the material shot.

- **General to the particular**: Much of camera/recorder location work will not be scripted. There may be a rough treatment outlined by the presenter or a written brief on what the item should cover but an interview may open up new aspects of the story. Without pre-planning or a shot list, camera technique will often revert to tried and trusted formulas. Telling a story in pictures is as old as the first efforts in film making. A safe rule-of-thumb is to move from the general to the particular – from wide shot to close-up. Use a general view (GV) to show relationships and to set the scene and then make the important points with the detail of close-ups. There must be a reason in editing to change shot and the cameraman has to provide a diversity of material to provide a cutting point.
- **Record of an event**: Information shots are specific. They refer to a unique event – the wreckage of a car crash, someone scoring a goal, a political speech. They are often non-repeatable. The crashed car is towed away, the politician moves on. The topicality of an event means that the camera technique must be precise and reliable, responding to the event with quick reflexes. There is often no opportunity for retakes.
- **Interpretative shots**: Interpretative or decorative shots are non-specific. They are often shot simply to give visual padding to the story. A typical example is a shot of an interviewee walking in a location before an interview. This shot allows the dubbed voice-over to identify who the interviewee is and possibly their attitude to the subject. The shot needs to be long enough to allow information that is not featured in the interview to be added as a voice-over. The interviewee leaves frame at the end of the shot to provide a cutting point to the interview.

112

Basic advice on structure

- When shooting an event or activity, have a rough mental outline of how the shots could be cut together and provide a mixture of changes in camera angle, size of shot and camera movement.
- Change of shot must be substantial, either in camera position or in shot size.
- Avoid too restricted a structure in type of shot – give some flexibility to the editor to reduce or expand the running time (e.g. do not stay on the same size shot of a speaker for the whole of his conference speech. Provide audience cutaways after the speech.)
- Provide some type of establishing shot and some general views (GVs) that may be useful in a context other than the immediate sequence.
- Provide the editor with a higher proportion of static shots to camera movement. It is difficult to cut between pans and zooms until they steady to a static frame and hold.
- For news, keep camera movement short with a greater proportion of small significant moves that reveal new (essential) information. Avoid long inconsequential pans and zooms.
- When shooting unrehearsed events, steady the shot as soon as possible and avoid a sequence of rapid, very brief shots.
- Get the 'safe' shot before attempting the ambitious development.
- Try to find relevant but non-specific shots so that voice-over information (to set the scene or the report) can be dubbed on after the script has been prepared.
- In general, wide shots require a longer viewing time than big close-ups.

Composition

One of the skills required in camerawork is the ability to provide shots that hold the interest and attention of the audience. Although the content of the shot such as a house, animal or personality may be the initial reason why a viewer's interest is captured by an image, the method of presentation, the composition of the shot, is also a vital factor in sustaining that interest.

What is composition?
Composition is the principal way of making clear the priorities of a shot. It emphasizes the main subject and eliminates or subdues competing elements of visual interest. There must be a reason for framing up any shot; good composition enables that reason to be transmitted to the viewer. Good visual communication is achieved by good composition.

'I see what you mean!'
There is usually a reason why a shot is recorded on tape or film. The purpose may be simply to record an event or the image may play an important part in expressing a complex idea. Whatever the reasons that initiate the shot, the cameraman should have a clear understanding of the purpose behind the shot.

After establishing why the shot is required, and usually this will be deduced purely from experience of the shot structure of the programme format, the cameraman will position the camera, adjust the lens angle, framing and focus. All four activities (as well as knowledge of programme formats) rely on an understanding of the visual design elements available to compose a shot within the standard television framing conventions. Effective picture making is the ability to manipulate the lens position and the lens angle within a particular programme context.

Primary decisions
The seven primary decisions to be made when setting up a shot are: camera angle, lens angle, camera distance, camera height, frame, subject in focus and depth of field. For example, a square-on shot of a block of flats ((a) opposite), can have more visual impact if the camera is repositioned to shoot the building obliquely ((b) opposite). Shooting two sides of a subject creates a more interesting dynamic arrangement of horizontal lines. This is changing the camera angle. The convergence of the horizontal lines can be emphasized by choosing the widest angle of the zoom, and repositioning the camera low and close to the subject. This is changing lens angle, camera distance and camera height. How the building is now framed, how much of the structure is within the depth of field of the chosen aperture, and which part of the building is chosen to be in focus will all affect the visual design of the shot. A building can have a radically different appearance by choosing how to employ the seven basic camera parameters. Lighting is another powerful design element in shot composition (see pages 172–85).

114

Positioning the lens

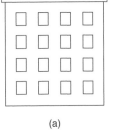

(a)

(b)

Physically changing the lens position and altering the lens angle controls the appearance and the information contained in a shot. One essential skill required by a cameraman is the ability to visualize a shot from a lens angle in any position in space without the need to move the camera to that position in order to discover its visual potential.

Composition summary

A shot is composed to emphasize the most important subject in the frame by placement using control of background, lens angle, height, focus, shot size, movement, etc. The cameraman makes certain that the eye is attracted to that part of the frame that is significant and seeks to avoid the main subject conflicting with other visual elements in the frame. Here is a partial checklist of the do's and don'ts of composition:

- The camera converts three dimensions into two dimensions. Try to compensate for the loss of the third dimension by looking for ways to represent depth in the composition.
- Avoid dividing the frame into separated areas by strong vertical and horizontal elements unless this is a specific required effect.
- Check the overall image, particularly background details (e.g. no chimneys/posts growing out of foreground subjects' heads).
- Keep important action away from the edge of the frame, but avoid repeating square-on, symmetrical eye-level centre-of-frame shots.
- Offset the dominant interest and balance this with a less important element.
- Fill the frame if possible with interest and avoid large plain areas that are there simply because of the aspect ratio of the screen. If necessary, mask off part of the frame with a feature in the shot to give a more interesting composition.
- Emphasize the most important element in the frame by its position using control of background, lens angle, height, focus, shot size, movement, etc. Make certain that the eye is attracted to the part of the frame that is significant and avoid conflict with other elements in the frame.
- Selective focus can control the composition. Pulling focus from one plane to another directs attention without reframing.
- Attempt some visual mystery or surprise but the stronger the visual impact the more sparingly it should be used. Repeated zooming results in loss of impact and interest.

Rule of thirds

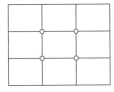

4:3 aspect ratio

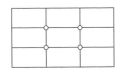

16:9 aspect ratio

The rule of thirds proposes that an attractive balance can be achieved by placing the main subject on one of the intersections of two equally spaced lines horizontally in the frame and two lines equally spaced in the vertical.

Visual conventions

Standard shot sizes

Because so much of television programming involves people talking, a number of standard shot sizes have evolved centred on the human body. In general, these shot sizes avoid cutting people at natural joints of the body such as neck, elbows, knees. Normal interview shots include (see figures opposite):

- **CU (close-up):** Bottom of frame cuts where the knot of tie would be.
- **MCU (medium close-up):** Bottom of the frame cuts where the top of a breast pocket of a jacket would be.
- **MS (medium shot):** Bottom of frame cuts at the waist.

Other standard shot descriptions are:-

- **BCU (big close-up):** The whole face fills the screen. Top of frame cuts the forehead. Bottom of the frame cuts the edge of chin avoiding any part of the mouth going out of frame (rarely used in interviews).
- **LS (long shot):** The long shot includes the whole figure.
- **WS (wide shot):** A wide shot includes the figure in a landscape or setting.
- **O/S 2s (over-the-shoulder 2-shot):** Looking over the shoulder of a foreground figure framing part of the head and shoulders to another participant.
- **2-shot, 3-shot, etc.:** Identifies the number of people in frame composed in different configurations.

Closed frame

One of the early Hollywood conventions was to compose the shot so that it contained the action within the frame and then by cutting, followed the action in distinct, complete shots. Each shot was self-contained and refers to only what is seen and shuts out or excludes anything outside of the frame. This is the *closed frame* technique and is structured to keep the attention only on the information that is contained in the shot. If there is any significant reference to a subject outside of the frame, then there is an additional shot to cover the referred subject. This convention is still followed in many different types of programme format. For example, in a television cooking demonstration, the demonstrator in medium close-up (MCU) may refer to some ingredient they are about to use which is outside the frame. Either the MCU is immediately loosened to reveal the ingredient or there is a need to record a cutaway shot of the ingredient later.

The open frame

The *open frame* convention allows action to move in and out of the frame. An example would be a character in a hallway who would be held on screen whilst in dialogue with someone who is moving in and out of frame entering and leaving various rooms which are unseen. Their movement while they are out of frame is implied and not cut to as separate shots. The *open frame* does not disguise the fact that the shot is only a partial viewpoint of a much larger environment. This convention considers that it is not necessary for the audience to see the reality beyond the shot in order to be convinced that it exists.

Standard shot sizes

BCU (big close-up)
Whole face fills screen. Top of frame cuts
forehead. Bottom of frame cuts chin

CU (close-up)
Bottom of frame cuts where
knot of tie would be

MCU (medium close-up)
Bottom of frame cuts where
top of breast pocket of a jacket would be

MS (medium shot)
Bottom of frame cuts at
the waist

LS (long shot)
Long shot includes whole
figure

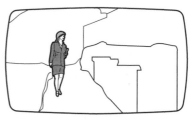

WS (wide shot)
Wide shot includes figure in
a landscape or setting

Note: Precise framing conventions for these standard shot descriptions vary with directors and cameramen. One person's MCU is another person's MS. Check that your understanding of the position of the bottom frame line on any of these shots shares the same size convention for each description as the director with whom you are working.

With profile shots, where people are looking out of frame, give additional space in the direction of their gaze for 'looking room'. Similarly when someone is walking across frame, give more space in front of them than behind.

Give consistent headroom for the same sized shots decreasing the amount with CUs and BCUs. Always cut the top of the head rather than the chin in extreme close up.

The eyes are the centre of attention in shots of faces. A good rule-of-thumb is to place them one third from the top of the frame.

Depiction of space

The composition of a shot is affected by the distance of the camera from the subject and the lens angle that is used. This will make a difference to the size relationships within the frame. The size relationship of objects in a field of view is known as the perspective of mass. Put simply, the closer an object is to us, the larger it will appear and vice versa. The image of an object doubles in size whenever its distance is halved. This is a simple fact of geometric optics and it applies to a camera as it does to the eye. Adjusting the camera distance and the lens angle can provide the size relationships required for a composition.

The wide-angle/narrow-angle effect

Size relationships or the perspective of mass can be confused with the wide-angle effect and the narrow-angle effect. To increase the size of a background figure in relation to a foreground figure it is common practice to reposition the camera back and zoom in to return to the original framing (see figure at top of page 119). The size relationships have now altered. It is not the narrower angle that produced this effect but the increased distance from the camera. By moving away from the two figures we have altered the ratio between lens and first figure and lens and second figure. It is a much smaller ratio and therefore the difference in size between the two of them is now not so great. When we zoom in and revert to the original full frame for foreground figure we keep the new size relationships that have been formed by camera distance. The two figures appear to be closer in size. Choosing which combination of camera distance and lens angle is used therefore has a significant effect on the depiction of space within a shot.

■ **Wide-angle effect:** A wide-angle lens working close to the main subject allows more of the foreground subject to be in frame but increases the ratio between foreground and background object size. It is this combination that produces distortion when used too close to the face (a 'Pinocchio' nose). A wide-angle zoom is very useful in confined surroundings, especially if attempting to interview someone in a crowd of journalists and photographers. By being close to the interviewee, masking by other people (such as fellow photographers) is prevented as there is insufficient room between lens and subject.
■ **Narrow-angle effect:** A part of our perception of depth depends on judging size relationships. The smaller we perceive a known object, the further we judge it to be from us. The size relationships produced by a very narrow-angle lens at a distance from the subject produces the illusion of squeezing the space between equal size figures. The camera distance from the subject produces the size relationships whilst the long focal length lens provides the magnification of the foreground and background. The space between the subjects in frame appears to be condensed. A common example is shooting a crowded pavement from a great distance on a long lens. The effect is that all people moving towards camera appear to be equal size and the time taken for them to change size, as they appear to be approaching the lens, appears to be abnormal.

Perspective of mass

Shot A   Shot B

In Shot A the camera is close to the presenter. In Shot B, to make the background subject (Big Ben) more dominant, the camera has moved back and zoomed in to match the presenter's size in Shot A.

The 'internal space' has been rearranged by changing the camera distance to presenter and it now appears as if the subject and the clock are much closer together. This creates a potential problem because it is very easy for members of the public to walk unwittingly between lens and presenter when working on a long lens. There will be a large gap between camera and presenter (>6 m) for Shot B.

Note: Lenses on DV format cameras may not have the focal length marked and the operator must always be aware of which part of the zoom range is selected and be able to recognize the visual effect of the chosen combination of camera distance/focal length. Do not just simply set up the camera from any viewpoint and zoom in to find the required framing. Think about how much depth you require in that specific shot and select the appropriate camera distance and adjust the zoom accordingly.

Natural perspective

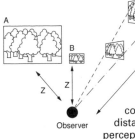

A shot can be set up with the camera at any distance from the subject and by varying the lens angle of the zoom the required framing can be achieved. But which lens angle will create natural perspective? Which combination of lens angle and camera distance most closely resembles human perception if the camera was replaced by an observer at the same point as the lens? The usual attempt to answer this question starts with the concept of the displayed image as a 'window in the wall'. The viewer looks through the 'window' and sees precisely the same scene as depicted by the lens angle/camera distance image. In practical everyday programme production the quest for 'natural perspective' is not achievable because it depends on two unknown factors. The correct viewing distance for natural perspective depends on the size of image displayed and the viewing distance of that image. This combination will vary between viewer and viewer although averages could be deduced based on average size of TV set and average size of sitting rooms.

(continued on page 121)

119

Camera movement

Invisible movement

There is the paradox of creating camera movement to provide visual excitement or visual change whilst attempting to make the movement 'invisible'. Invisible in the sense that the aim of the technique is to avoid the audience's attention switching from the programme content to the camerawork. This is achieved when camera movement matches the movement of the action and good composition is maintained throughout the move. The intention is to emphasize subject–picture content, rather than technique. Intrusive and conspicuous camera movements are often used for specific dramatic or stylistic reasons (e.g. pop promotions), but the majority of programme formats work on the premise that the methods of programme production should remain hidden or invisible.

Motivation

A camera move is usually prompted either:

- to add visual interest;
- to express excitement, increase tension or curiosity;
- to provide a new main subject of interest;
- to provide a change of viewpoint.

A camera move is therefore a visual development that provides new information or creates atmosphere or mood. If the opening and closing frames of a move, such as a zoom in, are the only images that are considered important, then it is probably better to use a cut to change shot rather than a camera move.

Match the movement to the mood or action

Two basic conventions controlling camera movement are, first, to match the movement to the action so that the camera move is motivated by the action and is controlled in speed, timing and degree by action. Second, there is a need to maintain good composition throughout the move. A camera move should provide new visual interest and there should be no 'dead' area between the first and end image of the movement.

When to reframe

There are broadly two types of camera movement: functional (the camera is moved to keep the subject in frame) and decorative (the camera is moved to provide variety and interest or to explain an idea). A common dilemma is when to reframe a subject who is swaying in and out of reasonable framing. The shot may be too tight for someone who can only talk when they move or they may make big hand movements to emphasize a point. The solution is to loosen off the shot. It is seldom a good idea to constantly pan to keep someone in frame as inevitably you will be 'wrong-footed' and compensate for an anticipated movement that does not happen.

Movement within the shot and lens angle

A small movement in a close-up can be the equivalent of a big movement in long shot. A full figure, three pace walk towards a wide-angle lens will create a much bigger change in size than the equivalent full figure walk towards a 25° lens. The 'internal space' of the lens in use becomes a critical consideration when staging action for the camera.

Basic advice for movement

■ Try to disguise camera movement by synchronizing with subject movement. Start and stop the movement at the same time as the subject.

■ When zooming, hold one side of the frame static as a 'pivot point' rather than zooming in to the centre of the frame.

■ Try to find a reason to motivate the zoom and to disguise the zoom. Use a combination of pan and zoom.

■ Panning and zooming are done to show relationships. If the beginning of the shot and the end of the shot are interesting but the middle section is not, it is better to cut between the start of the shot and the end frame rather than to pan or to zoom. Begin and end on a point of interest when panning. If the end of the shot is uninteresting why pan to it? Have a reason for drawing attention to the final image of a pan.

■ Pace the pan so that the viewer can see what the camera is panning over. Hold the frame at the beginning and end of the pan.

■ Use dominant lines or contours to pan across or along. Find some subject movement to motivate the pan.

■ When panning movement, leave space in the frame in the direction the subject is moving.

Natural perspective (continued from page 119)
The screen size of the reproduced image (see lower figure on page 119), will increase proportionally to the viewing distance if the original perspective experienced by the observer at distance 'z' from the subject is to be duplicated. The viewing distance 'z' of screen A is too close to reproduce a 'natural' perspective and would simulate a 'wide-angle' look at that viewing distance. Screen B would simulate a 'narrow-angle' viewpoint because the screen size is too small for viewing distance 'z'.

Controlling composition

The choice of lens angle and resulting composition should not be accidental unless there is no alternative camera position. The internal space of a shot often underlines the emotional quality of the scene. 'Normal' perspective for establishing shots is often used where the intention is to plainly and straightforwardly describe the locale. A condensed or an expanded space on the other hand may help to suggest the mood or atmosphere of the action. A long lens positioned at a distance from a cramped interior will heighten the claustrophobia of the setting. Subject size ratios will be evened out from foreground to background and movement to and away from camera will show no significant change in size and therefore give a subjective impression that no distance has been traversed. A wide-angle lens close to the subject will increase space, emphasize movement and, depending on shot content, emphasize convergence of line and accentuate the relative size of same size figures at different distances from the lens.

Control of background
Compositional priority can be given to a foreground subject by limiting the depth of field by ND (neutral density) filter or shutter but the greatest control is by choice of camera position, lens angle, camera distance and foreground subject position. Consideration must also be given to how the shot will be intercut and often a matching background of similar tonal range, colour and contrast has to be chosen to avoid a mismatch when intercutting. Too large a tonal difference between intercut backgrounds will result in obtrusive and very visible cuts. Visual continuity of elements such as direction of light, similar zones of focus and the continuity of background movement (e.g. crowds, traffic, etc.) in intercut shots have also to be checked.

The subjective influence of camera height
Lens height will also control the way the audience identifies with the subject. Moving the horizon down below a person makes them more dominant because the viewer is forced to adopt a lower eyeline viewpoint. We are in the size relationship of children looking up to adults. A low lens height may also de-emphasize floor or ground level detail because we are looking along at ground level and reducing or eliminating indications of ground space between objects. This concentrates the viewer's interest on the vertical subjects. A high position lens height has the reverse effect. The many planes of the scene are emphasized like a scale model. Usually it is better to divide the frame into unequal parts by positioning the horizon line above or below the mid-point of the frame. Many cameramen intuitively use the rule of thirds (see page 115) to position the horizon. A composition can evoke space by panning up and placing the line low in frame. Placing a high horizon in the frame can balance a darker foreground land mass or subject with the more attention grabbing detail of a high key sky. It also helps with contrast range and exposure.

Tracking and zooming

Zooming in

Tracking in

Foreground and background size relationship is a product of camera distance. How the subject fills the frame is a product of lens angle. This is the crucial distinction between tracking and zooming. Tracking the camera towards or away from the subject alters size relationships – the perspective of mass. Zooming the lens preserves the existing relative size relationships and magnifies or diminishes a portion of the shot. In the above figures, the man seated behind the presenter remains the same size (relative to foreground subject) when the camera zooms into the presenter. If the camera tracks into the presenter it alters the size relationship between foreground and background and the background figures become smaller relative to the foreground subject.

The purpose of the shot

The position of the lens and which lens angle is selected depend on the purpose of the shot, which may be one or a number of the following:

- to emphasize the principal subject;
- to provide variation in shot size;
- to give added prominence to the selected subject;
- to provide more information about the subject;
- to provide for change of angle/size of shot to allow unobtrusive intercutting;
- to allow variety of shot and shot emphasis;
- to create good shot composition;
- to favour the appearance of the performer;
- to alter the internal space in the shot;
- to alter size relationships in shot;
- to improve the eyeline;
- to comply with the lighting rig or natural light.

Programme production

Live multi-camera production technique uses a number of cameras which are switched to in turn to show different viewpoints of an event. This production method allows the material to be transmitted as it occurs or to be recorded for future transmission. If it is recorded then the material can be edited before transmission. Single camera coverage is usually recorded and the material receives extensive editing before transmission. This is similar to the film technique where one shot is recorded and then the single camera moved to another position or location to record another shot. The shots can be recorded out of sequence from their subsequent edited order. This type of production method is very flexible but does require more time in acquiring the material and in editing. An additional advantage of the single video camera is that it can be linked into a programme by satellite, land line or terrestrial link and be used as a live outside visual source. Pictures are nearly always accompanied by audio, either actuality speech, music, or effects of the subject in shot, or sound is added in post-production. The old cliché that television is a visual medium is a half truth. In nearly every circumstance, the viewer wants to hear, as well as see, what is transmitted. Pictures may have a greater initial impact, but sound frequently adds atmosphere, emotion, and space to the image.

Two types of programming

Programmes can be roughly divided into those that have a content that has been conceived and devised for television and those programmes with a content that cannot be preplanned, or are events that take place independent of television coverage. Many programmes have a mixture of both types of content.

If it is scripted for television, then the production is under the direct control of the production team who can arrange the content as they wish. The time scale of what happens on the screen is under their supervision and can be started and stopped as required. If it is an event that would happen independent of TV such as a sports event, then the production team will have to make arrangements to cover the event as it unfolds in its own time scale.

The creation of 'invisible' technique

As we discussed in the section on basic camera technique (page 110), the ability to find ways of shooting subjects and then editing the shots together without distracting the audience was learnt by the commercial cinema over a number of years. Television production mostly follows this technique. A number of standard conventions are practised by all members of the production team with a common aim of disguising their specific craft methods in order to maximize the audience's involvement with the programme content. If the audience becomes aware, for example, of audio transitions, change of shot or the colour cast on a presenter's face, they are unlikely to be following developments in the programme.

Production terms

Actuality event: Any event that is not specifically staged for television that exists in its own time scale.

Ad-lib shooting: Impromptu and unrehearsed camera coverage.

Camera left: Left of frame as opposed to the artiste's left when facing camera.

Camera right: Right of frame as opposed to the artiste's right when facing camera.

Canting the camera: Angling the camera so that the horizon is not parallel to the bottom of the frame.

Caption generator: Electronic equipment that allows text to be created and manipulated on screen via a keyboard.

Crossing the line: Moving the camera to the opposite side of an imaginary line drawn between two or more subjects after recording a shot of one of the subjects. This results in intercut faces looking out of the same side of frame and gives the impression that they are not in conversation with each other.

Cue: A signal for action to start, i.e. actor to start performing.

Cutaway: Cutting away from the main subject or master shot to a related shot.

Down stage: Moving towards the camera or audience.

Dry: Describes the inability of a performer either to remember or to continue with their presentation.

Establishing shot: The master shot which gives the maximum information about the subject.

Eyeline: The direction the subject is looking in the frame.

Grip: Supporting equipment for lighting or camera equipment. Also the name of the technicians responsible for handling grip equipment, e.g. camera trucks and dollies.

GV: General view; this is a long shot of the subject.

High angle: Any lens height above eye height.

High key: Picture with predominance of light tones and thin shadows.

Locked-off: Applying the locks on a pan and tilt head to ensure that the camera setting remains in a pre-selected position. Can also be applied to an unmanned camera.

Long lens: A lens with a large focal length or using a zoom at or near its narrowest angle of view.

Low angle: A lens height below eye height.

Low key: Picture with a predominance of dark tones and strong shadows.

Piece to camera: Presenter/reporter speaking straight to the camera lens.

Planning meetings: A meeting of some members of the production staff held for the exchange of information and planning decisions concerning a future programme.

Point-of-view shot: A shot from a lens position that seeks to duplicate the viewpoint of a subject depicted on screen.

Post-production: Editing and other work carried on pre-recorded material.

Prompters: A coated piece of glass positioned in front of the lens to reflect text displayed on a TV monitor below the lens.

Recces: The inspection of a location by production staff to assess the practicalities involved in its use as a setting for a programme or programme insert.

Reverse angle: When applied to a standard two-person interview, a camera repositioned 180° to the immediate shot being recorded to provide a complementary shot of the opposite subject.

Shooting off: Including in the shot more than the planned setting or scenery.

The narrow end of the lens: The longest focal length of the zoom that can be selected.

Tight lens: A long focal length primary lens or zoom lens setting.

Upstage: Moving further away from the camera or audience.

Virtual reality: System of chroma key where the background is computer generated.

Voice-over: A commentary mixed with effects or music as part of a sound track.

Vox pops (vox populi): The voice of the people, usually consist of a series of impromptu interviews recorded in the street with members of the public.

Wrap: Completion of a shoot.

See also other definitions in the Glossary, page 216.

Customary technique

Programme genres employ different production techniques. Sports coverage has shot patterns and camera coverage conventions, for example, different to the conventions used in the continuous coverage of music. Knowledge of these customary techniques is an essential part of the camerawork skills that need to be acquired. There is usually no time for directors to spell out their precise requirements and most assume that the production team is experienced and understands the conventions of the programme being made. The conventions can concern technique (e.g. news as factual, unstaged events, see page 130), or structure – how the programme is put together. A game show, for example, will introduce the contestants, show the prizes, play the game, find a winner and then award the prizes. The settings, style of camerawork, lighting and programme structure are almost predictable and completely different from a 30-minute natural history programme. It is almost impossible to carry over the same technique and style, for example, of a pop concert to a current affairs programme. Each production genre requires the customary technique of that type of format although crossover styles sometimes occur.

Attracting the audience's attention
Whatever the nature of the programme, the programme makers want an audience to switch on, be hooked by the opening sequence and then stay with the programme until the closing credits. There are a number of standard techniques used to achieve these aims. The opening few minutes are crucial in persuading the audience to stay with the programme and not switch channels. It usually consists, in news and magazine style programmes, of a quick 'taster' of all the upcoming items with the hope that each viewer will be interested in at least one item on the menu. Either existing material will be cut to promote the later item or very often 'teasers' will be shot specifically for the opening montage. Whether in this fast opening sequence or in the main body of the programme, most productions rely on the well tried and trusted formula of pace, mystery and some form of storytelling.

Story
The strongest way of engaging the audience's attention is to tell them a story. In fact, because film and television images are displayed in a linear way, shot follows shot, it is almost impossible for the audience not to construct connections between succeeding images whatever the real or perceived relationships between them. The task of the production team is to determine what the audience needs to know, and at what point in the 'story' they are told. This is the structure of the item or feature and usually takes the form of question and answer or cause and effect. Seeking answers to questions posed at the top of the programme, such as 'what are the authorities going to do about traffic jams?' or 'how were the pyramids built?', involves the viewer and draws them into the 'story' that is unfolding. Many items are built around the classical structure of exposition, tension, climax, and release.

126

Pivot point

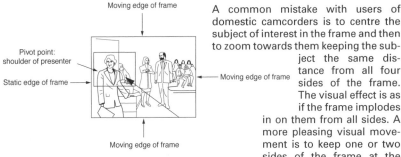

Moving edge of frame

Pivot point: shoulder of presenter

Static edge of frame

Moving edge of frame

Moving edge of frame

A common mistake with users of domestic camcorders is to centre the subject of interest in the frame and then to zoom towards them keeping the subject the same distance from all four sides of the frame. The visual effect is as if the frame implodes in on them from all sides. A more pleasing visual movement is to keep one or two sides of the frame at the same distance from the subject for the whole of the movement. Preselect one or two adjacent sides of the frame to the main subject of the zoom and whilst maintaining their position at a set distance from the main subject of the zoom allow the other three sides of the frame to change their relative position to the subject. Keep the same relationship of the two adjacent frame edges to the selected subject during the whole of the zoom movement. The point that is chosen to be held stationary in the

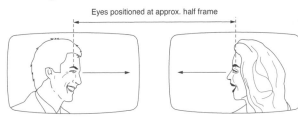

frame is called the pivot point. Using a pivot point allows the subject image to grow progressively larger (or smaller) within the frame whilst avoiding the impression of the frame contracting in towards them.

Looking room

Eyes positioned at approx. half frame

One of the compositional conventions of camerawork with profile shots, where people are looking out of frame, is to give additional space in the direction of their gaze for 'looking room'.

Similarly when someone is walking across frame, give more space in front of them than behind.

Headroom

Headroom is the space allowed above the head when framing a face. The amount of headroom will vary depending on the size of shot. In close-ups and big close-ups there will be no headroom. In long shots the amount of headroom will depend on location and composition. In general, the wider the shot the greater the headroom. It is only feasible to match headroom in medium close-ups and medium shots, other size shots will be framed on their individual merits.

Standard camerawork

Anyone new to camerawork will face the same learning curve as someone new to driving a car. They will be preoccupied with acquiring the basic skills of being fully conversant with the camera controls, focusing, framing and making certain they produce a technically competent image. Beyond the 'L plate' stage comes the recognition that there are many different ways of shooting a story.

Visual conventions

TV and film camerawork technique does not operate in a vacuum – there are past stylistic influences, contemporary variations and innovations caused by new production equipment. Most of these influences affect how productions are made but are rarely analysed by the practitioners. There have been changes in technique styles over the years so that it is not too difficult to identify when a TV production was shot. Retro fashion is always popular in commercials production and often prompts mainstream programme makers to rediscover discarded 'old-fashioned' techniques.

Equipment innovation

Equipment and technique interact and many programme formats have been developed because new hardware has become available. Kitchen drama in the 1960s was shot in a different way from previous styles of TV drama when ring-steer pedestals were developed and were able to move into the small box sets required by the subject matter and able to navigate the furniture. Steadicam and the Technocrane introduced a whole new look to camera movement and hand-held cameras reshaped breakfast shows and pop music videos. The new small DV format cameras are now opening up different stylistic methods of documentary production.

Two types of camerawork

An objective representation of 'reality' in a news, documentary or current affairs production uses the same perennial camerawork techniques as the subjective personal impression or the creation of atmosphere in fictional films. A football match appears to be a factual event whereas music coverage may appear more impressionistic. In both types of coverage there is selection and the use of visual conventions. Football uses a mixture of close-ups and wide shots, variation of lens height, camera position, cutaways to managers, fans, slow motion replays, etc., to inject pace, tension and drama to hold the attention of the audience. Music coverage will use similar techniques in interpreting the music, but with different rates of pans and zooms motivated by the mood and rhythm of the music. If it is a pop promo, there are no limits to the visual effects the director may feel is relevant. All TV camerawork is in one way or another an interpretation of an event. The degree of subjective personal impression fashioning the account will depend on which type of programme it is created for.

Invisible technique

To cut from this shot...

to this shot...

you need this shot to show change of direction
otherwise there would be a visual jump in the flow of shots

Keeping the audience informed of the geography of the event is the mainstay of standard camera technique. Shots are structured to allow the audience to understand the space, time and logic of the action and each shot follows the line of action to maintain consistent screen direction so that the action is completely intelligible.

Alternative styles

There is an alternative camerawork style to the standard 'invisible technique' already discussed. Camera movement is often restlessly on the move, panning abruptly from subject to subject, making no effort to disguise the transitions and deliberately drawing attention to the means by which the images are brought to the viewer. This breaking down or subverting of the standard convention of an 'invisible' seamless flow of images was created from a number of different influences.

The camera surprised by events

When camcorders came into widespread use in broadcasting in the early 1980s, they were first used for news gathering before entering into general programme making. On-the-shoulder 'wobblyscope' became the standard trademark when covering impromptu action. War reporting or civil unrest was presented in news bulletins with the nervous 'tic' of a hand-held video camera. Realism appeared to be equated with an unsteady frame. Cinema verité in the early 1960s linked on-the-shoulder camerawork with a new flexibility of movement and subject but many film directors adopted the uncertainty of an unsteady picture to suggest realism and authenticity (e.g. Oliver Stone in *JFK* (1991)). Many productions mimic the camera movement of ENG news coverage which because the subject matter is unknown and unstaged is frequently 'wrong footed' when panning or zooming. Holding unpredictable action within the frame results in a different visual appearance to the calculated camera movement of a rehearsed shot. The uncertainty displayed in following impromptu and fast developing action has an energy which these productions attempt to replicate. Hand-held camerawork became the signature for realism.

Naïveté

Ignorance of technique may seem to be a curious influence on a style but the growth of the amateur use of the video camera has spawned a million holiday videos and the recording of family events which appear remarkably similar in appearance to some visual aspects of production shot in the 'camera surprised by events' style. The user of the holiday camcorder is often unaware of main-stream camera technique and usually pans and zooms the camera around to pick up anything and everything that catches their attention. The result is a stream of fast moving shots that never settle on a subject and are restlessly on the move (i.e. similar to the production style of *NYPD Blue*). Video diaries have exploited the appeal of the 'innocent eye'. Many broadcast companies have loaned camcorders to the 'man in the street' for them to make video diaries of their own lives. The broadcasters claim that the appeal of this 'camcorder style' is its immediacy, its primitive but authentic image. It is always cut though by professional editors who use the same conventional entertainment values of maximizing audience interest and involvement as any other programme genre.

News camerawork

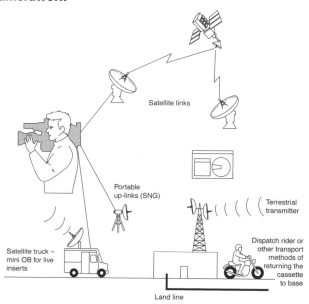

Satellite links

Portable up-links (SNG)

Terrestrial transmitter

Satellite truck – mini OB for live inserts

Dispatch rider or other transport methods of returning the cassette to base

Land line

Video news journalism covers a wide spectrum of visual/sound reports which use a number of camerawork conventions. A loose classification separates hard news stories, which aim to transmit an objective, detached account of an event (e.g. a plane crash), from those soft news stories which incline more towards accounts of lifestyle, personality interviews and consumer reports. Acceptable camera technique and style of shooting will depend on content and the aim of the report. For example, a politician arriving to make a policy statement at a conference will be shot in a fairly straightforward camera style with the intention of simply 'showing the facts'. An item about a fashion show could use any of the styles of feature film presentation (e.g. wide-angle distortion, subjective camerawork, canted camera, etc.). The political item has to be presented in an objective manner to avoid colouring the viewer's response. The fashion item can be more interpretative in technique and presentation in an attempt to entertain, engage and visually tease the audience. A basic skill of news/magazine camerawork is matching the appropriate camerawork style to the story content. The main points to consider are:

- the need to provide a technically acceptable picture;
- an understanding of news values and matching camerawork style to the aims of objective news coverage;
- structuring the story for news editing and the requirements of news bulletins/magazine programmes;
- getting access to the story and getting the story back to base.

Returning the material

Getting the news material back to base can be by transport, land line, terrestrial or satellite link or foldaway SNG equipment. The important thing is to get the material to base fast with supporting information (if a reporter is not at the location) in a form (the cassette clearly marked) that can be rapidly edited. Use a separate tape for the reporter's voice-over and a 5-minute tape for cutaways to speed up editing. Use a new tape for each story so that the stories can be cut independently if required.

131

News

There is no universally acceptable definition of news. A wide diversity of stories can be seen every day as the front page lead in newspapers. The only generalization that can be made in television is that news is usually considered to be those topical events that need to be transmitted in the next immediate news broadcast. Access, rapid working methods, a good appreciation of news values and the ability to get the material back, edited and on the air are the main ingredients of 'hard news' camerawork. There is no specific agreed technique in camera/recorder news coverage although there are a number of conventions that are widely accepted. People almost always take precedence over setting as the principal subject of news stories. Faces make good television if they are seen in context with the crisis. Where to position the camera to get the shot that will summarize the event is a product of experience and luck although good news technique will often provide its own opportunities.

Objectivity

A television news report has an obligation to separate fact from opinion, to be objective in its reporting, and by selection, to emphasize that which is significant to its potential audience. These considerations therefore needed to be borne in mind by a potential news cameraman as well as the standard camera technique associated with visual storytelling. Although news aims to be objective and free from the entertainment values of standard television story telling (e.g. suspense, excitement, etc.) it must also aim to engage the audience's attention and keep them watching. The trade-off between the need to visually hold the attention of the audience and the need to be objective when covering news centres on structure and shot selection. As the popularity of cinema films has shown, an audience enjoys a strong story that involves them in suspense and moves them through the action by wanting to know 'what happens next?' This is often incompatible with the need for news to be objective and factual. The production techniques used for shooting and cutting fiction and factual material are almost the same. These visual story telling techniques have been learned by the audiences from a lifetime of watching fictional accounts of life. The twin aims of communication and engaging the attention of the audience apply to news as much as they do to entertainment programmes.

Access

One crucial requirement for news coverage is to get to where the story is. This relies on contacts and the determination to get where the action is. Civil emergencies and crisis are the mainstay of hard news. Floods, air/sea rescue, transport crashes, riots, fire and crime are news events that arise at any time and just as quickly die away. They require a rapid response by the cameraman who has to be at the scene and begin recording immediately before events move on. Equipment must be ready for instantaneous use and the cameraman must work swiftly to keep up with a developing story.

News story

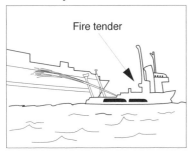

(a) Container ship on fire

(b) Container ship and fire tender, closer view

(c) Cruise ship in port, showing damage

(d) Disappointed holidaymakers

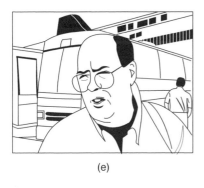

(e)

(f)

The above figures illustrate a news story reporting on a collision at sea between a container ship and a cruise ship. (a) shows the container ship on fire. Access is vital in news coverage and the cameraman must attempt to get to a position where the vital shot that summarizes the story can be recorded. (b) is shot on the container ship showing the 'geography' of the item of cargo and fire tender. (c) shows the damaged cruise ship in port and (d) is the disappointed holidaymakers leaving the ship while it is repaired. (e) is an interview with one of the passengers giving his experience of the collision and (f) is a piece-to-camera by the reporter (with an appropriate background) summarizing the story and posing questions of who/what was to blame.

Interviews

The interview is an essential element of news and magazine reporting. It provides for a factual testimony from a participant or witness to an event. Interviews can be shot in a location that reinforces the story and possibly gives more information to the viewer about the speaker (e.g. office, kitchen, garden, etc.). The staging of an interview usually involves placing the interviewee against a suitable background that may echo the content or reinforce the identity of the guest. Exterior interviews are easier to stage when there is a continuity of lighting conditions such as an overcast day or where there is consistent sunshine. The natural lighting will have to cater for three shots and possibly three camera positions – an MCU of the interviewee, a similar sized shot of the interviewer and some kind of 2-shot or 'establishing' shot of them both. If it is decided to shoot the interview in direct sunlight, then the interview needs to be positioned with the sun lighting both 'upstage' faces (i.e. the camera is looking at the shaded side of the face) using a reflector to bounce light into the unlit side of the face. The position of the participants can be 'cheated' for their individual close shots to allow a good position for modelling of the face by the sun. Because of the intensity of sunlight and sometimes because of its inconsistency, it is often preferable to shoot the interview in shade avoiding backgrounds which are in the full brightness of the sun.

Staging an interview

An interview is usually shot using a combination of basic shots which are:

- an MS, MCU or CU of the interviewee;
- a matched shot of the interviewer asking questions or reacting to the answers (usually shot after the interview has ended);
- a 2-shot which establishes location and relationship between the participants or an over-the-shoulder 2-shot looking from interviewer to interviewee.

After the interview has been shot, there is often the need to pick up shots of points raised in the interview (e.g. references to objects, places or activity, etc.). In order for normal 'invisible' editing to be applied, the shots should match in size and lens angle between interviewee and interviewer.

Crossing the line

There may be a number of variations in shots available depending on the number of participants and the method of staging the discussion/interview. All of these shot variations need to be one side of an imaginary line drawn between the participants. To intercut between individual shots of two people to create the appearance of a normal conversation between them, three simple rules have to be observed. First, if a speaker in a single is looking from left to right in the frame then the single of the listener must look right to left. Second, the shot size and eyeline should match (i.e. they should individually be looking out of the frame at a point where the viewer anticipates the other speaker is standing). Finally, every shot of a sequence should stay the same side of an imaginary line drawn between the speakers.

Interview technique

Interviewer　　Interviewee

(a) Camera
position for
MCU interviewee

(b) Camera position
for MCU interviewer
and o/s 2-shot

(c) Camera position
for wide 2-shot

- Set interviewee's position, first ensuring good background and lighting.
- Then set interviewer beside camera lens (a) to achieve a good eyeline on the interviewee.
- It is useful for editing purposes to precede the interview with details of name and title of the interviewee.
- Remind the reporter and interviewee not to speak over the end of an answer.
- Do not allow interviewee to speak over a question.
- Agree with the journalist that he/she will start the interview when cued (or take a count of 5) when the camera is up to speed.
- Record the interviewee's shot first, changing size of shot on the out-of-frame questions.
- Reposition for the interviewer's questions and 'noddies' (b). An over-the-shoulder 2-shot from this position can be useful to the editor when shortening the answers.
- Match the MCU shot size on both participants.
- Do cutaways immediately after interview to avoid changes in light level.
- Always provide cutaways to avoid jump cuts when shortening answers.
- A wide 2-shot of the two participants talking to each other (without sound) can be recorded after the main interview if the shot is sufficiently wide to avoid detecting the lack of lip sync if the shot is used for editing purposes in mid-interview (c).
- Watch that the background to an establishing 2-shot is from a different angle to any cutaway shot of the subject. For example, a wide shot of the ruins of a fire is not used later for the background to an interview about the fire. This causes a continuity 'jump' if they are cut together.
- Think about sound as well as picture, e.g. avoid wind noise, ticking clocks or repetitive mechanical sound, etc., in background.
- Depending on the custom and practice of the commissioning organization that cut the material, use track 1 for v/o and interview, and use track 2 for effects.
- Indicate audio track arrangements on the cassette and put your name/story title on the tape.

135

Live inserts

The ability to broadcast live considerably increases the usefulness of the camera/recorder format. As well as providing recorded news coverage of an event, a single camera unit with portable links can provide live 'updates' from the location. As the camera will be non-synchronous with the studio production, its incoming signal will pass through a digital field and frame synchronizer and the reconstituted signal timed to the station's sync pulse generator. One advantage of this digital conversion is that any loss of signal from the location produces a freeze frame from the frame store of the last usable picture rather than picture break-up.

Equipment

Cameras with a dockable VTR can attach a portable transmitter/receiver powered by the camera battery in place of the VTR. The camera output is transmitted 'line of sight' to a base antenna (up to 1000 m) which relays the signal on by land line, RF link or by a satellite up-link. Other portable 'line of sight' transmitters are designed to be carried by a second operator connected to the camera by cable.

When feeding into an OB scanner on site, the camera/recorder operator can receive a return feed of talkback and cue lights, whilst control of its picture can be remoted to the OB control truck to allow vision control matching to other cameras. It can therefore be used as an additional camera to an outside broadcast unit. In this mode of operation it can supply recorded inserts from remote parts of the location prior to transmission. During transmission the camera reverts to being part of a multi-camera shoot. Unless there is very rapid and/or continuous repositioning, mount the camera on a tripod.

Good communications are essential for a single camera operator feeding a live insert into a programme. Information prior to transmission is required of 'in and out' times, of duration of item and when to cue a 'front of camera' presenter if talkback on an ear piece is not available. A small battery-driven 'off air' portable receiver is usually a valuable addition to the standard camera/recorder unit plus a mobile phone.

A single camera insert can be a very useful programme item in a fast breaking news story, providing location atmosphere and immediacy, but because it is a single camera any change of view must be achieved 'on shot'. This may involve an uncomfortable mixture of panning and zooming in order to change shot. If the story is strong enough, then absorbing content will mask awkward camera moves. Alternatively, a cut back to the studio can allow quick reframing at the location.

If two cameras are used, some method of switching between them is employed via a small field vision mixing panel operated by the director. Because this is a very simple set-up there will be no cue lights fed to the cameras and the operators will therefore need to be informed when they are 'on' and 'off' shot by radio talkback. Cameras need to be jointly white balanced and matched in exposure before the insert.

Geosynchronous orbit

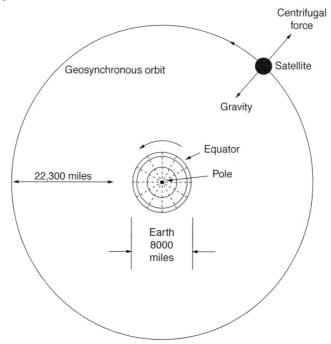

In order that an SNG unit can continuously transmit an unbroken signal without constantly realigning its dish aerial, the satellite must be placed in an orbit stationary above the earth. This is achieved by placing the satellite in an orbit 22,300 miles from the earth where it is held in place by the balance between the opposing force of the gravity pull of the earth against the centrifugal force pulling it out into space. Geosynchronous orbit (GEO) satellites revolve at the same rotational speed as the earth and appear stationary from the earth's surface. Signals can be transmitted to and from them with highly directional antennas pointed in a fixed direction. It is the satellites' fixed position in relation to earth that has allowed the growth of small, portable dish transmitters.

Orbital arcs

The number and position of the satellites located in this orbital arc 23,300 miles above the earth are regulated by a number of world-wide authorities. The satellites are positioned, after the initial launch, by a gas thruster which ensures they keep their position 2° from adjacent satellites. Frequencies used for communications transmission are grouped into Ku band (10.7–18 GHz) and C band (3.7–4.2 GHz). The Ku band is almost universally used for portable SNG service because the antennas are smaller for a given beam width due to the shorter wavelength, and the freedom from interference to and from microwave systems.

There are problems with transmission paths to satellites positioned close to the horizon and therefore some orbital slots are more favourable than others. A minimum elevation angle of 10° to 20° for Ku band is required to avoid difficulty in clearing buildings, trees, and other terrestrial objects, atmospheric attenuation, and electrical noise generated by heat near the earth's surface.

Magazine items

Like news, magazine items often attempt to capture spontaneous action and present an event objectively. But whereas news is generally topical information of the day, shot on the day, magazine themes and issues are shot over a period of time. A news item may have a duration of less than 30 seconds while a 'feature' report can run for 3 to 5 minutes. All these factors have a bearing on the camera techniques that are used on the different genres.

News attempts to emphasize fact rather than opinion although journalistic values cannot escape subjective judgements. Feature items can use fact, feeling and atmosphere, argument, opinion, dramatic reconstruction and subjective impressions which can be very similar to standard feature film storytelling. Non-topical items can be filmed and edited, and often shelved as stand-by or they can be used to balance the programme when required. Without the immediate pressure to transmit, they can have more considered post-production (e.g. the addition of music and effects).

Diary events

Many topics that are featured in news and magazine programmes are known about a long time before the event occurs. These 'diary' events allow forward planning and efficient allocation of people and time. They also provide the opportunity for advanced research and a location shoot can be structured and more considered.

Even if a 'diary' item is considered to be predictable and straightforward, be flexible on the day and be prepared for the unexpected (e.g. an unexpected demonstration by protesters in the middle of a VIP tour).

Abstract items

Many issues dealt with by factual programmes are often of an abstract nature which at first thought have little or no obvious visual equivalent. Images to illustrate such topics as inflation can be difficult to find when searching for visual representations. Often the solution, with the above example, is to fall back on clichéd shots of shoppers and cash tills with a great deal of voice-over narration providing the explanations.

Whatever the nature of a news story there must be an on-screen image, and whatever is chosen, that picture will be invested by the viewer with significance. That significance may not match the main thrust of the item and may lead the viewer away from the topic. For example, a story about rising house prices may feature a couple looking at a house for sale. To the viewer, the couple can easily, inadvertently, become the subject of the story. Consider the relevance of all details in the shot, and have a clear idea of the shape of the item, its structure, and what it is communicating.

Music coverage with a single camera

Non-sync close-ups

Non-specific cutaways

Continuous sound track

A first priority of single camera coverage of a musical item is to make certain there is a well-balanced continuous sound track of the complete piece.

Master shot

Record a master shot with a continuous sound track of the whole musical item. This can take the form of a wide shot of the musicians (or a closer shot in the case of a solo musician), with a couple of camera repositions to give variety to the shot if you are certain the moves can be covered by cutaways or you provide a continuously usable shot.

Avoid using the camera-mounted microphone on music or you risk a selective musical balance, depending where the camera is centre framed.

Second performance

On a second performance of the music, provide the editor with a variety of close shots such as faces (non-singing) that can be cut into the master even if slightly out of sync, but avoid shots of fingering on instruments that may have to be precisely matched up to sync sound – especially keyboards and timpani. If there are vocals, record a third performance featuring complete choruses of singers. These may or may not be usable, depending on the type of music and the ability to cut between takes.

Cutaways

Non-performance shots of the artistes in any location can also help the editor, plus decorative shots of nature, light and location objects.

Documentary ethics

A documentary about two young men contained a sequence of them climbing a fence into a compound and apparently stealing wooden pallets and a wheelbarrow. The director admitted this was staged with the permission of the owner of the yard. He claimed this was done to avoid the unit being involved in an illegal act. He justifies the reconstruction because he claimed the theft would have taken place even if they were not being filmed. This is a common excuse for what is in effect a 'reconstruction'. If the protagonists were likely to do some kind of action, they can be asked to perform it or act out a similar sequence because it is in character. If 'reconstruction' had been supered over the robbery it would have made the documentary less convincing to the viewer because there is no point in watching a poor piece of fiction as the impact and interest of the sequence was premised on the belief that it was 'real'. Is the viewer watching a 'real' event if the director stages what the participants normally do?

The viewing public have only just woken up to the fact that most documentaries are staged in some way or other. 'Reality' programmes are very popular with viewers, but the question facing any would-be documentary cameraman or director is 'how much manipulation does it take to put "reality" onto the TV screen?'

Objectivity

Like news, documentary often attempts to capture spontaneous action and present a slice of life avoiding influencing the subject material with the presence of the camera. But there is also the investigative form of documentary; an exposé of social ills.

Whereas news is generally topical information of the day, shot on the day, to be transmitted on that day, documentary themes and issues are shot over a period of time. The documentary format is often used to take a more considered look at social concerns than may have occurred in the form of a quick specific event in a news bulletin.

Conventional documentary style

A standard documentary structure, popular for many years, involves an unseen presenter (often the producer/director) interviewing the principal subject/s in the film. From the interview (the questions are edited out), appropriate visuals are recorded to match the interviewee comments which then becomes the voice-over. A professional actor is often used to deliver an impersonal narration on scientific or academic subjects. The choice of the quality of the voice is often based on the aim to avoid an overt personality or 'identity' in the voice-over whilst still keeping a lively delivery.

The camera can follow the documentary subject without production intervention, but often the individual is asked to follow some typical activity in order for the camera to catch the event, and to match up with comments made in previous interviews.

Documentary reconstruction

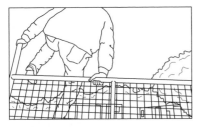 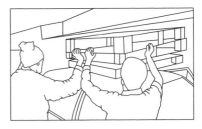

A documentary purporting to follow (without intervention) the criminal activity of two young men breaking into and stealing from a builder's yard. The director of the documentary had got prior permission from the owner to allow this to happen. Was this sequence fact or fiction?

Stylized documentary

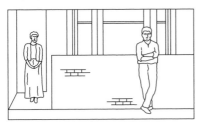 

Documentary styles

Television documentary attempts to deal with the truth of a particular situation but it also has to engage and hold the attention of a mass audience. John Grierson defined documentary as 'the creative treatment of actuality'. How much 'creativity' is mixed in with the attempt at an objective account of the subject has been a subject of debate for many years.

'Verité' as a style

The mini DV camera format has allowed the 'verité' style to proliferate. This type of documentary attempts to be a fly-on-the-wall by simply observing events without influence. It over-relies on chance and the coincidence of being at the right place at the right time to capture an event which will reveal (subjectively judged by the film maker at the editing stage) the nature of the subject. With this style, the main objective of being in the right place at the right time becomes the major creative task. There is often an emphasis on a highly charged atmosphere to inject drama into the story. It may use minimum scripting and research other than to get 'inside' where the action is estimated to be. The style often incorporates more traditional techniques of commentary, interviews, graphics, and reconstruction, using hand-held camerawork and available light technique.

Wildlife

Documentaries featuring the habitat and lives of animals are a perennially popular form of documentary. They often involve long and painstaking observation and filming to get the required footage added to some very ingenious special effects set-ups. A programme about the Himalayan black bear also featured a sequence of the bear hunting for honey on a tree trunk that was filmed in Glasgow Zoo. The director said it would have been impossible to film it in the wild and it was needed because it made the sequence stronger. It is commonplace in wildlife programmes to mix and match wild and captured animals.

Docusoap

The spontaneous style of ordinary people observed strives for 'realism' and neutral reportage but gives no clues to what has been reconstructed. The viewer is sucked into a totally believable account. Many professional film makers protest that the viewer understands their subterfuge and fabrication and they are forgiven for the sake of entertainment, involvement and pace. But do viewers understand the subtleties of programme making? The viewer needs to question what they are shown, but as 'invisible' techniques are designed to hide the joins, how can the viewer remind themselves at each moment that they are watching a construct of reality? A documentary crew followed a woman who repeatedly failed her driving test. One sequence involved the woman waking her husband in the middle of the night with her worries. Did the viewer question if the crew had spent each night in the bedroom waiting on the off-chance that this was going to happen or did they immediately think 'this is a fake – a reconstruction'?

Secret filming

Secret filming allows evidence to be collected that is obtainable by no other method – it is an unglamorous version of crime. Its raw appearance feels closer to reality but there is the danger of becoming obsessed with the form of surveillance/secret filming, and how something was shot becomes more important than the reason it was shot. The stylized conventions of secret filming and the imitation of raw footage such as 'grained up' images, converting colour images to black and white, shaky camerawork and the appearance of voyeurism is a developed programme 'style'.

Video diary format takes the viewer back to themselves, back to the routine and the ordinary which becomes novel and new because it is unlike 'reality' portrayed in the fiction programmes. It allows people to put forward their own idiosyncrasies which differ from documentaries made by TV professionals. Are people spending too much time watching 'reality', leaving no time for their own reality?

Surveillance compilations

The other programme fashion is a proliferation of surveillance camera compilations. These use police car chases, city centre fixed cameras of street crime, etc. This 'reality' TV also includes secret filming and the self-documentation of video diaries. The very roughness of surveillance images guarantees total authenticity. The appeal of this video reality TV is that it is perceived as real – it is not recreation. New technology can go where TV cameras have never been before.

There is in fact a new lust for authenticity – no interpretation, just a flat statement of reality. Programme production has been able to achieve increasing standards of glossiness which can be contrasted with the charge of rawness – the jolt of raw footage which is unmediated – a direct access to the real without modification.

Video diaries

Video diary format takes the viewer back to themselves, back to the routine and the ordinary which becomes novel and new because it is unlike 'reality' portrayed in the fiction programmes. It allows people to put forward their own idiosyncrasies which differ from documentaries made by TV professionals.

Privacy and the mini DV camera

As mini DV cameras can be positioned anywhere and provide continuous coverage, the question raised is do our lives belong to ourselves or can they be just another product for public display and consumption?

If video cameras are used to record more and more of the ordinary and mundane parts of people's lives, will their life only exist through their recordings? Will they only experience their life by watching a playback of it on a TV screen as holidaymakers experience their holidays through a viewfinder and then later through a snapshot album?

Camerawork and editing

It is part of broadcasting folklore that the best place to start to learn about camerawork is in the edit booth. Here, the shots that have been provided by the cameraman have to be previewed, selected and then knitted together by the editor into a coherent structure to explain the story and fit the designated running time of the item in the programme. Clear story telling, running time and structure are the key points of editing and a cameraman who simply provides a endless number of unrelated shots will pose problems for the editor. A cameraman returning from a difficult shoot may have a different version of the edit process. A vital shot may be missing, but then the editor was not there to see the difficulties encountered by the news cameraman. And how about all the wonderful material that was at the end of the second cassette that was never used? With one hour to transmission there was no time to view or to cut it, claims the editor.

In some areas of news and magazine coverage this perennial exchange is being eliminated by the gradual introduction of portable field editing. It is no longer the case of handing over material for someone else 'to sort out'. Now the cameraman is the editor or the editor is the cameraman. This focuses under 'one hat' the priorities of camerawork and the priorities of editing. The cameraman can keep his favourite shot if he can convince himself, as the editor, that the shot is pertinent and works in the final cut.

Selection and structure

Editing is selecting and coordinating one shot with the next to construct a sequence of shots which form a coherent and logical narrative. There are a number of standard editing conventions and techniques that can be employed to achieve a flow of images that guide the viewer through a visual journey. A programme's aim may be to provide a set of factual arguments that allows the viewer to decide on the competing points of view; it may be dramatic entertainment utilizing editing technique to prompt the viewer to experience a series of highs and lows on the journey from conflict to resolution; or a news item's intention may be to accurately report an event for the audience's information or curiosity.

The manipulation of sound and picture can only be achieved electronically, and an editor who aims to fully exploit the potential of television must master the basic technology of the medium. To the knowledge of technique and technology must be added the essential requirement of a supply of appropriate video and audio material. As we have seen in the section on camerawork, the cameraman, director or journalist need to shoot with editing in mind. Unless the necessary shots are available for the item, an editor cannot cut a cohesive and structured story. A random collection of shots is not a story, and although an editor may be able to salvage a usable item from a series of 'snapshots', essentially editing is exactly like the well-known computer equation which states that 'garbage in equals garbage out'.

Camerawork priorities and editing priorities

Order of shooting   Edited order

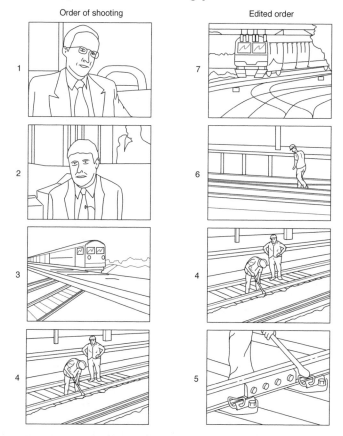

A topical news story (for example an item on rail safety) is required for the early evening bulletin on the day it becomes news. The camera crew and reporter have a very limited time to shoot the material and then get it back to base for editing (e.g. a total of less than 6 hours). The editor with the reporter is also constrained for time in the afternoon (e.g. 3 hours) before the item is transmitted. Time management is important for both groups.

The shooting order depends on availability of material, such as interviews, driving time between locations, and access to locations. Then the cassettes must be returned to base.

In the example story, the interviews (1 and 2) are shot first because the essential participants are available, and also because their comments may provide developments to the story.

Visual support for the comments and the reporter's eventual voice-over are then shot (3–7) at two locations before recording the reporter's 'piece to camera' for the ending (8) (see page 147).

The editor and reporter rearrange the material ensuring there are no visual jumps and the shots follow the points being made in the interviews, and the 'piece to camera'. The archive material of a rail crash (9) is found and inserted to support the main thrust of the item which is rail safety.

Editing technology

Video tape editing started with a primitive mechanical cut and join system on 2-inch tape. As tape formats changed more sophisticated electronic methods were devised but the proliferation of recording formats (including the introduction of disk) meant that nearly all formats have their individual designated editing systems or they need to be dubbed to the preferred editing format. In news programmes and in many other types of programming there is also the need to use library material which may be originated on a superseded and/or obsolete format. The lack of the simple standardization of film (i.e. it is either 35 mm or 16 mm with the complication of changing aspect ratios) has meant that a number of different video editing systems have been devised, mostly using the same basic editing methods but taking place in a variety of recording formats. To add to the variety of contemporary formats and the back catalogues of material are the conversion and compression problems posed by the transition from analogue to digital television. An edit suite or field edit system is therefore defined by its analogue or digital format and whether the shot selection is achieved in a linear or non-linear form.

Selective copying

Recorded video material from the camera almost always requires rearrangement and selection before it can be transmitted. Selective copying from this material onto a new recording is the basis of the video editing craft. Selecting the required shots, finding ways to unobtrusively cut them together to make up a coherent, logical, narrative progression takes time. Using a linear editing technique (i.e. tape-to-tape transfer), and repeatedly re-recording the analogue material exposes the signal to possible distortions and generation losses. Some digital VTR formats very much reduce these distortions. An alternative to this system is to store all the recorded shots on disk or integrated circuits to make up an edit list detailing shot order and source origin (e.g. cassette number, etc.) which can then be used to instruct VTR machines to automatically dub across the required material, or to instruct storage devices to play out shots in the prescribed edit list order.

On tape, an edit is performed by dubbing across the new shot from the originating tape onto the out point of the last shot on the master tape. Simple non-linear disk systems may need to shuffle their recorded data in order to achieve the required frame to frame whereas there is no re-recording required in random access editing, simply an instruction to read frames in a new order from the storage device.

Off-line editing allows editing decisions to be made using low-cost equipment to produce an edit decision list, or a rough cut, which can then be conformed or referred to in a high-quality on-line suite. A high-quality/high-cost edit suite is not required for such decision making, although very few off-line edit facilities allow settings for DVEs, colour correctors or keyers. Low-cost off-line editing allows a range of story structure and edit alternatives to be tried out before tying up a high-cost on-line edit suite to produce the final master tape.

Camerawork priorities and editing priorities (continued from page 145)

Order of shooting   Edited order

The audio is very often just as complex as the reordering of the visuals and needs careful planning and the provision of the right points and length.

Sound and vision need to be provided which will allow the editor to cut to the required time slot in the running order in the time he/she has available to edit the material.

Insert and assembly editing

There are two types of linear editing:

- **Insert editing** records new video and audio over existing recorded material (often black and colour burst) on a 'striped' tape. **Striped tape** is prepared (often referred to as blacking up a tape) before the editing session by recording a continuous control track and timecode along its complete length. This is similar to the need to format a disk before its use in a computer. This pre-recording also ensures that the tape tension is reasonably stable across the length of the tape. During the editing session, only new video and audio is inserted onto the striped tape leaving the existing control track and timecode already recorded on the tape, undisturbed. This minimizes the chance of any discontinuity in the edited result. It ensures that it is possible to come 'out' of an edit cleanly, and return to the recorded material without any visual disturbance. This is the most common method of video tape editing and is the preferred alternative to assemble editing.
- **Assemble editing** is a method of editing onto blank (unstriped) tape in a linear fashion. The control track, timecode, video and audio are all recorded simultaneously and joined to the end of the previously recorded material. This can lead to discontinuities in the recorded timecode and especially with the control track if the master tape is recorded on more than one VTR.

Limitation of analogue signal

The analogue signal can suffer degradation during processing through the signal chain, particularly in multi-generation editing where impairment to the signal is cumulative. This loss of quality over succeeding generations places a limit to the amount of process work that can be achieved in analogue linear editing (e.g. multi-pass build-ups of special effects). This limitation can be reduced by coding the video signal into a 4:2:2 digital form (see page 28).

Compression and editing

As we discussed in Compression (page 26), passing on only the difference between one picture and the next means that at any instant in time, an image can only be reconstructed by reference to a previous 'complete' picture. Editing such compressed pictures can only occur on a complete frame.

Provided the digital signal is uncompressed, there is no limit to how many generations of the original are 'rerecorded' as each new digital generation of the original material is a clone rather than a copy. Imperfections introduced in the editing chain are not accentuated except where different compression systems are applied to the signal in its journey from acquisition to the viewer. Nearly all digital signals from the point of acquisition are compressed. Care must be taken when editing compressed video to make certain that the edit point of an incoming shot is a complete frame, and does not rely (during compression decoding) on information from a preceding frame (see page 29).

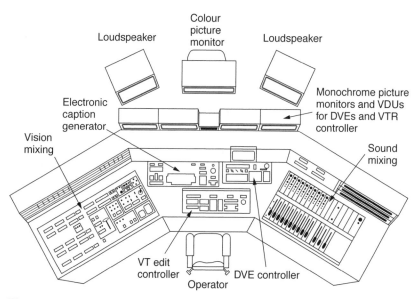

Loudspeaker

Colour picture monitor

Loudspeaker

Electronic caption generator

Monochrome picture monitors and VDUs for DVEs and VTR controller

Vision mixing

Sound mixing

VT edit controller

Operator

DVE controller

The technical requirements for an edit

- Enter the replay timecode in and out points into the edit controller.
- Enter the record tape timecode in-point.
- Preview the edit.
- Check sync stability for the pre-roll time when using time-of-day timecode.
- Make the edit.
- Check the edit is technically correct in sound and vision and the edit occurs at the required place.
- When two shots are cut together, check that there is continuity across the cut and the transition (to an innocent eye) is invisible.

Timecode and editing

Editing requires the required shot to be quickly located on the appropriate tape (linear editing) or by code or description on a disk (non-linear editing). Identification of shots becomes of paramount importance especially in high-speed turnaround operations such as news. Many non-news productions use a log (dope sheet) which records details of shots and the start/finish timecode. News editing usually has to rely on previewing or pre-selection (if there is time) by a journalist. Video editing can only be achieved with precision if there is a method of uniquely identifying each frame. Usually at the point of origination in the camera (see page 92), a timecode number identifying hour, minute, second and frame is recorded on the tape against every frame of video. This number can be used when the material is edited, or a new series of numbers can be generated and added before editing. A common standard is the SMPTE/EBU which is an 80-bit code defined to contain sufficient information for most video editing tasks.

There are two types of timecode: record run and free run.

Record run

Record run only records a frame identification when the camera is recording. The timecode is set to zero at the start of the day's operation, and a continuous record is produced on each tape covering all takes. It is customary practice to record the tape number in place of the hour section on the timecode. For example, the first cassette of the day would start 01.00.00.00, and the second cassette would start 02.00.00.00. Record run is the preferred method of recording timecode on most productions.

Free run

In free run, the timecode is set to the actual time of day, and when synchronized, is set to run continuously. Whether the camera is recording or not, the internal clock will continue to operate. When the camera is recording, the actual time of day will be recorded on each frame. In free run (time-of-day), a change in shot will produce a gap in timecode proportional to the amount of time that elapsed between actual recordings. These missing timecode numbers can cause problems with the edit controller when it rolls back from an intended edit point, and is unable to find the timecode number it expects there (i.e. the timecode of the frame to cut on, minus the pre-roll time).

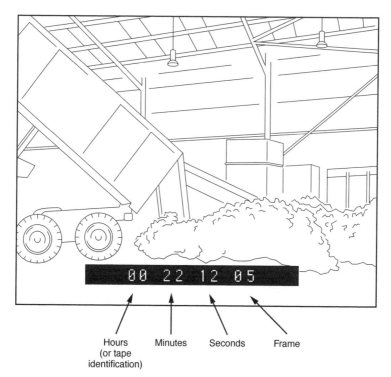

Hours   Minutes   Seconds   Frame
(or tape
identification)

Code word: Every frame contains an 80-bit code word which contains 'time bits' (8 decimal numbers) recording hours, minutes, seconds, frames and other digital synchronizing information. All this is updated every frame but there is room for additional 'user bit' information.

User-bit: User-bit allows up to 9 numbers and an A to F code to be programmed into the code word which is recorded every frame. Unlike the 'time bits', the user-bits remain unchanged until re-programmed. They can be used to identify production, cameraman, etc.

Problems with DV format timecode

DV recording format cameras are intended for the non-broadcast consumer market and their timecode facility is often less complex than standard broadcast formats. When recording a new shot, the timecode circuit picks up the new code from the previous shot. If the previous shot has been previewed and then the tape has been parked on blank tape (a prudent practice to avoid over-recording existing material), the timecode will read the 'blank tape' and assume it is at the start of a new reel. The code will revert to 00.00.00.00. This can cause problems in editing as there will be more than one shot with the same timecode. Standard broadcast format cameras have an edit search button to butt the next recording hard up against the existing recording. This provides a seamless cut between the two shots but DV format cameras may have a break in timecode if either a gap is left between two shots or the cassette has been removed and replaced in the camera.

Continuity editing

As well as the technological requirements needed to edit together two shots, there are subtle but more important basic editing conventions to be satisfied if the viewer is to remain unaware of shot transition. It would be visually distracting if the audience's attention was continually interrupted by every change of shot.

Moving images in film or television are created by the repetition of individual static frames. It is human perception that combines the separate images into a simulation of movement. One reason this succeeds is that the adjacent images in a shot are very similar. If the shot is changed and new information appears within the frame (e.g. what was an image of a face is now an aeroplane), the eye/brain takes a little time to understand the new image. The greater the visual discrepancy between the two shots, the more likely it is that the viewer will consciously notice the change of shot.

A basic editing technique is to find ways of reducing the visual mismatch between two adjacent images. In general, a change of shot will be unobtrusive:

- if the individual shots (when intercutting between people) are matched in size, have the same amount of headroom, have the same amount of looking space if in semi-profile, if the lens angle is similar (i.e. internal perspective is similar) and if the lens height is the same;
- if the intercut pictures are colour matched (e.g. skin tones, background brightness, etc.) and if in succeeding shots the same subject has a consistent colour (e.g. grass in a stadium);
- if there is continuity in action (e.g. body posture, attitude) and the flow of movement in the frame is carried over into the succeeding shot;
- if there is a significant change in shot size or camera angle when intercutting on the same subject or if there is a significant change in content;
- if there is continuity in lighting, in sound, props and setting and continuity in performance or presentation.

As we have already identified, the basis of all invisible technique employed in programme production and specifically in continuity editing is to ensure that:

- shots are structured to allow the audience to understand the space, time and logic of the action so each shot follows the line of action to maintain consistent screen direction to make the geography of the action completely intelligible;
- unobtrusive camera movement and shot change directs the audience to the content of the production rather than the mechanics of production;
- continuity editing creates the illusion that distinct, separate shots (possibly recorded out of sequence and at different times) form part of a continuous event being witnessed by the audience.

Cutaways and cut-in

(a) Antiques expert talking about the detail in a piece of pottery

(b) Listener reacting to expert

(c) Close-up of the vase

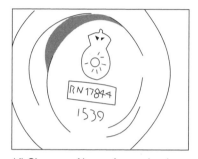

(d) Close-up of base of vase showing manufacturer's mark

A cutaway literally means to cut away from the main subject (a) either as a reaction to the event, e.g. cutting to a listener reacting to what a speaker is saying (b), or to support the point being made.

A cut-in usually means to go tighter on an aspect of the main subject. In the above example, the antiques expert talking in mid-shot (a) about the detail in a piece of pottery would require a cut-in close shot of the vase (c) to support the comment, and an even closer shot (d) to see a manufacturer's mark on the base of the piece for the item to make sense to the viewer. Without these supporting shots, the item relies on what is being said to the viewer (similar to a 'radio' description) rather than what the viewer can see for themselves.

Perennial techniques

The skills and craft employed by the film editor to stitch together a sequence of separate shots persuades the audience that they are watching a continuous event. The action flows from shot to shot and appears natural and obvious. Obviously the craft of editing covers a wide range of genres up to and including the sophisticated creative decisions that are required to cut feature films. However, there is not such a wide gap between different editing technique as first it would appear.

Rearranging time and space

When two shots are cut together the audience attempts to make a connection between them. For example, a man on a station platform boards a train. A wide shot shows a train pulling out of a station. The audience makes the connection that the man is in the train. A cut to a close shot of the seated man follows, and it is assumed that he is travelling on the train. We see a wide shot of a train crossing the Forth Bridge, and the audience assumes that the man is travelling in Scotland. Adding a few more shots would allow a shot of the man leaving the train at his destination with the audience experiencing no violent discontinuity in the depiction of time or space. And yet a journey that may take two hours is collapsed to 30 seconds of screen time, and a variety of shots of trains and a man at different locations have been strung together in a manner that convinces the audience they have followed the same train and man throughout a journey.

Basic editing principles

This way of arranging shots is fundamental to editing. Space and time are rearranged in the most efficient way to present the information that the viewer requires to follow the argument presented. The transition between shots must not violate the audience's sense of continuity between the actions presented. This can be achieved by:

- **Continuity of action:** action is carried over from one shot to another without an apparent break in speed or direction of movement (see figures opposite).
- **Screen direction:** each shot maintains the same direction of movement of the principal subject (see the cut from (a) to (b)).
- **Eyeline match:** the eyeline of someone looking out of frame should be in the direction the audience believes the subject of the observation is situated. If they look out of frame with their eyeline levelled at their own height, the implication is that they are looking at something at that height.

There is a need to cement the spatial relationship between shots. Eyeline matches are decided by position (see Crossing the line, page 134), and there is very little that can be done at the editing stage to correct shooting mismatches except flipping the frame to reverse the eyeline which alters the continuity of the symmetry of the face and other left/right continuity elements in the composition such as hair partings, etc.

Screen direction

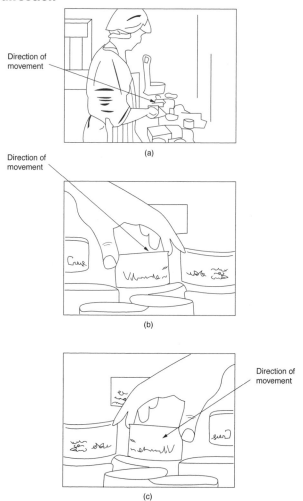

Direction of movement

(a)

Direction of movement

(b)

Direction of movement

(c)

In a medium shot, for example (a), someone is wrapping a small cheese and placing it on the work surface. A cut to a closer shot of the table (b) shows the cheese just before it is laid on the table. Providing the cheese position relative to the table and the speed of its movement in both shots is similar, and there is continuity in the table surface, lighting, hand position, etc., then the cut will not be obtrusive. A cut on movement is often the preferred edit convention. A close shot that crosses the line (c) will not cut.

Matching shots

Matching visual design between shots
The cut between two shots can be made invisible if the incoming shot has one or more similar compositional elements as the preceding shot. The relationships between the two shots may relate to similar shape, similar position of dominant subject in the frame, colours, lighting, setting, overall composition, etc. Any similar aspects of visual design that are present in both shots (e.g. matching tone, colour or background) will help smooth the transition from one shot to the next. There is, however, a critical point in matching identical shots to achieve an unobtrusive cut (e.g. cutting together the same size shot of the same individual), where the jump between almost identical shots becomes noticeable. Narrative motivation for changing the shot (e.g. 'What happens next? What is this person doing?' etc.) will also smooth the transition.

Matching temporal relationships between shots
The position of a shot in relation to other shots (preceding or following) will control the viewers' understanding of its time relationship to surrounding shots. Usually a factual event is cut in a linear time line unless indicators are built in to signal flashbacks, or, very rarely, flashforwards. The viewer assumes the order of depicted events is linked to the passing of time. The duration of an event can be considerably shortened to a fraction of its actual running time by editing if the viewers' concept of time passing is not violated. The standard formula for compressing space and time is to allow the main subject to leave frame, or to provide appropriate cutaways to shorten the actual time taken to complete the activity. While they are out of shot, the viewer will accept that greater distance has been travelled than is realistically possible.

Matching spatial relationships between shots
Editing creates spatial relationships between subjects which need never exist in reality. A common example is a shot of an interviewee responding to an out-of-frame question followed by a cut to the questioner listening and nodding attentively. This response, filmed possibly after the interviewee has left the location, is recorded for editing purposes in order to shorten an answer or to allow a change of shot size on the guest. The two shots are normally accepted by the viewer as being directly connected in time and the attentive 'nodding' is perceived as a genuine response to what the guest is saying. Cause and effect patterns occur continuously in editing.

Any two subjects or events can be linked by a cut if there is an apparent graphic continuity between shots framing them, and if there is an absence of an establishing shot showing their physical relationship.

Disguising the join between two shots can be achieved by:

- matching by visual design (i.e. shot composition);
- matching spatial relationships;
- matching rhythm relationships;
- matching temporal relationships;
- cutting on action;
- cutting on dialogue or sound.

Basic visual transitions include:

- **A cut,** the simplest switch between shots. One image is instantaneously replaced by another image.
- **Dissolve or mix** (also known as a cross-fade) allows the incoming shot to emerge from the outgoing shot until it replaces it on screen. Sometimes both images are held on screen (a half-mix) before completing the transition. The time taken for the dissolve to make the transition from one image to the next can vary depending on content and the dramatic point the dissolve is making. The proportion of each image present at any point in the mix can be varied, with one image being held as a dominant image for most of the dissolve.
- **Fade** is similar to a mix except only one image is involved and either appears from a blank/black screen (fade-in) or dissolves into a blank/black screen (fade-out). A fade-in is often used to begin a sequence whilst a fade-out marks a natural end to a sequence.
- **Superimposition** is when one image (often text, such as the name of the speaker in shot) is superimposed on top of another image. Name-super text is usually faded-in or wiped-in, held so that it can be read, and then faded-out, cut-out or wiped-out.
- **Wipes and pattern wipes** provide an edge that moves across the screen between the outgoing image and the incoming image. The edge may be soft or bordered (a soft-wipe, or a border-wipe) to add to the transition visually.
- **Split screen** is when two different images are held on screen separated by a hard or soft edge wipe.
- **Digital video effect (DVE):** When a picture is digitalized the image is formed by millions of separate parts called pixels. These pixels can be endlessly rearranged to produce a variety of random and mathematically defined transitions such as geometric wipes, spins, tumbles, squeezes, squashing, and transitions from one image to another simulating the page of a book, for example, being turned to introduce the next image.
- **Colour synthesizers:** A method of producing coloured captions and other effects from a monochrome source. The synthesizers rely on an adjustable preset video level to operate a switch, and usually two or three levels can be separated and used to operate colour generators and produce different colours. The switching signal is usually derived from a caption generator.
- **Chroma key:** A method of combining two images to achieve the appearance of a single image. This technique requires a switch to be inserted in the signal chain which will electronically select the appropriate image. Blue is commonly chosen as the colour to be used as the separation key but other colours can be employed.

Rhythm

The editor needs to consider two types of rhythm when cutting together shots; the rhythm created by the rate of shot change, and the internal rhythm of the depicted action. Each shot will have a measurable time on screen. The rate at which shots are cut creates a rhythm which affects the viewer's response to the sequence. For example, in a feature film action sequence, a common way of increasing the excitement and pace of the action is to increase the cutting rate by decreasing the duration of each shot on screen as the action approaches a climax. The rhythms introduced by editing are in addition to the other rhythms created by artiste movement, camera movement, and the rhythm of sound. The editor can therefore adjust shot duration and shot rate independent of the need to match continuity of action between shots; this controls an acceleration or deceleration in the pace of the item. By controlling the editing rhythm, the editor controls the amount of time the viewer has to grasp and understand the selected shots. Many productions exploit this fact in order to create an atmosphere of mystery and confusion by ambiguous framing and rapid cutting which deliberately undermines the viewer's attempt to make sense of the images they are shown.

Another editing consideration is maintaining the rhythm of action carried over into succeeding shots. Most people have a strong sense of rhythm as expressed in running, marching, dancing, etc. If this rhythm is destroyed, as, for example, cutting together a number of shots of a marching band so that their step becomes irregular, viewers will sense the discrepancies, and the sequence will appear disjointed and awkward. When cutting from a shot of a person running, for example (see figure opposite), care must be taken that the person's foot hits the ground with the same rhythm as in the preceding shot, and that it is the appropriate foot (e.g. after a left foot comes a right foot). Sustaining rhythms of action may well override the need for a narrative 'ideal' cut at an earlier or later point.

Alternatives to 'invisible technique'

An alternative editing technique, such as, for example, pop promotions, use hundreds of cuts, disrupted continuity, ambiguous imagery, etc., to deliberately visually tease the audience, and to avoid clear visual communication. The aim is often to recreate the 'rave' experience of a club or concert. The production intention is to be interpretative rather than informative (see Alternative styles, page 130). There are innovations and variations on basic technique, but the majority of television programme productions use the standard editing conventions to keep the viewer's attention on the content of the programme rather than its method of production. Standard conventions are a response to the need to provide a variety of ways of presenting visual information coupled with the need for them to be unobtrusive in their transition from shot to shot. Expertly used, they are invisible and yet provide the narrative with pace, excitement, and variety.

Cutting to rhythm

In the example illustrated, the editor will need to solve several basic editing problems when cutting together a sequence of shots following a cross-country runner in a race:

■ The running time of the item will be of a much shorter duration than the actual event, and if shot on one camera, there will be gaps in the coverage. Ways have to be found to cut together a compressed account of the race.

■ The editor must ensure that standard visual conventions of continuity of action and screen direction are carried over from one shot to the next without an apparent break in speed or direction of movement so that the viewer understands what is happening (e.g. no instant reversal of direction across the screen).

■ The editor will have to maintain the continuity of arm and leg movement between shots, avoiding any jump in the rhythm of movement.

■ Possibly the rate of cutting may be increased towards the end of the race to inject pace and tension.

■ Added to all of the above will be the need to match the continuity of background so that the designated runner appears to have run through a 'logical' landscape.

Cutting to music (see also page 139)

It helps when cutting to music to have an appreciation of music form, but the minimum skill that is required to be developed by an editor is a feel for pace and tempo, and an understanding of bar structure. Most popular music is created around a 16 or 32 bar structure and the cutting rate and time of the cut happening will relate to this bar structure. Listen to a wide range of music and identify the beat and changes in phrase and melody. A shot change on the beat (or on the 'off' beat) will lift the tempo of the item. Shot changes out of sync with the tempo, mood or structure of the music will neither flow nor help the images to meld together.

Types of edit

There are a number of standard editing techniques that are used across a wide range of programme making. These include:

- **Intercutting editing** can be applied to locations or people. The technique of intercutting between different actions that are happening simultaneously at different locations was discovered as early as 1906 to inject pace and tension into a story. Intercutting on faces in the same location presents the viewer with changing viewpoints on action and reaction.
- **Analytical editing** breaks a space down into separate framings. The classic sequence begins with a long shot to show relationships and the 'geography' of the setting followed by closer shots to show detail, and to focus on important action.
- **Contiguity editing** follows action through different frames of changing locations. The classic pattern of shots in a 'western' chase sequence is where one group of horsemen ride through the frame past a distinctive tree to be followed later, in the same framing, by the pursuers riding through shot past the same distinctive tree. The tree acts as a 'signpost' for the audience to establish location, and as a marker of the duration of elapsed time between the pursued and the pursuer.
- **Point-of-view shot.** A variant of this, which establishes the relationship between different spaces, is the point-of-view shot. Someone on-screen looks out of one side of the frame. The following shot reveals what the person is looking at. This can also be applied to anyone moving and looking out of frame, followed by their moving point-of-view shot.

Previewing

The restraints of cutting a story to a specific running time, and having it ready for a broadcast transmission deadline, is a constant pressure on the television editor. Often there is simply not enough time to preview all the material in 'real' time. Usually material is shuttled through at a fast-forward speed stopping only to check vital interview content. The editor has to develop a visual memory of the content of a shot and its position in the reel. One of the major contributions an editor can make is the ability to remember a shot that solves some particular visual dilemma. If two crucial shots will not cut together because of continuity problems, is there a suitable 'buffer' shot that could be used? The ability to identify and remember the location of a specific shot, even when spooling and shuttling, is a skill that has to be learnt in order to speed up editing.

Solving continuity problems is one reason why the location production unit need to provide additional material to help in the edit. It is a developed professional skill to find the happy medium between too much material that cannot be previewed in the editing time available, and too little material that gives the edit no flexibility if structure, running time, or story development changes between shooting and editing the material.

Cutting on movement

A change of shot requires a measurable time for the audience to adjust to the incoming shot. If the shot is part of a series of shots showing an event or action, the viewer will be able to follow the flow of action across the cut if the editor has selected an appropriate point to cut on movement. This will move the viewer into the next part of the action without them consciously realizing a cut has occurred. An edit point in the middle of an action disguises the edit point.

Cutting on movement is the bedrock of editing. It is the preferred option in cutting, compared to most other editing methods, provided the sequence has been shot to include action edit points. When breaking down a sequence of shots depicting a continuous action, there are usually five questions faced by the editor:

- What is visually interesting?
- What part of a shot is necessary to advance the 'story' of the topic?
- How long can the sequence last ?
- Has the activity been adequately covered on camera?
- Is there a sufficient variety of shots to serve the above requirements?

Cutting on exits and entrances

One of the basic tenets of perennial editing technique is that each shot follows the line of action to maintain consistent screen direction so that the geography of the action is completely intelligible. Cutting on exits and entrances into a frame is a standard way of reducing the amount of screen time taken to traverse distance. The usual convention is to make the cut when the subject has nearly left the frame. It is natural for the viewer, if the subject is disappearing out of the side of the frame, to wish to be shown where they are going. If the cut comes after they have left the frame then the viewer is left with an empty frame and either their interest switches to whatever is left in the frame or they feel frustrated because the subject of their interest has gone. Conversely, the incoming frame can have the subject just appearing, but the match on action has to be good otherwise there will be an obtrusive jump in their walking cadence or some other posture mismatch. Allowing the subject to clear the frame in the outgoing shot and not be present in the incoming shot is usually the lazy way of avoiding continuity mismatches. An empty frame at the end of a shot is already 'stale' to the viewer. If it is necessary, because there is no possibility in the shots provided of matching up the action across the cut, try to use the empty frame of the incoming shot (which is new to the viewer) before the action begins, to avoid continuity problems. This convention can be applied to any movement across a cut. In general, choose an empty frame on an incoming shot rather than the outgoing shot unless there is the need for a 'visual' full stop to end a sequence, e.g. a fade-down or mix across to a new scene.

Frequently cameras are intercut to follow action. It is important to know when to follow the action and when to hold a static frame and let the action leave the frame. For example, a camera framed on an MCU of someone sitting could pan with them when they stood up but this might spoil the cut to a wider shot. A camera tightening into MCU may prevent a planned cut to the same size shot from another camera.

Fact or fiction

The editing techniques used for cutting fiction and factual material are almost the same. When switching on a television programme mid-way, it is sometimes impossible to assess from the editing alone if the programme is fact or fiction. Documentary makers use story telling techniques learned by audiences from a lifetime of watching drama. Usually, the indicator of what genre the production falls into is gained from the participants. Even the most realistic acting appears stilted or stylized when placed alongside people talking in their own environment. Another visual convention is to allow 'factual' presenters to address the lens and the viewer directly, whereas actors and the 'public' are usually instructed not to look at camera.

- **Communication and holding attention:** The primary aim of editing is to provide the right structure and selection of shots to communicate to the audience the programme maker's motives for making the programme, and, second, to hold their attention so that they listen and remain watching.
- **Communication with the audience:** Good editing technique structures the material and identifies the main 'teaching' points the audience should understand. A crucial role of the editor is to be audience 'number one'. The editor will start fresh to the material and he/she must understand the story in order for the audience to understand the story. The editor needs to be objective and bring a dispassionate eye to the material. The director/reporter may have been very close to the story for hours/days/weeks – the audience comes to it new and may not pick up the relevance of the setting or set-up if this is spelt out rapidly in the first opening sentence. It is surprising how often, with professional communicators, that what is obvious to them about the background detail of a story is unknown or its importance unappreciated by their potential audience. Beware of the 'I think that is so obvious we needn't mention it' statement. As an editor, if you do not understand the relevance of the material, say so. You will not be alone.
- **Holding their attention:** The edited package needs to hold the audience's attention by its method of presentation (e.g. method of storytelling – what happens next, camera technique, editing technique, etc.). Pace and brevity (e.g. no redundant footage) are often the key factors in raising the viewer's involvement in the item. Be aware that visuals can fight voice-over narration. Arresting images capture the attention first. The viewer would probably prefer to 'see it' rather than 'hear it'. A successful visual demonstration is always more convincing than a verbal argument – as every successful salesman knows.
- **Selection:** Editing, in a literal sense, is the activity of selecting from all the available material and choosing what is relevant. Film and video editing requires the additional consideration that selected shots spliced together must meet the requirements of the standard conventions of continuity editing.

Reconstruction

An early documentary, John Grierson's 'Drifters' (1929), included sequences which were shot on the beach with a 'mock-up' of a boat with fresh fish bought from a shop. Grierson described documentary as 'the creative treatment of reality' and suggested that documentary style should be 'in a fashion which strikes the imagination and makes observation a little richer'.

Creative treatment of reality

A contemporary television documentary followed a woman who had repeatedly failed her driving test. One sequence depicted her waking her husband at night for him to test her knowledge of driving. A shot of a bedroom clock suggested it was 2.15 am. Was the clock set and lit for this 'night time' shot? Was the production unit in the couple's bedroom at night? Was this fact or fiction?

Wildlife programmes

A close-up crabbing shot of geese in a wild life programme was obtained by patiently training the geese, from a young age, to fly alongside a car. After training, the shot was easily obtained. Within the context of the film, it appeared as if the geese were filmed in their natural habitat. Was this shot fact or reconstruction?

163

What the editor requires

Providing cutting points

Most interviews will be edited down to a fraction of their original running time. Be aware of the need for alternative shots to allow for this to happen.

Brief the presenter/journalist to start talking when you cue (i.e. approximately 5/6 seconds after start of recording) and to precede the interview with the interviewee's name and status to 'ident' the interview. Also ask them not to speak over the end of an answer or allow the interviewee to speak over the start of a question. If necessary, change framing during questions but not answers unless you make the camera movement smooth and usable.

Cutaways

Make sure your 2-shots, cutaways, reverse questions, noddies, etc., follow the interview immediately. Not only does this save the editor time in shuttling but light conditions may change and render the shots unusable. Match the interviewee and interviewer shot size. If the interview is long, provide cutaways on a separate tape. Listen to the content of the interview, which may suggest suitable cutaways.

Think about sound as well as pictures

If the interview is exterior, check for wind noise and shield the microphone as much as possible by using a windshield or using the presenter's/interviewee's body as a windbreak. Check background noise, particularly any continuous sound such as running water which may cause sound jumps in editing. Record a 'wild track' or 'buzz track' of atmosphere or continuous sound after the interview to assist the editor.

Backgrounds

If an interview is being conducted against a changing background (e.g. a tennis match or a busy shopping arcade) reverse questions must be shot because a 2-shot, shot after the interview will not match. If an interview or 'presenter to camera' is staged in front of a discussed building or object (e.g. crash scene) which is an essential part of the item, make certain that cutaways of the building or object are sufficiently different in angle and size to avoid jump cuts.

Eyeline and frame

Alternate the direction the interviewees are looking in the frame so that the editor can create the feeling of a dialogue between consecutive speakers and to avoid jump cuts between subjects who are looking in the same direction.

Thinking about editing when shooting (continued on page 167)

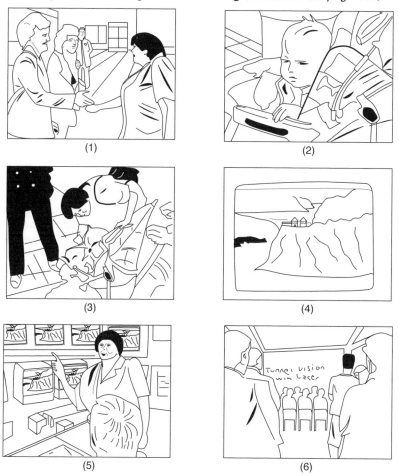

(1)

(2)

(3)

(4)

(5)

(6)

A news item about a politician's visit may eventually be given a running order time of less than 25 seconds. In reality the visit may have taken 2 or 3 hours. The news coverage needs to include the essential points of the visit but also to provide the editor with maximum flexibility in the final cut. The shooting ratio must be low enough to have adequate material but not over-long so that the editor cannot preview and cut the material in the time available.

The sound will be voice-over explaining the purpose of the visit with actuality sound of interview comments (9) and (10) finishing with an interview with the politician (12). The politician's speech (8) will be a précis on the voice-over (see page 167).

The cameraman can help the editor by providing buffer shots to allow the politician to be seen in the various locations (1), (3), (5), (8) and (12) with no jump cuts (see page 167).

165

Telling a story

The story telling of factual items is probably better served by the presentation of detail rather than broad generalizations. Which details are chosen to explain a topic is crucial, both in explanation and engagement. Many issues dealt with by factual programmes are often of an abstract nature which, at first thought, have little or no obvious visual representation. Images to illustrate topics such as inflation can be difficult to find when searching for precise representations of the diminishing value of money. The camera must provide an image of something, and whatever it may be, that something will be invested by the viewer with significance.

That significance may not match the main thrust of the item and may lead the viewer away from the topic. Significant detail requires careful observation at location, and a clear idea of the shape of the item when it is being shot. The editor then has to find ways of cutting together a series of shots so the transitions are seamless, and the images logically advance the story. Remember that the viewer will not necessarily have the same impression or meaning from an image that you have invested in it. A shot of a doctor on an emergency call having difficulty in parking, chosen, for example, to illustrate the problems of traffic congestion, may be seen by some viewers as simply an illustration of bad driving.

A linking theme
Because the story is told over time, there is a need for a central motif or thread which is easily followed and guides the viewer through the item. A report, for example, on traffic congestion may have a car driver on a journey through rush hour traffic. Each point about the causes of traffic congestion can be illustrated and picked up as they occur, such as out-of-town shoppers, the school run, commuters, traffic black spots, road layout, etc. The frustrations of the journey throughout the topic will naturally link the 'teaching points', and the viewer can easily identify and speculate about the story's outcome.

Time
With the above example, as the story progresses over time, the attitude of the driver will probably change. He/she may display bad temper, irritation with other road users, etc. There will be a difference over time and without time there is no story. Finding ways of registering change over time is one of the key activities of editing. Choosing shots that register the temperament of the driver by using small observational details (providing the cameraman has shot the detail) reveals the story to the viewer. The main topic of the item is traffic congestion and its wear and tear on everyday life. It can be effectively revealed by focusing on one drive through a narrated journey rather than generalizations by a presenter standing alongside a traffic queue.

Thinking about editing when shooting (*continued from page 165*)

(7)   (8)

(9)   (10)

(11)   (12)

The cameraman can help the editor to condense time and place by:

- Shot (2): remembering to provide a shot of the child the politician was talking to after the politician has left. This avoids a jump between (1) and (3) (see page 165).
- Shot (4): providing a shot of the TV screen the politician is standing in front of in (5). This allows the introduction of a new location without a jump. The transition can also be smoothed by the content of the voice-over (see page 165).
- Shot (6) (see page 165): a long shot from the back of the hall allows the politician to move to a new location and the cutaway audience shots (7) and (11) allow the section to fit the allowed duration of the voice-over avoiding any lip-sync clash.
- The cameraman has provided different eyelines for two conflicting comments about the politician. The interviewee (9) is staged looking left to right. The interviewee shot (10) is staged looking right to left which makes a natural cut between them as if they were in conversation but holding different viewpoints. They are matched in size and headroom.
- The final interview shot (12) is a selected key point comment by the politician following on the voice-over summing-up the visit.

167

Structuring a sequence

The chosen structure of a section or sequence will usually have a beginning, a development, and a conclusion. Editing patterns and the narrative context do not necessarily lay the events of a story out in simple chronological order. For example, there can be a 'tease' sequence which seeks to engage the audience's attention with a question or a mystery. It may be some time into the material before the solution is revealed, and the audience's curiosity is satisfied. Whatever the shape of the structure it usually contains one or more of the following methods of sequence construction:

- A **narrative** sequence is a record of an event such as a child's first day at school, an Olympic athlete training in the early morning, etc. Narrative sequences tell a strong story and are used to engage the audience's interest.

- A **descriptive** sequence simply sets the atmosphere or provides background information. For example, an item featuring the retirement of a watchmaker may have an introductory sequence of shots featuring the watches and clocks in his workshop before the participant is introduced or interviewed. Essentially, a descriptive sequence is a scene setter, an overture to the main point of the story, although sometimes it may be used as an interlude to break up the texture of the story, or act as a transitional visual bridge to a new topic.

- An **explanatory** sequence is, as the name implies, a sequence which explains either the context of the story, facts about the participants or event, or to explain an idea. Abstract concepts like a rise in unemployment usually need a verbal explanatory section backed by 'visual wallpaper' – images which are not specific or important in themselves, but are needed to accompany the important narration. Explanatory sequences are likely to lose the viewer's interest, and need to be supported by narrative and description. Explanatory exposition is often essential when winding-up an item in order to draw conclusions or make explicit the relevance of the events depicted.

The shape of a sequence

The tempo and shape of a sequence, and of a number of sequences that may make up a longer item, will depend on how these methods of structuring are cut and arranged. Whether shooting news or documentaries, the transmitted item will be shaped by the editor to connect a sequence of shots either visually, by voice-over, atmosphere, music, or by a combination of any of them. Essentially the cameraman or director must organize the shooting of separate shots with some structure in mind. Any activity must be filmed to provide a sufficient variety of shots that are able to be cut together following standard editing conventions (e.g. avoidance of jump cuts, not crossing the line, etc.), and enough variety of shot to allow some flexibility in editing. Just as no shot can be considered in isolation, every sequence must be considered in context with the overall aims of the production.

168

Descriptive shots, narrative shots, explanatory shots

Shot 1 (descriptive) sets the atmosphere for the item – early morning, countryside location.

Shot 2 is still mainly descriptive but introduces the subject of the narration.

Shot 3 (narrative) goes closer to the subject who remains mysterious because he
is in silhouette – the story begins in voice-over.

Shot 4 (narrative) the subject's face is revealed but not his objective.

Shot 5 (narrative) the subject is now running in city streets – where is he running
to?

Shot 6 (narrative) the subject is followed inside an office building running down
a corridor.

Shot 7 (narrative) the subject enters, now in office clothes.

Shot 8 (explanatory) the subject explains, in an interview, his ambition to run in
the Olympics, etc., and a voice-over rounds off the story.

Editing an interview

The interview is an essential element of news and magazine reporting. It provides for a factual testimony from an active participant similar to a witness's court statement; that is, direct evidence of their own understanding, not rumour or hearsay. They can speak about what they feel, what they think, what they know, from their own experience. An interviewee can introduce into the report opinion, beliefs and emotion as opposed to the reporter who traditionally sticks to the facts. An interviewee therefore provides colour and emotion into an objective assessment of an event and captures the audience's attention.

How long should a shot be held?
The simple answer to this question is as long as the viewer needs to extract the required information, or before the action depicted requires a wider or closer framing to satisfy the viewer's curiosity, or a different shot (e.g. someone exiting the frame) to follow the action. The on-screen length also depends on many more subtle considerations than the specific content of the shot.

As discussed above, the rhythm of the editing produced by rate of shot change, and the shaping of the rate of shot change to produce an appropriate shape to a sequence, will have a bearing on how long a shot is held on screen. Rhythm relies on variation of shot length, but should not be arbitrarily imposed simply to add interest. As always with editing, there is a balance to be struck between clear communication, and the need to hold the viewer's interest with visual variety. The aim is to clarify and emphasize the topic, and not confuse the viewer with shots that are snatched off the screen before they are visually understood.

The critical factor controlling on-screen duration is often the shot size. A long shot may have a great deal more information than a close shot. Also, a long shot is often used to introduce a new location or to set the 'geography' of the action. These features will be new to the audience, and therefore they will take longer to understand and absorb the information. Shifting visual information produced by moving shots will also need longer screen time.

A closer shot will usually yield its content fairly quickly, particularly if the content has been seen before (e.g. a well-known 'screen' face). There are other psychological aspects of perception which also have a bearing on how quickly an audience can recognize images which are flashed on to a screen. These factors are exploited in those commercials which have a very high cutting rate, but are not part of standard news/magazine editing technique.

Content and pace

Although news/magazine editing is always paring an item down to essential shots, due consideration should always be given to the subject of the item. For example, a news item about the funeral of a victim of a civil disaster or crime has to have pauses and 'quiet' on-screen time to reflect the feelings and emotion of the event. Just as there is a need to have changes of pace and rhythm in editing a piece to give a particularly overall shape, so a news bulletin or magazine running order will have an overall requirement for changes of tempo between hard and soft items to provide balance and variety.

Cutting an interview

A standard interview convention is to establish who the interviewee is by superimposing their name and possibly some other identification (e.g. farmer, market street trader, etc.) in text across an MCU of them. The interview is often cut using a combination of basic shots such as:

- an MS, MCU or CU of the interviewee;
- a matched shot of the interviewer asking questions or reacting to the answers (usually shot after the interview has ended);
- a 2-shot which establishes location and relationship between the participants or an over-the-shoulder 2-shot looking from interviewee to interviewer;
- the interviewee is often staged so that their background is relevant to their comments.

The interview can follow straightforward intercutting between question and answer of the participants, but more usually, after a few words from the interviewee establishing their presence, a series of cutaways are used to illustrate the points the interviewee is making. A basic interview technique requires the appropriate basic shots:

- matched shots in size and lens angle (see Camerawork section, pages 110–23);
- over-the-shoulder (o/s) shots;
- intercutting on question and answer;
- cutaways to referred items in the interview;
- 'noddies' and reaction shots (NB reaction shots should be reactions, that is, a response to the main subject);
- cutaways to avoid jump cuts when shortening answers.

Television lighting

The most important element in the design of television images is light. Apart from its fundamental role of illuminating the subject, light determines tonal differences, outline, shape, colour, texture and depth. It can create compositional relationships, provide balance, harmony and contrast. It provides mood, atmosphere and visual continuity. Light is the key pictorial force in television production.

The basic requirement to provide adequate light for a correctly exposed picture with the required depth of field can easily be achieved. Video cameras are sufficiently sensitive to provide an acceptable exposure under almost any found lighting condition. But whereas the television technical requirements of exposure, appropriate colour temperature and contrast range may be readily satisfied, the resultant image may be a muddle of competing areas of light and shade that do not communicate the intended 'visual message' of the shot. The control of light to guide the audience's attention and to communicate production requirements plays a crucial part in the creation of any film or TV image. In almost every situation, visual communication can be more effective by choosing the camera position or staging participants with reference to found light or, if necessary, by adding some form of additional light.

The nature of light

Using a visual medium is choosing to communicate through pictures and in television, the end result of manipulating lens, camera position and lighting must be images that are compatible with human perception. A basic understanding of how we see the world will help when devising the lighting and composition of a shot. There are significant differences between how the eye responds to a scene and how a camera converts light into an electrical signal. Lighting must take account of these differences and make the appropriate adjustments.

One aim of lighting is to create a range of tones, either to conform to the contrast ratio of television or to express a production requirement. The relative brightness of a reflective surface is a subjective perceptual construct depending on the brightness levels of surrounding surfaces. Human perception responds to equal changes in brightness levels in a logarithmic manner and this can be mimicked by changes in grey scale step brightness. As we have discussed in Colour temperature (page 64) the eye continually adapts to changes in colour and has a much wider ability than a video camera to see detail in shadows through to highlights.

172

Measurement of light

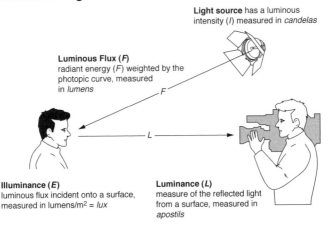

Light source has a luminous intensity (*I*) measured in *candelas*

Luminous Flux (*F*)
radiant energy (*F*) weighted by the photopic curve, measured in *lumens*

Illuminance (*E*)
luminous flux incident onto a surface, measured in lumens/m² = *lux*

Luminance (*L*)
measure of the reflected light from a surface, measured in *apostils*

Inverse square law

Doubling the distance from light to subject quarters the level of illumination (lux) falling on the subject.

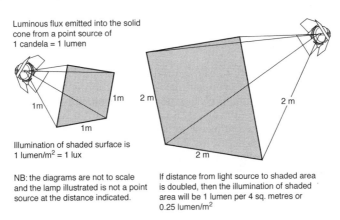

Luminous flux emitted into the solid cone from a point source of 1 candela = 1 lumen

Illumination of shaded surface is 1 lumen/m² = 1 lux

NB: the diagrams are not to scale and the lamp illustrated is not a point source at the distance indicated.

If distance from light source to shaded area is doubled, then the illumination of shaded area will be 1 lumen per 4 sq. metres or 0.25 lumen/m²

Cosine law

If the angle of a light beam to a surface it is illuminating is less than 90°, the illuminance of that surface is reduced by a factor equal to the cosine angle of incidence, e.g. for 30° angle of incidence, illuminance is reduced to 86% (cosine 30° = 0.86).

Incident light meter

These meters are designed to measure the light falling on the subject. To calculate the ratio between key and fill, place the meter close to the face of subject and point in turn at the key light and the fill. The ratio of the two readings will provide the contrast ratio of light on the face.

173

Characteristics of light

Like clay in a potter's hand, the four characteristics of light, quality (hard or soft), direction (frontal, side, back, underlit, top lit, etc.) source (available light, additional lights), and colour can be manipulated by the lighting cameraman to achieve the precise requirements for a specific shot. The auto features on a camera are often unable to discriminate the priorities of a shot and must be over-ridden, so likewise, to simply accept the effects of a found lighting situation is to disregard the most powerful part of image making. Available or 'found' light is any combination of sunlight and/or artificial light that illuminates any potential location.

Quality

The quality of light produced by a natural or an artificial light source is often categorized as 'hard' or 'soft'. A 'point' source (i.e. a small area of light at a distance from the subject) produces a single hard-edged shadow. An unobscured sun or moon is a hard light source. Hard lighting reveals shape and texture and when produced by a lamp, can be shaped and controlled to fall precisely on the required part of the frame. Shadow areas of an image (the absence of light or very low light levels) often play an essential part in the composition and atmosphere of a shot. Lighter and darker areas within the frame help to create the overall composition of the shot and to guide the attention of the viewer to certain objects and actions. Shadows on a face (modelling, see page 181) reveal structure and character.

A soft source of light can be produced by a large area of light (relative to the subject) and produce many overlapping soft-edged shadows and tends to destroy texture. It is not so controllable as hard light but is often used to modify the effect of hard light, for example, by bouncing sunlight off a large area reflector to fill in the shadow created by sunlight falling on the subject.

How much light is used and where it is focused also sets the 'key' of the image. A brightly lit shot with little or no shadow is termed a high key picture and is usually considered cheerful and upbeat. An image with large areas of shadow and very few highlights is termed a low key image and appears sombre, sinister or mysterious.

Direction

The direction from which any part of an image is lit affects the overall composition and atmosphere of a shot (see also Lighting a face, page 180). Frequently when setting lamps for a shot, the position and therefore the direction of illumination is controlled by the perceived 'natural' source of light (e.g. window or table lamp in an interior).

Source

Early film was lit by natural light. Artificial light sources were introduced for greater production flexibility and economic reliability (e.g. to keep filming whatever the weather). A system of lighting faces (often the most common subject in feature films) was devised using a key light to model the face, soft light to modify the key light effect and a backlight to separate the face from its backing. Three-point lighting is still extensively practised although the use of a backlight has fallen out of fashion in feature film making. The quest for a 'natural' look to an image produced a fashion for using large areas of bounced light. Modelling on a face was reduced or eliminated and the overall image produced was softer and less modelled. To heighten realism, and because of the availability of very sensitive cameras, many shots were devised using available light. This is often necessary when shooting documentaries because not only does rigging lights take time and unsettle participants but being filmed under bright lights is inhibiting and counter-productive to the aim of recording unmediated 'actuality'.

The fourth aspect of lighting is colour, which is discussed on page 177. See also mixed light, page 184.

Brightness

How 'bright' one subject appears compared to another and the perceived changes in brightness is a function of perception. In an interior, a face against a window during the day will appear to be dark. With the same illumination on the face against a window at night, the face will appear to be bright. Colours appear to be lighter against a dark background and darker against a light backing.

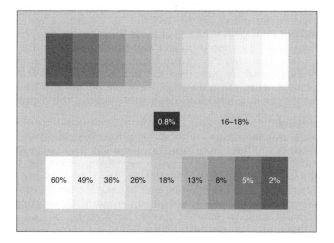

A grey scale chart is designed to mimic perception by having a series of grey tones starting at peak white and decreasing by $1/\sqrt{2}$ to produce equal changes in brightness to the eye. This logarithmic progression is similar to the ear's response to equal changes in sound level (see page 188). Starting at 60% reflectivity and decreasing by $1/\sqrt{2}$ (0.5 of one stop) produces (in this design of grey scale) 9 wedges with 0.8% black represented by a chip in the chart lined with black non-reflective flock paper or velvet. The background is often 16–18% reflectance to simulate average scene brightness.

Lighting levels

How light is shaped, balanced and distributed within a shot plays a vital part in television production but there are a number practical considerations when deciding the overall level of light that is to be used. These include:

- satisfying exposure requirements which depend on camera sensitivity;
- creating an appropriate depth of field;
- providing a good environment for artists' performance;
- heat generation, ventilation, number of luminaires available, total capacity and cost of the power supply.

Camera sensitivity

Camera sensitivity is usually quoted by camera manufacturers with reference to four interlinking elements – a subject with peak white reflectivity, scene illumination, f number, and signal-to-noise ratio for a stated signal. It is usually stated as being the resulting f number when exposed to a peak white subject with 89.9 per cent reflectance lit by 2000 lux and also quoting the signal/noise ratio. For most current cameras this is f8, with some achieving f11 and better. The definition is based on the Japanese standard for peak white reflectivity of 89.9 per cent. The rest of the world mostly use a 60 per cent reflectance peak white based on the need to correctly expose (Caucasian) face tones without overloading (overexposing) on a peak white area. With a 60 per cent reflectance surface, 2000 lux will only allow it to be two thirds exposed therefore the illuminance has to be increased to 3000 lux to transpose the sensitivity rating to 60 per cent peak white operation. The sensitivity of the camera could be increased by simply greater and greater amplification of weak signals but this degrades the picture by adding 'noise' generated by the camera circuits. In many 'actuality' location work (e.g. news gathering, sports coverage, etc.), the gain of the head amplifiers can be increased if insufficient light is available to adequately expose the picture.

Depth of field

Lighting level will determine f number for correct exposure, which in turn will decide depth of field (see Zooming, page 50). The range of subjects in focus within the frame will have a significant effect on the visual appearance of the production. The chosen depth of field can therefore be a production design element as well having a crucial impact on the ability to find and hold focus in ad-lib camerawork. Other factors which affect exposure include shutter speed, lens range extenders, zoom ramping, filters, prompt devices and the lighting environment to accommodate performance and mood.

Mood and atmosphere

With highly sensitive cameras, it is possible to achieve correct exposure with very low light levels – levels which may appear to be darker than a brightly lit office corridor. This may be appropriate for some types of location work but it can have a depressing effect on other types of production. A location should be lit at a level that provides a good environment for participants and enhances their presentation. The opposite consideration, of high intensity key lights close to the eyeline, can also inhibit optimum performance and is usually avoided in documentary work.

Budget

Luminaires require a power supply and, in an enclosed space, some method of ventilation to extract the heat that tungsten lamps can generate. Also the number, hire cost of luminaires available to a production and the total capacity of the power supply and the deployment of the rig are practical controlling factors in lighting design.

Use of colour

The individual response to colour may be a product of fashion and culture – a learnt relationship – or may be an intrinsic part of the act of perception. People's colour preferences have been tested and in general western people choose in order of preference blue, red, green, purple, orange, yellow. This choice is modified when the colour is associated with an object that has a specific use. Below is a very generalized checklist of points to bear in mind when using colour:

- Many colours have a hot or a cold feel to them. Red is considered hot and blue is felt as cold. It will take other strong design elements within a shot to force a foreground blue object to exist in space in front of a red object. The eye naturally sees red as closer than blue unless the brightness, shape, chroma value and background of the blue is so arranged that in context it becomes more dominant than the desaturated, low brightness of the red.
- Colour effects are relative and no one set of guidelines will hold true for all colour relationships. For example, the intensity of a hot colour can be emphasized by surrounding it by cool colours. The intensity of the contrast will affect balance and to what part of the frame the eye is attracted.
- The perception of the apparent hue of any coloured object is likely to vary depending on the colour of its background and the colour temperature of the light illuminating it. Staging someone in a yellow jacket against green foliage will produce a different contrast relationship to staging the same person against a blue sky.
- Complementary contrast balance can be achieved by opposing a colour with its complementary. The complementary of red is green, the complementary of blue is orange, the complementary of yellow is violet. These complementary pairings consist of a hot and a cold colour. Complementaries placed alongside each other will appear to be more vivid and vital than colours that are adjacent in the colour wheel. Visual equilibrium however is not simply achieved by equal areas of complementary pairs. Blue needs a greater area to balance its complementary orange. Red needs approximately the same area of green whereas yellow needs a relatively small area of violet to achieve visual equilibrium.
- Colour can communicate experience or feeling by association. Red is often described as passionate, stimulating and exciting. Blue is seen as sad and depressing. Yellow is serene and gay whilst green is thought of as restful and stable. Strong prolonged stimulation of one colour has the effect of decreasing the sensitivity to that colour but sensitivity to its complementary is enhanced.
- The balancing of area and the shape of a coloured object has a strong impact on the unity of an image. A small area of intense colour can unbalance a composition and continually attract the eye. If its location coincides with the main subject of the shot then the right emphasis is achieved. If it exists near the edge of frame or away from the dominant subject then it acts as a second subject of interest and is a distraction.
- Paintings often achieve a strong visual impact by restricting the range of colours used. A limited palette of colours on a set can create unity and impact. A number of sequences in a variety show can each be given their own individual identity by using colours which complement or contrast with the artiste's costume colour.

177

Types of location luminaires

Reflector: A reflector board or sheet requires no power and takes up very little space. It is invaluable for fill-in lighting by bouncing light from daylight or lamp into shadow.

Battery lamps: These are fixed to the top of the camera and powered from the camcorder battery or, preferably, a separate battery belt. When working in daylight they require a dichroic filter to correct the colour temperature of the lamp to daylight. A dichroic is made of glass and is therefore more fragile than gel filters, but their advantage is that they transmit approximately 15 per cent more light than gels.

Flight kit (portable lighting kit): This is a two or three lamp kit that derived its name from its compact size small enough to fit into a metallized container for quick stowage and easy transportation.

Redhead: This is a 800 W lamp drawing 3.3 A, weighing 3 kg including barndoor and safety glass, with an output of approximately 6000 candelas (cd) flooded and 24 000 cd spotted and a wide beam angle >80°.

Blonde: This is a 2000 W lamp drawing 8.3 A and weighing 6 kg with barndoor and safety glass. It produces approximately 25,000 cd flooded and 150,000 cd spotted and a beam angle >80°. Because of their weight and flexibility and their low power consumption they can be rigged and derigged quickly and plugged into most domestic power supplies.

Discharge lamps: Discharge light sources such as HMI lamps produce light by ionizing a gas contained in the bulb. They have greater efficiency than tungsten, are lighter and cooler in operation and produce light which approximates to daylight. They require an EHT supply to ionize the gas and a current limiting device. This may be a simple inductive choke or in the form of a flicker free electronic ballast. A 1.2 kW HMI, which is one of the most useful lamps on a small unit, with conventional ballast, will draw 12 A when switched on but settle to 6.4 A when warmed up. It can therefore be used on a domestic 13 A ring main circuit providing no other lamps are connected when it is switched on.

With fluorescent lights, the use of high-frequency dimmable ballasts operating above 40 kHz provide a flicker free output and allow dimming with a simple 0–10 V control (or 100 kΩ potentiometer) to achieve reduction in lighting levels with little change in colour (unlike dimmed tungsten sources).

Pulsed light sources

Fluorescent tubes, HMI discharge lamps and neon signs do not produce a constant light output but give short pulses of light at a frequency depending on the mains supply. Using a 625 PAL camera lit by 60 Hz mains fluorescent (e.g. when working away from the country of origin mains standard) will produce severe flicker. Some cameras are fitted with 1/60th shutter so that the exposure time is one full period of the lighting. If a high shutter speed is used, the duration of the pulsed red, green and blue parts of the light spectrum may not coincide with the 'shutter' open and a colour drift will be observed to cycle usually between blue and yellow. It can be eliminated by switching the shutter off. FT sensors have a mechanical shutter which cannot be switched off and therefore the problem will remain. The problem with most fluorescent tubes is that they emit very little or no red and an excessive amount of green in comparison to daylight. For example, light from mercury vapour lamps is blue-green with no red in it, and no amount of filtering can add red to it. Unless red light can be added to the scene, there is no hope of getting a video image that looks normal. Conversely, low pressure sodium vapour lamps contain nothing but yellow light which cannot be colour corrected.

High-frequency fluorescent luminaires (cold lights)

Fluorescent luminaires are now being used for television programme production. Usually several lamps are grouped to produce a practical light source, hence they are soft sources. Control of the light beam shape is either by a fine structured 'egg-crate' or 'honeycomb' fitment. Improved phosphors have made the fluorescent lamp acceptable for television and film and are available to provide tungsten matching and daylight matching colour temperatures.

Filters and diffusers

- **Neutral density filters:** A recurring problem with location interiors is controlling and balancing the intensity of daylight from windows with the much lower light levels from lamps. Neutral density (ND) filters will reduce the level of daylight without changing its colour temperature. They are made of flexible gelatine or thin acrylic sheets and are available in a range of grades. They can also be combined with colour correction filters. The filters are fixed to windows in a method that will avoid being seen on camera. Although ND gel can buckle and produce flares, it is easily transportable in rolls. The acrylic sheet needs to be cut, is difficult to move and is expensive.
- **Plastic 'scrim'**, a perforated material silver on one side and black on the other, can also be used on windows (black side in) to act as a neutral density filter (0.6ND). It is more robust than ND gels and not so prone to flare. Check that its perforated pattern cannot be seen on camera.
- **Polarizing filters** on the camera lens reduce glare reflections, darken blue skies and increase colour saturation. They are useful in eliminating reflections in glass such as shop windows, cars and shooting into water. The filter must be rotated until the maximum reduction of unwanted reflection is achieved.
- **Spun or diffusion**, a fibreglass-type material, is used in front of lamps to diffuse or soften the light. It also reduces the lamp intensity. It can be used to cover partially a portion of the lamp's throw to soften edges and to produce a reduction in brightness in part of the shot. It is available in a range of grades and can be doubled up in use to increase diffusion.
- **Colour filters**: Polyester filters have a clear plastic base coated with a coloured pigment. Polycarbonate filters have the base material mixed with the pigment. They are referred to as high temperature (HT) filters and are not affected by heat as much as the polyester filters.
- **Colour correction filters** are used to correct the light sources to a common colour temperature, e.g. tungsten sources to daylight (5500K), daylight to tungsten (3200K) or to correct both sources to an intermediate value.
- **Barndoors** are metal flaps fitted to the front of the lamp lens and can be adjusted in a number of ways to keep light off areas in shot and to shape, soften and produce gradations on surfaces.

179

Lighting a face

As we discussed in Exposure continuity (page 76), in general, Caucasian face tones will tend to look right when a 'television white' of 60 per cent reflectivity is exposed to give peak white. As a generalization, face tones are approximately one stop down on peak white. But as well as achieving correct exposure, lighting a face also involves making decisions about how a specific face is to be portrayed. Most professional presenters know their 'good' side and their 'bad' side. This may be to do with blemishes or their nose line but usually it is because faces are asymmetrical about the centre-line. Depending on its position, the key light modelling will either make the shadowed side of the face appear to be narrower (to be avoided if it is already the narrow side of the face) or broader.

The lighting treatment must take into account blemishes ('key' into the blemish), emphasizing or adjusting the overall shape of the face, the shape of the jaw line, the line of the eyes, the line of the mouth, etc. If a subject with a bent nose is keyed the same way as the bend of the nose, this will exaggerate the nose bend. If keyed in the opposite direction it will tend to straighten out the bend. The American cinematographer Gordon Willis used top lighting on Marlon Brando in *The Godfather* to help reduce Brando's jowls but this also had the effect of putting his eyes in shadow and making him more mysterious and threatening. Presenters with deep set eyes can lose contact with their audience unless a way is found to get light on to their eyes. A catch light reflected in the eyes often lifts the personality of the face and allows the viewer 'eye contact' with the most important part of the face.

Location lighting may only have to accommodate one face and one camera position, but the shot may include a natural lighting source such as a window or the direct light from the sun (see Mixed light, page 184). Ideally, the aim is to light artistes separately to their backgrounds as this enables control of the lighting of both areas to be achieved.

Three-point lighting

Key light

A single strong directional light gives the best modelling and structure to a shot. The key light provides the necessary exposure and brings out the three-dimensional aspects of the subject. As we have discussed, when keying faces, the decisions to be made are: where should the nose shadow fall (or should there be a nose shadow?), are deep-set eyes lit, does the angle and position of the key suit the structure of the subject's face, are there reflections in spectacles, and are any facial imperfections exaggerated or concealed? Does it throw unwanted shadows on the background of the shot?

Fill

Wherever the key is placed, the strong shadows it creates need to be modified to reduce the contrast range and normally to lighten the mood of the shot. This is achieved by a fill light on the opposite side of the lens to the key. It is usually a soft source of light produced by a reflector or a diffused flooded lamp or an overcast sky but not direct sunlight. The key-to-fill ratio on the face is the contrast range and can be balanced by using a meter or estimated by eye to match the required mood of the shot. An average is between 2:1 and 3:1.

Backlight

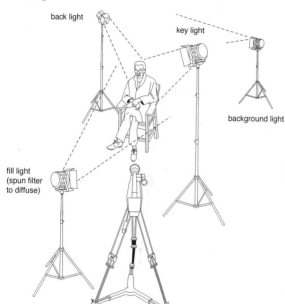

back light

key light

background light

fill light
(spun filter
to diffuse)

It is usually necessary to find some visual way of separating the subject from its background so that attention can be focused on the subject. Check for suitable unobtrusive background detail when positioning camera and subject and use a hard light source directed from behind the subject to highlight the head. This will give sparkle to the hair and rim light the shoulders. Try to avoid too high an intensity – the backlight should hardly be perceptible.

Background light

To avoid people being shot in limbo, some light needs to be directed to the space behind them. The aim should be to light sufficient background to provide some indication of location whilst avoiding overpowering the foreground. A lit background gives space and mood to the shot but on location, ensure that it conforms to the main source of light.

Colour correction

Whether shooting interior or exterior, a fundamental problem with location work is dealing with a mixture of light of different colour temperatures. If the light remains uncorrected, faces and subjects may have colour casts which look unnatural and distracting. The two most common light sources on location are daylight, which has a range of colour temperatures but averages around 5600K, and tungsten light which is often produced by lamps carried to the location which are approximately 3200K.

Colour correction filters
There are two basic types of correction filter used when attempting to combine mixed lighting of tungsten and daylight.

- An orange filter which converts daylight to tungsten and is most often seen attached to windows for interior shots.
- A blue filter which converts tungsten to daylight and is often used on tungsten lamps.

Any correction filter will reduce the amount of light it transmits and therefore a balance must be struck between colour correction and sufficient light for adequate exposure. A filter for full colour conversion from daylight to tungsten will have a transmission of only 55 per cent which means nearly half of the available light is lost. A filter for full colour correction from tungsten to daylight has an even smaller transmission factor of 34 per cent – it cuts out nearly two thirds of the possible light from a lamp. This is a more serious loss because whereas daylight is usually more than adequate for a reasonable exposure, reducing the light output of a lamp (say a redhead) by blue filtering to match daylight may leave an interior lit by blue-filtered lamps short of adequate light.

All light sources at same colour temperature
The choice when shooting an environment which has a mixture of daylight and tungsten is to decide whether to correct all sources to daylight or all sources to tungsten. If the choice is tungsten, any window which is in shot or producing light which is reaching the shot requires filtering. It needs a full orange filter squeegeed onto the glass or fastened by double-sided tape onto the frame. Orange filters can be obtained which have additional light reduction by combining with neutral density filters. This is helpful when attempting to balance out a very bright window with the interior lit by lamps.

Daylight
If the choice is to light by daylight, then all lamps must be blue filtered to correct them to daylight (5600K) and a careful check made on any table lamps or domestic lighting which may influence the shot. The disadvantage of choosing daylight is the reduction in light output due to the filters and the increased contrast range between subjects lit by a combination of daylight and colour corrected tungsten. Neutral density filters without colour correction can be used on windows to reduce the intensity of daylight and to achieve exposure on external detail.

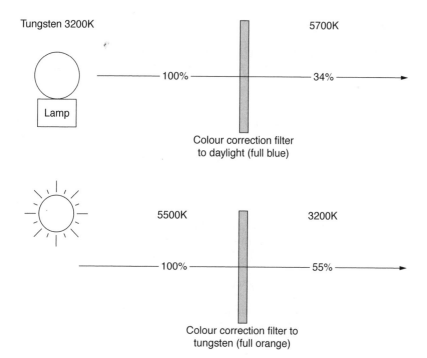

Tungsten 3200K

5700K

Lamp

100%

34%

Colour correction filter
to daylight (full blue)

5500K

3200K

100%

55%

Colour correction filter to
tungsten (full orange)

Mixed light

A recurring location item is the interior interview. It usually requires shots of the interviewee seated in his or her office or house being questioned by a presenter.

Interview position

There are a number of questions to be answered before deciding camera position and interview position:

- Is there a colour temperature difference and balance between daylight entering from windows and the light provided by added lamps?
- Do windows need to be in shot?
- Does the interview position allow a variety of shot to sustain a long interview if required?
- Can the relationship of people be shown?
- Is the environment of the interviewee important to the interview?
- Does the background to the shot give more information about the topic?
- Is there a comfortable distance between participants to allow them to relate to each other?
- Is there sufficient space in the chosen location and how convenient is it to relight and reposition for reverses?

The first decision to make is whether to go tungsten or daylight. If daylight is consistent and there is no direct sunlight on the proposed interview area, then colour correcting for daylight is the best option, using daylight as the main source.

If sunlight is entering the room and if it is intermittent, then avoid windows in frame and light by tungsten filtering or curtaining out the large changes in brightness from the sun.

Position the camera close to the shoulder of the interviewer with the lens at approximately seated eye-level to get a good eyeline on the interviewee. Light for that position checking for a good fill ratio and if the background is adequately lit. Switch off any fluorescent lighting, if possible, and check sound level for background noise. Check exposure, white balance and voice levels and record the interview. Only reframe on interviewee during questions unless a move has been agreed. Keep the camera recording after the interview has ended. Sometimes, a vital comment is made at the end.

After confirming that no more questions are to be asked, reposition the camera for a 2-shot checking that there has been no significant change of posture or any other continuity links between single and 2-shot. Record the 2-shot with the interviewer repeating some of the questions.

Reposition and relight for the interviewer's questions and noddies, staying on the same side of the imaginary line between interviewer and interviewee as the shot of the interviewee.

Electrical safety

More haste

Location recording is often a scramble to rig, record, wrap and move on to the next set-up. There is always the urgency to get the job done, but, as pressurized as this may be, it is never expedient to cut corners on safety. A couple of minutes saved by not making safe a cable crossing the top of a flight of stairs may result in injury and many hours of lost time. You have a responsibility to ensure that the condition and the method of rigging lamps and cables at a location is safe to yourself and to members of the public.

Periodically check the earthing and safety of your lamps. Make certain the safety glass or wire is fitted and not damaged in any way. Check the condition of cables for frayed or worn insulation and that they are earthed correctly.

HMIs

Discharge light sources such as HMI lamps produce light by ionizing a gas contained in the bulb. Because of a high bulb pressure they are liable to explode and they also produce a harmful level of ultraviolet radiation. Therefore all discharge sources must be fitted with a glass filter as a safety glass. Usually an inter-lock will prevent the supply of EHT if the safety glass is broken or missing.

Check that any HMI you are using has a safety glass fitted.

Location electrical supplies

It is important to check the power supply fuse rating and the condition of the wiring before using a domestic supply. Blown fuses can waste time but burnt out wiring could start a fire. Also check cable runs, especially around doors and tops of stairs. Check where you place lamps. They get hot and so will anything touching them.

Care and consideration

If you need to attach any material to windows, use masking tape or low-tack tape so that you leave the paintwork as you found it. Remember, you may want to return to that location. If you have ever followed a TV crew that caused problems onto a site, you will appreciate that loss of goodwill from the public makes for a very hard day's shoot. People appearing on television for the first time may be nervous or excited. You may be under pressure to get the job done and onto the next set-up. When working with the public, their safety and your safety are equally important.

Accidents and disasters

Police or authorities in control of an accident locale or disaster area may exclude you from the location if you are not wearing a protective (hard) hat and luminous 'vest'. The requirement is in the interests of your safety as well as the interests of other people working on that site.

Programme production and audio

Many news and magazine items are shot by a single operator. The cameraman is responsible for pictures, lighting and audio. This section of the manual deals with audio that is recorded in this way although this does not mean the control of audio should be passed over to the ubiquitous auto-gain. No cameraman would be happy with a camera that had no viewfinder, simply an auto composition/auto shot selection button. This is the visual equivalent of auto-gain – allowing the camera to make all the audio decisions.

Television programme sound can have a significant emotional effect on the audience and yet remain quite unnoticeable. Sound does not simply complement the image, it can actively shape how we perceive and interpret the image. Most TV crafts such as lighting, camerawork and editing use a form of invisible technique which achieves its effects without the audience being aware that any artifice has been employed. The production contribution of sound is usually the most unobtrusive and difficult for the audience to evaluate – until it is badly done. Visual awareness appears to take precedence over audible awareness and yet intelligibility, space and atmosphere are often created by sound. The selection and treatment of audio shapes our perception and can be used to focus our attention just as effectively as the selection of images.

Match the sound to the pictures
This is a fairly obvious requirement but whereas image content can be quickly assessed, it often needs a trained ear to identify the complete sound spectrum being recorded. The shot may be someone in medium close-up talking. The sound may include in equal proportion the person's voice, unseen traffic and a noise from a children's playground. If the cameraman's attention is simply focused on the speaker, the competing background sound is ignored until the cassette gets into post-production. Audio post-production is a good training ground for location sound.

In many ways, recording audio on location is a bigger challenge than the facilities available in a purpose-built studio. There are many problems that are created simply by lack of time, equipment limitations and the production convention that sound follows picture. It is rare that good sound conditions are decided on before the selection of the shot and yet sound and image are often of equal importance and need equal attention.

What can be fixed later?
Although remedial work is possible in editing and dubbing, if post-production begin their work with good quality audio and a range of location sounds (wild tracks to provide flexibility in the edit), they can add to the original tracks rather than be faced with a challenge of salvaging something usable. 'Fix it in editing' is as bad a work convention in audio as it is in video.

Audio manipulation

The selection and treatment of sound in a production shapes the perception of the audience and involves a range of audio techniques. These include:

- **Adjustment of loudness** in order to emphasize production content; to indicate priority (e.g. dialogue louder than background traffic); to exploit the dynamic range of sound (e.g. quiet contrasted with loud passages in orchestral music).
- **Pitch** is a subjective quality of the frequency of sound vibrations and each frequency band, similar to colour, has associated feelings.
- **Timbre** is the tonal quality of a sound as judged by the ear. It describes the texture or feel of a sound, and can be manufactured for specific production purposes (e.g. the use of distort for a telephone voice).
- **Reverberation** is the reflections from surfaces and can be artificially created by using digital delay to the audio signal to simulate the effect of audio echo to suggest environment. Audio delay is also required when a visual source has been delayed by a frame store or satellite link. The sound is delayed to match the timing of the image.
- **Fades and mixes** mark the transition between sound sources, production sections or complete programmes. The rate at which a sound dies away can be highly evocative.
- **Sound effects** heighten realism, add space and atmosphere, reinforce the action, and can guide the audience to a new situation or scene. Combining sound effects can create an aural impression that is greater than its parts.
- **Smooth transitions** between contrasting images can be created by effects or music.
- **Anticipation** or preparing the audience for change can be achieved by sound leading picture (e.g. the sound of the incoming scene beginning at the end of the outgoing scene).
- **Sound perspective** focuses the attention of the audience on the visual space depicted (e.g. close-up sound for foreground action, distant sound for long shot). Sometimes dialogue clarity is more important than the realism of sound perspective especially in news and news features. The sound level of orchestral instruments in close-up, for example, are not normally boosted to match picture content. The overall orchestral balance is an integral part of the performance and therefore takes precedence.
- **Off-stage sound** suggests space and a continuing world beyond the frame of the image. It can also be used to introduce or alert the audience to new events. Sound from an unseen source creates space and mystery.
- **Narration** voice-over acts in a similar way to the thoughts of a reader. Careful balance between voice, effects, and music combine to give a powerful unity and authority to the production.
- **Music** is a sound source that has immense influence on the audience's response. It can create pace, rhythm, emotion, humour, tension, and requires a very subtle balance to weave the music in and out of effects and speech in order to create unity in the final production.
- **Silence** is an attribute of sound that has no visual equivalent. It emphasizes or enhances a production point but only in a sound film can silence be used for dramatic effect.

The nature of sound

What is sound?

When there is a variation of air pressure at frequencies between approximately 16 to 16,000 Hz, the human ear (depending on age and health) can detect sound. The change in air pressure can be caused by a variety of sources such as the human voice, musical instruments, etc. Some of the terms used to describe the characteristics of the sounds are:

Sound waves are produced by increased air pressure and rarefaction along the line of travel.

Frequency of sound is the number of regular excursions made by an air particle in 1 s (see figure opposite).

Wavelength of a pure tone (i.e. a sine wave, see figure opposite) is the distance between successive peaks.

Harmonics are part of the sound from a musical instrument which are a combination of frequencies that are multiples of the lowest frequency present (the fundamental).

Dynamic range is the range of sound intensities from quietest to loudest occurring from sound sources. This may exceed the dynamic range a recording or transmission system is able to process without distortion.

Decibels: Our ears do not respond to changes in sound intensity in even, linear increments. To hear an equal change in intensity, the sound level must double at each increase rather than changing in equal steps. To match the ear's response to changes in sound intensity, it is convenient to measure the changes in the amplitude of the audio signal by using a logarithmic ratio – decibels (dB). Decibels are a ratio of change and are scaled to imitate the ear's response to changing sound intensity. If a sound intensity doubles in volume then there would be a 3 dB increase in audio level. If it was quadrupled, there would be a 6 dB increase. To hear an equal change in intensity, the sound level must double at each increase rather than changing in equal steps.

Loudness is a subjective effect. An irritating sound may appear to be a great deal louder than a sound we are sympathetic to (e.g. the sound of a neighbour's cat at night compared to our own practice session on a violin!).

Phase of a signal becomes important when signals are combined. Signals in phase reinforce each other. Signals out of phase subtract from or cancel out each other (see figure opposite).

Pitch is the highness or lowness of the frequency of a note.

Wavelength and frequency

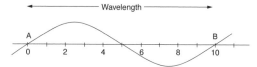

The time taken for a complete cycle of pure tone (A) to begin to repeat itself (B) is the frequency of the signal and is measured in cycles per second (Hz), e.g. 50 Hz = 50 cycles per second. Frequency is inversely proportional to wavelength. For example, a high-frequency sound source of 10,000 Hz produces sound with a short wavelength of 3.4 cm. A low-frequency sound source of 100 Hz produces sound with a longer wavelength of 3.4 m. Frequency multiplied by wavelength equals the speed of sound (335 m/sec) in cold air. It is faster in warm air.

Phase

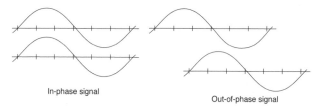

In-phase signal

Out-of-phase signal

Acoustics

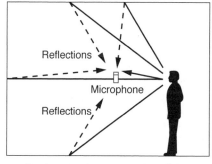

- **Reverberation** relates to the time delay before sounds reflected from the wall and other surfaces reach the microphone.
- **Standing waves** effect is due to the room having resonances where the parallel walls enhance certain frequencies.

Audio requires processing in order for it to be recorded or transmitted. This may include:

- **Equalization:** the process of adjusting the frequency response of the signal usually banded into control of high, medium and low frequencies. Switched filters are used to remove low-frequency rumble, etc.
- **Limiters:** these prevent the signal from exceeding a predetermined level.
- **Compression:** the dynamic range (see page 205) of some sound sources (e.g. an orchestral concert) can exceed that which can be transmitted. If manually riding the level is not always feasible, sound compression can be used. The aim is to preserve as much of the original dynamic range by judicious use of 'threshold' – the level at which compression starts; 'slope or ratio', which controls the amount of adjustment; and 'attack and release', which determines the speed at which the compression equipment will react to changes.

Digital audio

It is important to have a basic understanding of how the audio is converted into digital information so that errors are not made in setting up the equipment. The audio signal is sampled at a constant rate like a series of pulses. For each of these pulses, the level of the sound is checked and this value is given a number. This number is transferred into binary code and this code is recorded as the digital information. The actual recording is therefore a string of codes, each representing the level of the audio at a particular moment in time. In order to achieve a good frequency response, the sampling is carried out at a very high frequency; 48,000 samples per second (48 kHz) is used for most professional systems. The level of the sound to be converted into binary numbers must also have sufficient steps to ensure accuracy, which is called quantizing. With the 16-bit system employed by most camera/recorders, 65,536 finite levels can be represented. Put simply, this means that in order to encode and decode the signals, all the systems must operate at the same sampling rate and the signal level must never exceed the maximum quantization step or no value will be recorded.

Digital audio recording
Video recording resolved the problem of recording a much higher frequency spectrum than analogue audio on tape by means of a rotating record/replay head as well as moving the tape. Digital stereo audio needs to record at 1.4 MHz and the DAT (digital audio tape) system was developed to meet this criteria. For editing purposes, an identical analogue audio track is added (sometimes called cue track) as rocking a slow moving digital signal past a head produces no sound, unlike an analogue signal. The frequency response and signal-to-noise ratio of digital recorders are superior to analogue machines and repeated copying results in far less degradation. Drop out can be corrected and print through has less significance or is eliminated. Wow and flutter can be corrected by having a memory reservoir system from which data is extracted at a constant rate eliminating any variation in the speed at which it was memorized. In general, when a signal is converted to digital, there is more opportunity to accurately rebuild and rectify any imperfections (see Error correction opposite), and to allow signal manipulation.

Sampling and the conversion of the amplitude of each sample (quantizing) is carried out at precisely regulated intervals. The precision of these intervals must be faithfully preserved in order to accurately mimic the original analogue signal. The binary data produced by the quantization must be accurately timed. Coding converts the data into a regular pattern of signals that can be recorded with a clock signal. When the signal is replayed, the recorded clock information can be compared with a stable reference clock in the replay equipment to ensure the correct timing of the digital information. The timing and reference information not only ensures an accurate decoding of the signal, but also allows error correction techniques to be applied to the samples.

Simplified audio digital process

Sampling

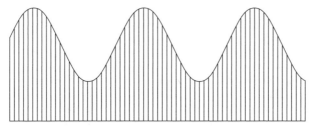

The analogue audio signal is split into samples at a fixed rate of 48,000 samples per second (48 kHz). The height (amplitude) of each sample (each vertical line in the figure) is then measured in a process known as quantizing. The high number of samples is to ensure that the analogue signal is faithfully mimicked because changes in signal amplitude between samples would be lost and distortion would occur in the digitalizing process. The sampling frequency needs to be at least twice the maximum audio frequency that it is required to reproduce. Filtering the audio signal is required to ensure that no audio exists at more than half the sample frequency.

Typical sampling rates that have been chosen include: for the transmission systems such as NICAM 728, the system design uses 32 kHz giving a practical limit to the audio of 15 kHz; for compact disc the rate has been set at 44.1 kHz whilst many broadcasting stations set the rate at 48 kHz.

Quantization

The amplitude of each sample needs to be converted into a binary number. The greater the range of numbers, the more accurately each sample can be measured. To simplify this measurement, each sample is converted into a whole number and the accuracy of this conversion will depend on how many divisions are chosen to make the representation. For example, the height of people could be measured in metres ignoring centimetres. There would be 2 metre high people or 3 metre high people and no heights in between. This would not reflect the variation in people's height. In quantization, if there are a greater number of levels used in the encoding process the decoded signal will be nearer to the original sound (see Binary counting, page 25).

Error correction

In addition to quantizing errors, other defects can occur in analogue/digital conversions.

- **Burst error** is the loss of a number of consecutive samples when recorded. It is possible to minimize this by arranging the data in a non-sequential order by a controlled code that can be reassembled in its correct temporal order when decoding. This effectively separates the missing data, ensuring that consecutive values are less likely to be lost.
- **Random error** is the loss of single samples due to noise or poor signal quality. Correction systems can either replace the missing sample with a copy of the preceding sample (although this is only useful for a very few consecutive samples), or replace it with an average of the preceding and succeeding data. If the error cannot be resolved the system will mute until sufficient samples are available for the conversion to continue.

Camcorder audio facilities

Most professional systems have four digital audio tracks. These all have the same specifications and can all be recorded with the picture or used for insert editing. The camera/recorder will have the ability to select any of these as mic or line inputs and will provide phantom voltages for the mics if required. On many digital camera/recorders, audio input/channel selections are not made with switches on the camera but are enabled via a menu displayed on an LCD screen positioned on the side of the camera. Many allow for adjustments such as noise reduction, bass filters, equalization, signal limiting, routeing to tracks 3 and 4, routeing to cue track, monitor signal and level, timecode adjustment. These settings can be memorized on scene files.

Cue track

As well as the four digital audio tracks, the digital formats also allow for a longitudinal audio cue track. This can be used for timecode or have a guide version of the sync, or feature audio to assist in editing. This track will be easier to listen to when the tape is being played at a non-standard speed whereas digital tracks will be decoded in bursts, omitting material when played faster than standard and repeating material when slower. The cue track can be recorded at any time, either with the picture or inserted separately. The information to be recorded on the cue track is normally set via the set-up menu in the viewfinder or on the camera/recorder output.

On the higher specification camera/recorders, a return output of audio from the camera/recorder to separate audio mixer no longer needs to come from the tiny headphone socket. Instead it is fitted with a male XLR socket on the rear of the camera. The track or mix of tracks and the level of the signal to be fed from this socket may also be adjusted via the menu-driven software on the camera/recorder.

Audio inputs

- **Mic (front):** When an audio channel is switched to this position, any microphone connected to the front audio input can be selected.
- **Mic (rear):** This position enables the user to plug a microphone into the connector at the rear of the camera. On some camera/recorders, a separate switch can be found under the mic input marked +48 V (phantom power) that supplies power to the microphone if required.
- **Line:** When an audio channel is switched to this position, an external audio mixer can be connected. All microphones to be used are connected and controlled via this mixer and its input sensitivity to the Betacam is 0 dB, that is known as line level. Line input can also be used for a feed from a public address system mixer before amplification.

192

Digital camera audio controls (position and facilities will vary depending on make and model)

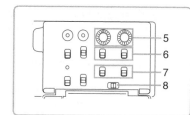

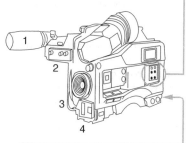

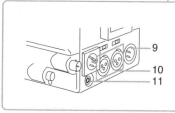

1 **On-camera microphone.**

2 **Audio channel recording level indicator switch**: This switch determines whether the recording level of audio channel is displayed on the viewfinder screen.

3 **On-camera microphone cable input.**

4 **MIC (microphone) AUDIO LEVEL control**: If the AUDIO IN switches are both set to FRONT, you can adjust the recording level of the microphone. If the AUDIO IND switch is set to ON, you can watch the audio level display in the viewfinder while adjusting the level.

5 **AUDIO LEVEL CH-1/CH-2** (audio channel 1 and channel 2 recording level) controls: These controls adjust the audio level of channels 1 and 2 when you set the AUDIO SELECT CH-1/CH-2 switches to MAN.

6 **AUDIO SELECT CH-1/CH-2** (audio channel 1 and channel 2 select) switches: These switches set the audio level adjustment for channels 1 and 2 to MANUAL or AUTO.

7 **AUDIO IN** (audio input) switches: These switches select the audio input signals for audio channels 1 and 2. The input signal source is either:

FRONT: The input signal source is the MIC IN connector.

REAR: The input signal source is the AUDIO IN CH-1/CH-2 connectors.

8 **CUE IN** (cue track input) switch: This switch selects the input signals for recording the cue track.

CH-1: Channel 1 input signal MIX; Mixed input signal of channels 1 and 2;

CH-2: Channel 2 input signal.

9 **AUDIO OUT** (audio output) connector (XLR type, 3-pin, male): This connector outputs the sound selected by the MONITOR switch.

10 **AUDIO IN CH-1/CH-2** (audio channel 1 and channel 2 input) connectors (XLR type, 3-pin, female) and LINE/MIC/+48 V ON (line input/microphone input/ external power supply +48 V on) selectors: These are the audio input connectors for channels 1 and 2, to which you can connect a microphone or other audio sources.

The LINE/MIC/+48 V ON selectors select the audio input signal source connected to these connectors, as follows:

LINE: Line input audio equipment.

MIC: A microphone with internal batteries.

+48 V ON: A microphone with an external power supply system.

11 **DC OUT** (DC power output) connector: This connector supplies power for a portable tuner. Do not connect anything other than a UHF portable tuner to this connector.

193

Microphones

Choosing which microphone to use in a specific production environment will require consideration to be given to some or all of the following factors affecting a microphone's performance:

- nature of the sound source (e.g. speech, pop group drums, bird song, etc.);
- matching the technical characteristics of the microphone to the sound source (e.g. frequency response, transient response, ability to handle high/low levels of sound (sensitivity) and directional properties);
- mechanical characteristics such as size, appearance, robustness, wind shields, affected by humidity, stability, reliability, etc.;
- compatibility – cable plugs, connectors and adaptors, matching electrical impedance, cable run required, interface with other audio equipment;
- powering arrangements (see condenser microphone opposite);
- programme budget, microphone cost/hire and availability.

Frequency response of a microphone

Microphones convert acoustical energy (sound waves) into electrical power, either by exposing one side of a diaphragm (pressure-operated) to air pressure variations or by exposing both sides of the diaphragm (pressure-gradient). Directional response of the microphone will depend upon which method is chosen or a combination of both and the physical design of the microphone. This is an important factor in the choice of microphone on location to avoid or reduce unwanted background sound. Response of the microphone is also related to frequency of the audio signal. Directional response can be plotted on a polar diagram which places the microphone in the centre of a circular graph indicating the sensitivity at each angle with respect to the front axis of the microphone (see polar diagram opposite).

There are three basic types of microphone: moving coil, ribbon, and condenser.

- **The moving coil or dynamic:** The polar diagram of this microphone can be omni-directional or cardioid, i.e. having a dead side to the rear of the microphone. This type of microphone can be used as a reporter's 'hand held' but care must be taken in its handling. They are less sensitive to wind noise than other microphones and are often fitted with wind protection within the body of the unit although they may need extra protection in extreme conditions, where foam windshields should be sufficient. Windshields give some protection against rain and provide the microphone with a waterproof cover for short periods.
- **The ribbon:** This microphone's polar response is 'figure of eight' – open front and rear, but closed to the sides. This microphone has been used mainly in radio studios with the interviewer and interviewee sitting across a table facing one another.

194

■ **The condenser:** The condenser microphone achieves the best quality of the three and requires a power supply to make it operate. This can be supplied by an 'in-line' battery supply although many condenser microphones can be powered directly from the camera or audio mixer unit, the supply being known as the 48 V phantom power. There are other forms of condenser microphone power supply known as 12 V A/B and T power. Always check that the mic power supply matches the microphone to be used *before* connection.

Microphone sensitivity

The sensitivity or output of a microphone is expressed in units of millivolt/Pascal (mV/Pa) but more commonly quoted in comparison to 0 dB line level in decibels (dB). The more negative the dB figure the less sensitive the microphone. For example, the output of a hand-held moving coil microphone will be in the region of −75 dB and is less sensitive than the output of a short condenser microphone which will be around −55 dB. Usually the camera microphone input sensitivity is around −70 dB, therefore most types of microphone can be used directly into the camera.

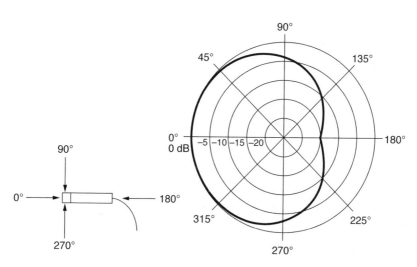

Power supplies to microphones

Before plugging a microphone into an audio input, check the position of the phantom power switch. Switch the supply to ON only if the condenser microphone requires a 48 V supply. For an 'in-line' condenser microphone (one fitted with a battery) check the condition and charge of the batteries in the microphone. Some condenser microphones require 12 V A/B, sometimes known as T power. These are not compatible with phantom systems as the voltage is supplied on different pins of the XLR connector. A convertor can be placed in the line, or the mic could be powered by a separate unit.

Basic audio kit

The directional response of a microphone is an important factor in the choice of microphone on location to avoid or reduce unwanted background sound. As well as quality headsets (single and double-sided), a basic audio kit could include:

- a pair of radio mics;
- a pair of condenser lapel microphones with clips or black gaffer tape for taping in place;
- a dynamic stick microphone – reliable and versatile;
- a short condenser rifle microphone which requires a shock mount, a foam windshield for interior use, a basket windshield for exteriors and a hairy cover for extreme wind conditions;
- microphone clamps and stands;
- XLR microphone cables and extensions;
- balance transformer.

For more specialist audio recording (e.g. music), other types of microphone can be hired. Every microphone used on an exterior location will need a purpose-designed windshield protection plus a clip or stand.

XLR connectors
XLR (eXternal, Live and Return) type connectors are used for all balanced microphone connections and balanced high-level signals. The connector has three pins – earth, live and return – and follows the convention that cable connectors with holes are inputs to the mixing/monitoring point. Connectors with pins point in the direction of the signal source.

Cables
Microphone cables should be screen balanced or star-quad design to avoid unwanted pick-up and flexible to avoid cable tangles. It is useful to have a selection of cables in various lengths such as 2, 4 and 6 metres. As well as the potential for pulling you off-shot, if operating hand-held with a connected audio cable, be aware of straining the camera audio input connector if the cable should get snagged.

Pool feeds
Press conferences, theatre performances, concerts, publicity presentations, etc., often provide a PA feed. This may be an unbalanced system and therefore a device called a direct injection (DI) box or balance transformer will be required. These usually have an unbalanced input fed with ¼-inch jack plugs and a balanced output on an XLR connector that can be plugged into the back of the camera. They may require internal batteries. An assortment of cable connectors and in-line adaptors is often invaluable when faced with a non-standard set-up. Alternatively, use a PA feed through an unbalanced cable, with appropriate attenuation to connect to the input of a radio transmitter. If there is only a single speaker at a press conference, a radio microphone in close proximity avoids cables trailing to the back of the hall, but pre-check that no other camera crew are using radio microphones on or close to the chosen frequency.

On-camera microphone

There are a number of disadvantages in mounting a microphone on a camera but it is expedient when covering news. Care must be taken not to transfer camera operational noise to the microphone and that when using a very narrow angle, to check that the sound the microphone is picking up matches the picture. High quality microphones should be used wherever possible. Usually the microphone supplied as an on-camera fixed microphone has filtering circuits which attenuate frequency response below approximately 250 Hz to help reduce wind noise. It is not practical to fit a large windshield on a microphone fixed to a camera (although small windshields are available) and so filtering helps to reduce wind noise and traffic noise. Check that the 'noise cancelling' (zoom noise, etc.) on-camera microphone is selected if the facility is available on the camcorder.

Phasing (acoustic)

If two people are close together and separately miked, it is possible, if one of them has a much louder voice than the other, to pick up the loudest voice on both microphones. This causes coloration or phase cancellation to the recorded sound because of the time delay proportional to the distance between the speakers. This can be avoided if each microphone level is only set at the correct level when that speaker is talking. This is not possible with a one-man operation and if the problem is serious either use a single stick microphone or record each voice on separate tracks with information for post-production to balance the two tracks to avoid coloration. This is called 'split-track' recording and is the preferred technique (if post-production time allows), since simply adding the two tracks together will not eliminate the original coloration problem.

Electronic phase checks

If a number of microphones are to be used together (e.g. four microphones for four speakers around a table), pre-check the rig by putting all the microphones together and use one microphone as a reference. Check as each of the other microphones are faded up that there is no loss of bass response. Any loss (electronic phase) could be caused by incorrect microphone manufacture or cable errors. The fault can be temporarily rectified by a phase lead, but the problem should be identified and repaired.

Proximity effect or bass tip-up

To avoid picking up background noise on location, someone might be requested to speak very close to the microphone. The effect with many microphones is to increase the lower frequencies or bass tip-up particularly with male voices. Some stick microphones are designed to reduce this effect for close working with singers but the trade-off with the design is to provide bass loss when working with the microphone at a more normal distance and is therefore not suitable for interviews.

Radio microphones

A radio microphone system consists of:

- a microphone which could be any type of microphone but for many television programmes is a personal or lapel microphone;
- a small FM transmitter carried by the programme participant (or it can be built into larger microphones) into which plugs the microphone;
- a short aerial attached to the transmitter;
- a receiver often mounted on the rear of the camera/recorder, powered by the camera's power supply and designed to receive the same frequency signal as the transmitter;
- an XLR connector cable from the radio receiver to a audio input on the camera usually at mic level (but check; some receiver outputs are at high level).

Personal radio mics have been designed to be small and unobtrusive and their appearance is usually acceptable for being seen in-vision. It is good practice, when using several radio mics, to have the same type and clip for uniformity in vision and for ease of maintenance if spares are required. Although the most common application of a radio mic is as a lapel/personal type microphone, any dynamic microphone can be attached to a radio transmitter when it is difficult to lay out cable, for example, at a press conference when shooting from the back of a room. The transmitter's range can be 50 metres or more depending on the site.

Choice of operating frequency

The power of the transmitter and its frequency is controlled by licence and legislation which varies between different countries. In the UK the maximum power is 10 milliwatts which gives an effective radiated power of 2 milliwatts. This is to ensure that their use does not conflict with other users of radio communications. Location radio mics usually transmit on the UHF or VHF (138–250 MHz) band, and in the UK the use of frequencies between 173.8 MHz and 175 MHz does not have to be licensed. Each radio mic transmitter at the same location will need to operate at a different frequency with some separation (minimum 0.2 MHz), otherwise they will interfere with each other. With the necessary 0.2 MHz channel separation, five VHF common frequencies are 173.8, 174.1, 174.5, 174.8 and 175.0 MHz. An essential design requirement for radio mic transmitters is that they must be crystal controlled to ensure that their transmitting frequency does not drift outside their specified limits.

Design features

Most radio microphone transmitters/receivers are fitted with some or all of the following facilities:

- the ability to send a 1 kHz tone to check continuity of transmission strength and an input gain on the receiver to balance the use of various microphones with a signal strength indicator;
- a transmitted 'low battery' inaudible warning signal;
- a 'compander' to compress the signal before transmission and expand the signal after reception to improve the signal-to-noise ratio and bandwidth. This is switchable at the receiver and transmitter and both must be either on or off;
- to avoid multipath reception (e.g. reflections from metal structures), 'dead spots' when the programme participant is moving, and signal cancellation by the interaction when a number of radio microphones are in operation, diversity systems are fitted. This involves having two receiving aerials and a circuit which switches to the strongest and least distorted signal path.

Lining-up and rigging a radio microphone

- Check the condition of the transmitter battery and fit a good quality alkaline battery. Be aware that nickel-cadmium rechargeable cells decay below operating voltage with very little notice.
- The microphone needs to be clipped or taped at about 200 mm from the mouth about mid-chest on a lapel, tie or adjacent clothing. Personal microphones are condenser microphones but some are more prone to wind noise or rustling clothes than others. Choose a design that is suitable for location work. Omni-directional personal microphones can be rigged pointing up or down. If the speaker is liable to look down and talk, breathing across the microphone (e.g. a cooking demonstration), point the capsule down. Use adhesive tape to secure the microphone when hidden under clothing to ensure that it cannot move and rub against the fabric. If they are to be fixed directly to the skin, use non-allergenic plaster or a sterilized strip.
- Obtain a sound level check and adjust the gain on the transmitter using the peak level indicator on the transmitter. An LED is often fitted which flashes to indicate the onset of limiting. Set the gain with normal voice level so that limiting occurs and then reduce the gain so that only unexpected peaks will limit.
- Rig the transmitter in a pouch, belt or pocket of the artiste so that it is visually unobtrusive and away from any metal objects carried by them. The aerial should either hang vertically down or taped upwards if the participant is sitting.
- The receiving aerial should also be upright and, if available, switch in zero level tone from the transmitter and set receiver level to zero level.
- Adjust the input audio level on the camera to read −20 dB on the digital audio level meter on the display panel.
- If time allows, ask the presenter/participant to talk and walk the anticipated area of movement. Check there is no interference to the signal path from large reflective surfaces. The receiver is fitted with a squelch circuit that mutes the output if there is insufficient signal strength. If this occurs try to identify the source of the problem, try a different frequency or modify the area of movement. It is better to prove the signal path in a rehearsal than discover problems on the recording, or worse, on transmission.
- Problems are often experienced with man-made fabrics causing noise and static. If the capsule is rigged below certain types of dense fabric, sound quality and level will not be satisfactory. If the rustling of clothing is picked up, a windshield or small cage can be fitted to keep the fabric away from the microphone. Avoid rigging personal microphones near necklaces or jewellery which could come into contact with the capsule if the artiste moves, causing bangs and clicks.

199

Microphone technique

Recording location audio, particularly in a one-man camera/recorder operating mode, poses many problems. This is a brief introduction to some of the solutions.

Pieces to camera
Probably the first choice for a shot of a presenter talking straight to the lens is to rig a radio personal microphone but a piece-to-camera can also be accomplished using a short rifle microphone protected from wind noise mounted on the camera provided the camera is not panned to or away from the presenter. If the shot is tighter than a medium close-up, a stick microphone can be held by the presenter just out of shot.

Voice-over recordings
If it is necessary to record a voice-over on location, try to ensure the audio quality will match any in-vision audio from the same presenter. Avoid interiors such as vehicles perhaps chosen to exclude background noise but which will colour the voice. Try to eliminate background effects which will be distracting and probably not match the pictures the commentary is laid over. The aim is to record a neutral sound that will supply information without distraction. Lip ribbons microphones have a sports quality convention where they are used to exclude high ambient spectator or event noise. They often sound misplaced in other production situations.

Effects
Recorded effects (often known as a wild track, buzz track or atmos) is invaluable in post-production to iron out audio mismatches. Audio 'jump cuts' in editing caused by an obtrusive background sound (e.g. running water, machinery, etc.) can be made less obvious and a single 'spot' effect may provide space and location atmosphere to the recorded images.

Help post-production by being consistent in level and quality when recording effects and provide as much information on the cassette as possible. When covering an event using a camera-mounted microphone, the sound perspective may not match the picture. An additional effects recording may help to remedy the difference provided it is of sufficient length to cover the cut item. An omni-directional microphone will provide all-round atmosphere. Avoid distinctive audio that is never seen in shot unless it is provided for atmosphere (e.g. church bells, train noise). It is often impossible to match specific locations with library audio material and a good, long, consistent effects track is extremely useful. Avoid auto-gain unless there is no opportunity of achieving a sound level before the event (e.g. a loud explosion). It is impossible to record such high-intensity sound level with a presenter's voice. The presenter must sop talking when the anticipated event happens (e.g. stop talking before switching on a food mixer). A moving coil microphone is useful for very loud, transient sounds. A hand clap near the microphone can be used to set gain if auto-gain is not selected.

Interview with a stick microphone

If there is no time to rig and line up radio mics, a presenter can conduct an interview with a stick mic (cardioid response) provided they move the microphone to favour whoever is speaking (including themselves), avoid inducing acoustic noise by rattling the connector (e.g. rings on fingers), and keep the microphone the correct distance from the speaker's mouth to get an acceptable balance between voice and any background noise. An omnidirectional stick microphone is easier to use as it can be kept stationary between two speakers if they are staged close together and the presenter favours the softer voice.

Recording an interview on one microphone

When recording an interview with the presenter holding one hand-held microphone, always listen to establish who has the prominent voice and get the presenter to favour the microphone towards the quieter of the two. The obvious danger arises when the presenter consistently moves the microphone from one person to the other. If he or she is incorrect in favouring the person who is talking, the result will be worse than not moving the microphone at all.

Recording an interview on two microphones

Route each microphone to a separate channel ('split-track' recording):

- Connect interviewee's microphone to Channel 1 and set level (see page 204).
- Connect interviewer's microphone to Channel 2 and set level.
- Only Channel 1 (interviewee's microphone) can be monitored in the viewfinder and adjusted from the front audio control. Usually the interviewee is more important and more likely to vary in level.
- Identify on the tape cassette track number and voice.

Microphone checklist

- Just as continuity of skin tone exposure is required for the presenter, so continuity of audio quality is required for his/her voice throughout the item/production. Try to be consistent with the audio treatment of the in-vision as well as the voice-over commentary.
- Poor acoustics (echo, boxy sound) can be partly overcome with close microphone techniques. They impart an identifiable quality to the voice and need to be maintained for the whole of the item.
- To avoid distraction and problems in editing, background sounds such as air-conditioners, refrigerators, telephones may need to be switched off. An effects track of any unavoidable background sound may assist in post-production.
- Highly directional microphones are not always the solution to poor separation between voice and background sound. They can still pick up traffic noise, aircraft, working machinery, etc., because often their directional ability is restricted to voices and higher frequencies.
- The ear/brain can filter out and ignore general ambient sound and concentrate on the audio source which is the subject of their attention (e.g. one voice in a crowd). Microphones have limited selection and no priorities in content selection. Similar to auto-exposure, the camera operator must do the thinking and select what type of audio is necessary for the shot. An understanding of polar patterns and operational characteristics will assist in the choice of microphone and placement.

Location sound

Auto-gain

Auto-gain can be considered the equivalent of auto-iris and needs to be used with the same caution. Auto-gain will respond to rapid increases of sound intensity by rapid reduction of recording level. This may often be undesirable.

An example would be while recording 'quiet countryside atmosphere', when someone close to the microphone controlled by auto-gain slams a car door. The result would be a very rapid attenuation of 'quiet countryside atmosphere', followed by an equally quick rise in gain after the car door noise has finished. There are similar problems when using auto-gain on a voice with background noise. When speaking, the auto-gain will adjust for correct voice level with lower level background sound. During dialogue pauses, the auto-gain will pump up the background sound. This variation will be unpleasant and cause problems in editing. Use auto-gain when there is no opportunity for obtaining a sound level before recording (e.g. an explosion; aircraft take-off) or when it is anticipated there will be sudden and large changes in sound level (e.g. a crowd cheering). Decide whether auto-gain will produce more problems than it solves.

Manual control

Manual control allows intelligent decisions to be made about level and will rely on the built-in limiter to take care of the unexpected sound overload. There are three basic requirements in sound control:

To keep within the dynamic range of the audio recording system (see page 205).

To adjust the recorded sound levels to suit the subject (e.g. match the sound perspective to the size of shot).

To maintain consistent sound level and quality over a number of shots or the result will be difficult to edit.

Wind noise

The major problem for outside location recording is wind noise. Most microphone manufacturers will produce windshields for their products in the shape of foam covers. Lapel or personal mics suffer badly from wind noise and their small windshields provided by the manufacturers are only of limited effect. It is usually possible to rig the mic under the clothing, provided the clothing is made of reasonable open fabric; cotton or wool garments are ideal. Care must be taken to prevent rustle from the fabric rubbing the mic which can be avoided by taping the mic in place rather than using the clips provided. Listen carefully to ensure that the fabric is not too thick, causing a loss of high frequency and resulting in muffled sound, although in strong winds a small loss of high frequency is more acceptable than serious wind noise.

Background noise

On location there is often the unwanted background noise of traffic, aircraft noise, machinery, etc. Try to back the microphone off from the background noise and use the presenter's body as an acoustic screen. Record a wild track of persistent noise to help in post-production. There are difficulties in editing with some types of background noise (i.e. a passing aircraft) and note that directional mics are only directional at high frequencies. Traffic noise on either side of the microphone's 'acceptance' angle may still be intrusive. Be watchful in the vicinity of airfields, military establishments or high-powered electronic equipment for radar/radio transmissions that may induce electrical interference in microphone cables.

An intermittent background sound such as a refrigerator motor cutting in and out during an extended recording session will cause problems in editing. Often cutaways of close-ups of the cooking process or pack shots of ingredients are recorded after the main demonstration. The background fridge motor noise may be on or off during these shots and when the package is edited, the motor sound will cause audio continuity problems. The simplest solution is to switch it off.

Audio levels

Sound monitoring

Monitoring audio quality is difficult in single person camera/recorder operations. If there is time, a double-sided headset can be used to check quality but more often time is at a premium and single-sided headsets (or none) are used. It is only by listening to the sound that an evaluation can be made. Audio level meters in the viewfinder and on the recorder side panel only asses loudness and do not identify the source of the sound. The least one can achieve with the intelligent use of a meter is to avoid a sound overload pushing the audio into the limiting circuit when its level exceeds the maximum permissible recording level. Beyond this point, the audio will be progressively distorted with no increase in loudness. Listening to the audio establishes production priorities (subject prominence, disturbing background, sound perspective, etc.). Metering the audio allows the correct technical requirements to be fulfilled. The very least that can done is to have an audible sound check to confirm that audio is being recorded. There is usually provision for a confidence audio check on the camera speaker by switching between the audio tracks or combining (mix). E-E (electronics to electronics) is a facility that allows a check to be made on the signal before it is recorded.

Audio meters

There are two types of mechanical meter used to measure analogue audio levels. A peak programme meter (PPM) measures peaks of sound intensity. A programme volume meter (VU) measures average level of sound and gives a better indication of loudness but at the expense of missing brief high-intensity peaks that could cause distortion. Many digital cameras are fitted with electronic bargraph metering. These may have LED, plasma or liquid crystal displays that appear to be continuous from top to bottom. These are peak response meters but some have the facility to switch their response to VU mode where they will imitate the scale and ballistic response of a VU meter.

Sound monitoring through the viewfinder

If you are using a single microphone, use track one (although check the post-production audio policy of the commissioning agent). Having connected the mic and selected mic position, turn the gain control at the side panel of the camera to maximum. Select the viewfinder for metering of audio. Obtain a sound level and adjust the front gain control on the viewfinder to register normal audio level on the viewfinder audio indicator. Reduce rear audio gain on side panel if sufficient attenuation cannot be achieved. You now have attenuation and gain should it be required on the front audio control.

Zero level voltage

Just as light is converted into a TV signal with a standard peak amplitude of 0.7 V so sound energy when it is converted into electrical energy requires a standard signal, a baseline voltage to which all changes can be referred. This is known as zero level and the standard voltage selected is 0.775 V – the voltage across 600 Ω (a common input and output impedance of audio equipment) when 1 mW is developed. 1000 Hz is the frequency of the standard zero level signal. Increasing or decreasing sound intensity will alter the level of this voltage.

Digital audio meters

The audio meter on a digital camera is very different to that on an analogue device as it shows values up to the maximum signal that can be encoded. This is calibrated from infinity (no signal) to zero (maximum level). It will also be noted that a line-up level (–20 dB) is marked with a solid diamond shape or square on the scale (see figure). This –20 dB point is used as the reference when aligning an external device such as a separate mixer. When taking a level prior to recording, it is safe to allow peaks to be well below 0 (maximum level). –12 dB to –8 dB is fine for normal peaks, ensuring the signal is properly encoded and the safety margin allows for any unexpected peak. Limiters are built into the system to prevent loss of signal should levels become too high, but as signal noise is not a problem (unlike analogue systems) holding the levels down is acceptable.

If the audio level is too high it will automatically be limited. Sound level increasing above this preset point will be progressively distorted with no increase in loudness. The gain of the audio system must be reduced at the point where the level is going into the clipper. Adjustment of level further down the audio chain will not correct the distortion.

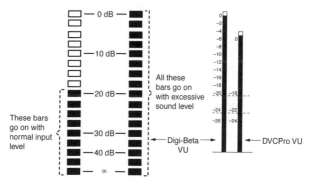

Zero level on Digi-Beta VU = 20 dB. On the DVCPro VU it is 18 dB.

Dynamic range

The intensity of sound is a function of the pressure variation set up in the atmosphere. Intensity is proportional to pressure squared. A microphone is used to convert sound energy into electrical energy and the voltage produced is proportional to the sound pressure. The range of intensities from quietest to loudest is the dynamic range of that sound situation. For example, the ratio of the loudest sound produced by an orchestra to the quietest sound can be as much as 60–70 dB in an orchestral performance. This dynamic range is greater than can be transmitted and therefore sound control and possibly sound compression is required when recording large variations in sound levels.

205

Stereo

Normal hearing provides depth and space, perspective and separation, effects and atmosphere by 360° spatial hearing. The ear/brain judges direction of sound by the time difference of sound arriving at the ear. This 'time of arrival' difference is what must be considered when recording and handling stereo audio signals. Television mono sound originates from a single speaker but television stereo sound attempts to provide an approximation of normal sound experience. Ambisonics or surround sound takes the stereo image further and allows signals to appear all around the listener. For television, ambisonic is commonly reproduced using five loudspeakers, one either side of the screen with a third placed under or over the screen and two further speakers placed behind the viewer. The ambisonic signals can be processed to feed a larger number of speakers. Many television sets in use are not equipped with stereo sound and therefore stereo transmissions must be compatible with mono reception.

Locating stereo sound

Effective stereo sound requires the 'on screen' sound to be augmented with 'off screen' sound. Stereo adds to the screen image sound, background sound located left or right of the screen whilst still being compatible with mono listening. If approximately 15° is the central wedge of sound image on screen, everything else that does not have an obvious geographical relationship to the picture is 'elsewhere'. A further complication is the variation in transmitted television formats which can be 4:3, 14:9 and 16:9. Sound which is 'off screen' for a 4:3 image may be 'on screen' for a 16:9 format. Stereo sound is not simply a technological enhancement but should be integral to the programme aims and production style.

Microphone placement

A stereo effect will occur if the time of arrival of an audio signal at a pair of coincident microphones is different and this difference is faithfully reproduced on two loudspeakers. This inter-channel difference can also be artificially replicated from a mono source by the use of a pan-pot which determines which proportion of the mono signal is directed to each stereo channel. The angle of acceptance of the two microphones, which are usually positioned 90° to each other, will depend on their polar diagrams and their position relative to the sound source. Similar to the angle of view of a lens, the closer the pair of microphones are to the sound source the better the sound image will fill the region between the monitoring loudspeakers. The sound can originate from a point source such as a voice (excluding reverberations, etc.) or occupy a wide physical area such as a symphony orchestra. As television stereo sound pick-up is normally required to match the field of view of the displayed image, the width of the sound image and the polar diagram of the microphones are important. For example, a figure-of-eight ribbon microphone close to a camera will pick up sound in front of as well as behind the camera.

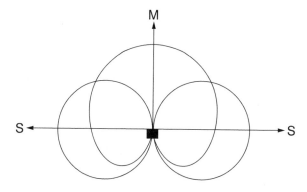

The middle and side (M and S) pair of microphones in the figure consists of a cardioid facing forward, providing the M (middle/main) signal or centre image and a figure-of-eight microphone providing the S (side) signal.

Advantages of the M and S technique in news and documentary production are:

■ the proportion of side component can be decided and adjusted away from pressure of location work;
■ a good mono signal is available if stereo problems occur in post-production;
■ the middle forward-facing microphone gives a clear indication of the direction the microphone is facing.

The main disadvantage for location work is that the S microphone (a figure-of-eight response) is prone to wind noise and rumble.

Points to consider when recording stereo sound on location exteriors when there is likely to be less control of placement and choice of microphone are:

■ Are the left-right position images correct relative to the picture?
■ Are there any time delays between picture and sound?
■ Are there any time delays between the left and right legs of a stereo signal producing a hollow sound, lacking clear imagery?
■ Do the sounds appear at the correct distance from the camera (perspective)?
■ Is the relationship between the primary sound sources and the background effects satisfactory, and is the effect of the acoustic suitable?
■ Does the sound match the picture?
■ Stereo sports coverage often uses very wide spaced positioned microphones rather than a co-incident pair on spectators to suggest an 'all round' atmosphere.
■ Spot effects of on-screen images (e.g. a cricketer hitting a ball) can be covered by an 'on-camera' microphone if it is continuously providing close shots of the main action.
■ Commentary will be central if the commentator is speaking in-vision or slightly off centre when out of vision.

Road craft

The audio/visual industry has a huge international turnover. For many millions of people, television is the prime means, and often the only choice of entertainment. Such a potentially profitable product requires tight budgetary control and efficient methods of production. Location camerawork is part of this industrial process and requires the standard professional disciplines of reliability, efficiency and consistent product quality. Quality is the result of good technique. Being reliable and efficient is a combination of the personal approach to the job and using and understanding technology. Road craft is preparing and maintaining the essential camera equipment needed for location production.

Start of day check
If you work with the same camera equipment each day and it is stored in a purpose-equipped vehicle, then you should know exactly what you are equipped with, its operational performance and its maintenance condition. In effect you have a set of production tools that are familiar and consistent. Many users of digital cameras do not have this continuity of equipment experience and may be faced with pool equipment shared by a number of people. The three questions that always need asking at the beginning of the day are: What is the nature of the day's shoot? What equipment is required? What is the condition of the equipment that is being taken to the shoot? There is never a complete answer to the first two questions (until after the event), but it should be possible to establish the condition of the camera and the consumables you are taking into the field.

■ Check that every item of equipment you need is there and remember to check over the equipment you bought to a location when you leave the location.
■ Check the state of charge of the batteries (see Batteries, page 212).
■ Check all mechanical parts for security and stability (e.g. tripod adaptor and the condition of the pan/tilt head).
■ Run the camera up and check scene file settings and lens operation.
■ Check and clean if needed the rear and front lens elements.
■ Check equipment and your own provision for foul weather protection.

Pool equipment
On an unfamiliar camera there are some time-consuming checks that need to be made before location day. These include checking that the auto-iris is functioning correctly (i.e. is the exposure setting accurate?), what signal level is the zebra exposure indicator set at, when were the recording heads last cleaned, and are there any malfunctioning facilities you should know about? Check, if possible, with the immediate previous user.

Sometimes, electronic equipment appears to be as idiosyncratic and as temperamental as some of the people you work with. A thorough knowledge of the technology involved, regular maintenance and equipment care will help to minimize equipment failure. People malfunction is outside the scope of this manual.

Lens cleaning

Remove lens and inspect rear element and filter wheel for finger marks or scratches. Refit lens if clean. A front-of-lens screw-in filter such as an ultraviolet (UV) is the best protection for the front element of a zoom. The cost of replacement if damaged is insignificant compared to the cost of repairing or replacing zoom front element. Lens tissue and breathing on the front-of-lens filter is the most common and the simplest method of removing rain marks or dust. Dirt and dust can be removed with an air blower or wiped off gently with a lens brush. Never vigorously rub lens surface or damage to the lens coating may result. With oil, fingerprints or water stains, apply a small amount of commercial lens cleaner to a lens tissue and clean in a circular movement from centre to edge of lens. Protect lens from driving rain. Dry off lens casing with a cloth and front element with lens tissue. Place lens in a plastic bag overnight, with a desiccant such as silica gel.

Pre-recording checks

Get into the habit of carrying out a routine check before each recording. All of the following checks may not be necessary on each shot and you may prefer to carry out your review in a different order.

- If the camera is mounted on a tripod, check the camera is level and the required friction adjusted. Check the condition of the front element of the lens.
- Switch power on and check state of battery charge and humidity warning indicator.
- Check if there is a tape cassette loaded and if the tape is unused, record 30 seconds of bars.
- Select colour correction filter according to colour temperature of light source.
- Check and set the timecode to the editing mode required.
- Frame and focus the shot required and check exposure and lighting.
- Check white balance.
- Select and plug-up required mic and obtain a test sound level and adjust recording level.
- Switch camera to standby, i.e. tape laced and ready to instantly record.
- Press RECORD button and wait at least 6 seconds before cueing essential action.

General operational notes

- Avoid recording from any 'power save' mode which usually means that the tape is not laced up and in contact with the head drum to conserve power. If the record button is pressed in this 'save' mode, there will be a small delay while the tape is laced and the recording achieves stability. This may result in a second or more of unusable picture. Always allow some run-up time before significant action to make certain that a stable edit can be achieved. Some formats require at least 5 seconds.
- Tape over any controls that are likely to be accidentally switched during operation (e.g. viewfinder brightness/contrast controls on viewfinder if they are likely to be knocked during lens operation).
- On some formats, camera power must be on to load or eject tape.
- A portion of the last shot can be previewed by using the RET button. The VTR will park after review awaiting next recording.
- The breaker button (if fitted) is designed to 'trip' out on a voltage overload to protect the camera. This seldom occurs and if it needs resetting more than once for no obvious reason, have the camera serviced.
- Usually, the cue lights on the front and back of the camera (which can be switched off) will light or blink while recording and will also light in sync with display panel warning lamps.

Camera mounts

One of the reasons conventionally proposed for using a tripod is that it allows the recording of video images without unintended camera movement or shake. This conforms to the 'invisible technique' style of programme making, where the emphasis is on programme content rather than the production techniques employed to present it. As we described in Alternative styles (page 130), the 'camera surprised by events' has become a popular camerawork style, where the camera nervously on the move, with unsteady framing, has sought to replicate unrehearsed news coverage. This may be a passing fashion or it may have become an established visual convention. Hand-held cameras shooting from the shoulder are difficult to hold on a steady frame when using the narrower end of the zoom. With some smaller DV format cameras, even using the stability of the shoulder is not feasible and they are difficult to hold steady for any length of time. This characteristic becomes a virtue if the 'unsteady' frame is equated with 'realism' and 'naturalism' and is a desirable production quality, but there are other types of production that require unobtrusive camerawork that can only be achieved with a tripod-mounted camera. With this type of production, shaky and unsteady pictures are not only difficult to disguise in the edit, but are seen as a distraction from the content of the shot.

Pan and tilt heads

A good pan and tilt head will have adjustment for the centre of gravity (C of G) of the combination of camera/recorder, lens and viewfinder in use. If the C of G is not adjusted then the camera will either be difficult to move from the horizontal or it will fall forwards or backwards. Adjustment of C of G balance should not be confused with mid-point balance, which involves positioning the camera and lens to find the point of balance on the head. If any additional accessories are added to the camera or lens (e.g. a pan bar with servo zoom control), then the balance needs to be readjusted. The friction or drag control of the head depends on the shot and personal preference. Using a very narrow lens for an extreme close shot may require much more friction than that needed to pan the camera smoothly when following rapid impromptu movement. Some cameramen prefer a heavy drag or 'feel' on the head so that there is weight to push against, whereas others remove all friction and the head can be panned at the slightest touch. The head should have provision for locking the camera in the pan and tilt mode when not in use, plus a fail safe system for locking the mounting plate attached to the base of the camera.

Tripods

If a tripod is to be of any value it must be quick to set up, rigid, with no tendency either for the legs to twist or flex. These essential design features need to be achieved with the lightest possible construction. It must have a good range of easily adjustable heights with an infallible locking clamp on each leg section. The feet of the tripod can be spikes which also fit into a spreader – a device to prevent the tripod legs from spreading out. The head-to-tripod connection can be a bowl fitting (100 mm or 150 mm), allowing the camera to be levelled using the built-in level bubble in the head, or a flat plate fixing which requires levelling to be carried out by adjusting one or more legs. A set of wheels can be exchanged for the spreader if the camera has flat, level ground to reposition on.

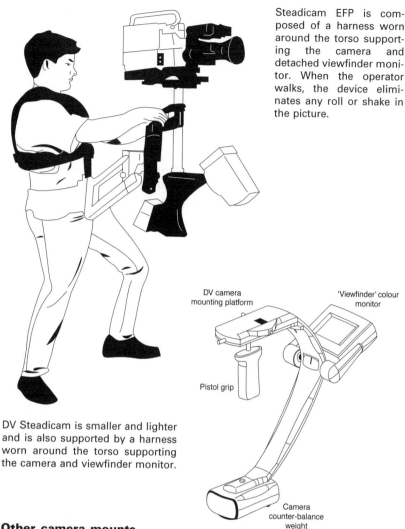

Steadicam EFP is composed of a harness worn around the torso supporting the camera and detached viewfinder monitor. When the operator walks, the device eliminates any roll or shake in the picture.

DV camera mounting platform

'Viewfinder' colour monitor

Pistol grip

DV Steadicam is smaller and lighter and is also supported by a harness worn around the torso supporting the camera and viewfinder monitor.

Camera counter-balance weight

Other camera mounts

There are a number of foldaway light portable dollies which can be packed and transported in a car. They consist of track and a wheeled base on which a tripod can be securely mounted. They require a tracker and sufficient time to level the track before shooting.

Clamps, gimbals and helicopter mounts provide stability when the camera is required to be mounted in moving vehicles, etc.

There is also provision to remote control pan and tilt, zoom and focus when the camera is mounted on a hothead (a servo-controlled pan/tilt head) at the end of a crane or when the camera needs to be placed in an inaccessible location without an operator.

There is a large range of dollies, arms and cranes that can be hired suitable for any size location or camera development shot.

Batteries

For many years nickel cadmium (Ni-Cad) batteries have been the standard power for portable video cameras. With the growth of portable computers and mobile phones, new battery technologies using nickel metal hydride (NiMH) and rechargeable lithium (Li-Ion or Li) have been developed but at present Ni-Cad batteries form the main proportion of professional video batteries in use. The camera/recorder is normally powered by a 13.2 V or 14.4 V nickel-cadmium rechargeable battery which is clipped to the back of the recorder. There are a range of different capacity batteries available to give extended running times or several batteries can be grouped together and worn on a belt. In general, digital recording requires more power than analogue recording.

- **Camera/recorder priorities:** Without power there can be no recording and battery life and reliability is an ever-present factor in a cameraman's working day. The basic criteria in assessing a battery for location camera/recorder work are:
  - What is the preferred and minimum acceptable run time?
  - What is the maximum power drain of the equipment?
  - How fast, how reliable and how safely can the battery be recharged?
  - What is the optimum size and weight to balance the camera?
  - Is there an accurate method of indicating battery power time remaining?
  - How much routine battery maintenance and service will be required?
  - What is the cost/estimated life of the battery system?
- **Camcorder power consumption:** Most camera/recorder units draw between 15 and 45 W and are usually powered by a 4-amp-hour battery which will on average provide 1–2 hours of continuous use depending on camera power consumption and the use of an on-camera light. As well as the chemistry of the battery design, the method of charging, discharging and temperature crucially affect the performance and life of the battery.
- **Battery voltage range:** Another crucial camera specification is the operating voltage range. Most cameras will specify a minimum voltage below which the camera will not operate and an upper voltage beyond which operating the equipment will cause damage or trigger the power breaker. The value of this power figure is stated, for example, as 12 V (–1 +5) which means that the camera will function over the voltage supply range of 11 V through to 17 V. Many battery manufactures provide a viewfinder indication of time remaining with the battery in use.
- **Fast charge/quick charge:** With ageing, individual cells in the battery charge and discharge at different rates. With a fast charge, the charger needs to assess when any cell has reached full charge and then drop the charging rate to the slow charge rate to prevent venting and overheating.
- **Shelf life:** A battery that has been charged and not used for a few days may not remain fully charged.
- **Temperature:** The Ni-Cad battery is affected by temperature. Temperatures below freezing (0°C) will not damage the cell but during discharge will seriously reduce the available capacity.

Battery checklist

- Identify each battery with a conspicuous number so that an accurate record can be kept of its charging cycles.
- Match charger to battery. Use battery manufacturer's recommended charger.
- Ensure that batteries are rotated and a set pattern of charging and usage is employed.
- Try to keep all batteries at room temperature. Avoid extreme temperatures on location by thermal insulation or shade.
- Keep batteries away from intense heat.
- Allow a battery to cool after heavy discharge before charging.
- Don't try to charge batteries that have been in extreme temperatures. Nickel-cadmium batteries must not be fast-charged when they are colder than 0°C. Wait until they are close to room temperature (65°F).
- The voltage of the battery is not a reliable way of assessing the state of charge of a battery.
- Unlike cameras/VTRs, many battery lamps have no power 'cut off' and could discharge a battery beyond a safe limit. Cells may be damaged if battery is discharged below 75% of its nominal voltage.
- Protect batteries from severe shock, vibration, high humidity, steam and rain. If battery should get very wet, shake out excess water and dry naturally in a warm place. Do not charge or use battery until it has fully dried.
- Take sufficient batteries to service a day's shoot. You may not be able to find suitable mains for re-charging.
- Don't subject batteries to rough usage. Any dents in the battery case may penetrate and ruin a cell.
- Conserve battery power by reverting to standby as often as possible; use manual zoom to set up shots; use separate battery for on-camera battery lamp.

Safety hazards when charging a battery

- **Cold temperature charging:** The fast charging of a cold battery is one of the most dangerous hazards associated with Ni-Cad batteries and can result in a violent explosion. When a Ni-Cad is fast charged at temperatures below +5°C (+41°F), the internal charging reaction cannot proceed normally and a significant portion of the charge current can be diverted into producing highly explosive hydrogen gas. A spark can ignite this gas causing an explosion that can turn the battery into a grenade. *Cold batteries must be allowed to reach room temperature before being placed on a charger.*
- **Fire hazards:** Ni-Cad batteries and chargers have been identified as the source of several fires and toxic smoke incidents over the years. One major TV network instructed their cameramen that batteries must not be charged in their hotel bedrooms. Most of these incidents are connected to fast chargers that failed to recognize when a battery reached full charge. The continuing current produces heat and eventually smoke or fire. This can be avoided by the use of a thermal fuse in the power circuit which will disconnect the battery from the charger if dangerous temperatures are detected.

   A similar fire hazard can also occur if there is a mismatch between the charger and battery on a slow charge. Always provide for air circulation around batteries and do not charge batteries in a bag or flight case.
- **Physical shock:** If a battery is internally damaged by physical impact or being accidentally dropped, internal wires can be short circuited and become red-hot elements causing the battery to burst into flames. Take every precaution to avoid subjecting batteries to violent physical impact.
- **Interactive battery charger:** Most of the above hazards can be avoided or eliminated by using an interactive charger that continuously interrogates the battery while charging.

Location safety

Individual responsibility

Health and safety legislation obliges you to take reasonable care of your own health and safety and that of others who may be affected by what you do or fail to do. You also have a responsibility to cooperate, as necessary, to ensure satisfactory safety standards. If you comply with the requirements for safety and something goes wrong, then your employer will be held to account. If you fail to comply, you may lose any claim for compensation for injury and could even be prosecuted as an individual. What you must do is:

- Follow the safety requirements and any instructions you are given, especially in relation to emergencies (e.g. know the location of fire exits).
- Ask for further information if you need it and report accidents (or a near miss!) and any dangerous situations or defects in safety arrangements.
- Do not interfere with or misuse safety systems or equipment.
- Work within the limits of your competence which means a knowledge of best practice and an awareness of the limitations of one's own experience and knowledge.

Assessing risk

The key to good, safe working practices is to assess any significant risk and to take action to eliminate or minimize such risks. The procedure is:

- identify precisely what is required in the production;
- identify any potential hazards in that activity;
- identify the means by which those risks can be controlled.

The key terms in risk assessment are:

- **Hazard:** the inherent ability to cause harm.
- **Risk:** the likelihood that harm will occur in particular circumstances.
- **Reasonably practicable:** the potential improvement in safety is balanced against the cost and inconvenience of the measures that would be required. If the costs and inconvenience do not heavily outweigh the benefits, then the thing is reasonably practicable and should be done.
- **Residual risk:** the risk remaining after precautions have been taken.

An example

It is proposed to shoot from a camera hoist near overhead power lines. The power lines are a **hazard**. Touching them could result in death. What is the likelihood (**risk**) that harm will occur in particular circumstances? There may be the risk of a high wind blowing the hoist onto the power lines. Is the weather changeable? Could a high wind arise? What is **reasonable and practical** to improve safety? The obvious action is to reposition the hoist to provide a usable shot but eliminate all risk of it touching the power lines. As weather is often unpredictable, the hoist should be repositioned as the costs and inconvenience do not heavily outweigh the benefits. There remains the **residual risk** of operating a camera on a hoist which can only be partially reduced by wearing a safety harness.

A checklist of potential location safety hazards

- **Boats**: It is essential to wear life lines and life-jacket when operating on a boat or near water such as on a harbour wall.
- **Confined spaces:** Check the quality of air and ventilation when working in confined spaces such as trenches, pipes, sewers, ducts, mines, caves, etc.
- **Children** are a hazard to themselves. When working in schools or on a children's programme, check that someone is available and responsible to prevent them touching or tripping over cables, floor lamps, camera mountings, etc.
- **Explosive effects and fire effects** must be regulated by a properly trained effects operator and special care should be taken with those effects that cannot be rehearsed.
- **Excessive fatigue** is a safety problem when operating equipment that could cause damage to yourself or others and when driving a vehicle on a long journey home after a production has finished.
- **Forklift trucks** must have a properly constructed cage if they are to carry a cameraman and camera.
- **Lamps:** All lamps should have a safety glass/safety mesh as protection against exploding bulbs. Compact source discharge lamps must always be used with a UV radiation protective lens. Lamps rigged overhead must be fitted with a safety bond. Check that lamp stands are secured and cabled to avoid being tripped over and that they are securely weighted at the base to prevent them being blown over.
- **Location safety:** In old buildings, check for weak floors, unsafe overhead windows, derelict water systems and that the electrical supply is suitable for the use it is put to. Check the means of escape in case of fire and the local methods of dealing with a fire. Check for the impact of adverse weather and in remote locations, the time and access to emergency services.
- **Noise:** High levels of location noise (machinery, etc.), effects (gunshots, explosions) as well as close working to foldback speakers can damage hearing. Stress will be experienced attempting to listen to talkback with a very high ambient noise. Wear noise-cancelling headsets. If wearing single-sided cans, use an ear plug in the unprotected ear.
- **Stunt vehicles:** Motor vehicles travelling at speed involved in a stunt are likely to go out of control. Leave the camera locked-off on the shot and stand well away from the action area in a safe position agreed with the stunt-coordinator.
- **Filming from a moving vehicle:** Cameras must be either securely mounted or independently secured on safety lanyards. Operators should be fitted with seat belts or safety harnesses attached to safety lines securely anchored.
- **Roadside working:** Wear high-visibility gear and get the police to direct traffic if required. Police may give permission for a member of the crew to direct traffic but motorists are not obliged to obey such instructions.
- **Adverse weather:** A cameraman setting out for the day needs to equip himself with a choice of clothing to match any changing weather conditions. Those who work regularly out of doors must make themselves aware of the risks involved and how to protect themselves against sunburn, skin cancer, heat stress and heat stroke, hypothermia, white finger and frost bite. A check on the effects of any extreme weather forecast must be assessed each day on exposed camera positions. Individual safety requires a personal assessment and only the individual on a scaffold tower or hoist can judge when it is time to call it a day and retreat from the threat of lightning.

Glossary

Actuality event Any event that is not specifically staged for television that exists in its own time scale.

A/D conversion Converting an analogue signal into a digital signal.

Ad-lib shooting Impromptu and unrehearsed camera coverage.

Alarm control Control of audible warning through speaker of camera/recorder of a fault condition in camera or VTR fault.

Aliasing Incorrect sampling due to input frequencies exceeding one half of the sampling rate.

Amplitude Maximum height of a waveform or signal.

Analogue signal A varying voltage signal.

Angle of view The horizontal angle of view of a specific focal length lens. Angle of view varies with a zoom lens.

ASA American Standards Association. A method of rating the speed of film. Replaced by International Standards Organisation, ISO, or Exposure Index, EI.

As-directed Unrehearsed camera coverage controlled at any moment by the director.

Aspect ratio The proportion of the picture width to its height.

Assembly edit Recording process where the video, audio and timecode are recorded, in sequence, to a blank tape.

Attenuation Reduction of signal level.

Auto-gain An electronic circuit which automatically adjusts audio recording level to keep within prescribed limits.

Auto-iris Automatic adjustment of the iris depending on main subject luminance.

Azimuth The azimuth on an audio tape machine is correct when the record head is at a right angle to the tape.

Back focus See Flange back.

Backlight Lamp used to separate subject from the background by rim lighting the subject from upstage.

Balance The relative level between sound sources or light sources.

Balanced line Connection of audio signals where the two signal paths are kept separate from earth.

Bandwidth The range of frequencies required for successful transmission of audio (20 kHz) or television (PAL 5.5 MHz).

Barndoors Hinged metal flaps on the front of a lamp used to control the spread of light.

Bars See Colour bars.

Bass Lower end of the frequency spectrum.

Battery lamp Small battery-powered lamp often mounted on top of the camera.

Betacam format 12.5 mm tape cassette video format recording, on two adjacent video heads, the luminance signal (Y) and a chroma signal consisting of a compressed time division multiplex of the colour difference signals (R − Y and B − Y).

Bias High-frequency signal added to the audio during the magnetic recording process.

216

Big close-up (BCU) A description of the size of a shot. When applied to the face, the frame only includes the point of the chin to mid-forehead.

Bit A unit of binary code.

Bitstream A series of binary digits.

Black balance Automatic adjustment of the black level of the camera.

Black level The amplitude of the television video signal representing the darkest past of the picture.

Black wrap Black anodized aluminium foil used to control spill light or shaping a light beam.

Blonde A 2000 W portable lamp.

BNC A twist-lock cable connector often used on monitor video cables.

Bouncing A method of transferring audio from one track to another. Also a method of obtaining a soft light source from a hard source.

Breaker button Automatic cut-out of power supply to electronic equipment if overload is detected.

Brightness A term often incorrectly used to mean luminance. Brightness is a subjective effect; it is how bright we see an object.

C-mount Standard broadcast video lens mount.

C10 rate A slow charge of constant current equal to 1/10th of the ampere-hour rating of the battery. A safe extended charge rate that will not produce a build up of oxygen.

Camera angle The position of the camera relative to the main subject in the shot.

Camera left Left of frame as opposed to the artiste's left when facing camera.

Camera right Right of frame as opposed to the artiste's right when facing camera.

Camera sensitivity Quoted in relation to a subject with peak white sensitivity, scene illuminance (lux), f number of lens and signal-to-noise ratio for a stated signal.

Candela The unit of measurement of the luminous intensity of a lamp.

Canting the camera Angling the camera so that the horizon is not parallel to the bottom of the frame.

Caption generator Electronic equipment that allows text to be created and manipulated on screen via a keyboard.

CCD A charge-coupled device; it converts light into electrical impulses which are compiled into the TV picture format.

Chroma Another name for saturation, a control usually found on monitors.

Chroma key An electronic process for inserting an artiste (foreground) into a background picture; also known as colour separation overlay (CSO) in the BBC.

Clean feed An audio source providing a programme participant with all audio signals but excluding own audio contribution.

Close-up (CU) Shot size. When applied to the face, the top of the frame rests on the top of the head and the bottom of the frame cuts at the position of a knotted tie if worn.

Coaxial cable Cable with a central conductor surrounded by a sheath of screening.

Coincident pair Two microphones that are effectively in the same position.

Coloration Unpleasant effect where sound is repeated with a small time delay. This may occur where two microphones pick up the same sound.

Colour balance See White balance.

Colour bars A special test signal used in colour television.

Colour temperature A convenient way to describe the colour of a light source by relating it to a black body radiator, e.g. heated poker, measured in Kelvins (K) after Lord Kelvin (physicist).

Component The individual or difference signals from the red, blue and green channels and luminance signal.

Composite The colour signals encoded (combined) with the luminance signal. Also, old definition for luminance signal plus synchronizing pulses.

Compression The process of reducing the amount of signal data that is required to be passed through a finite channel whilst endeavouring to maintain the quality of the originating signal. Also a method of reducing the range of audio levels.

Condenser A type of microphone using charged plates to transfer sound pressure changes into electrical signals.

Contrast ratio The ratio between the brightest part of the subject and the darkest part.

Control track A regular pulse recorded on video tape to identify the position of the video signal and tape speed.

Cosine law A law which follows the cosine 0°–90°.

Crash zoom Either an intentionally maximum speed zoom or an 'emergency' fast zoom to recompose 'on-shot'.

Crossing the line Moving the camera to the opposite side of an imaginary line drawn between two or more subjects after recording a shot of one of the subjects. This results in intercut faces looking out of the same side of frame and the impression that they are not in conversation with each other.

Cross talk Unwanted signal picked up between adjacent signal cables or from one audio track to another.

CSO Colour separation overlay – see Chroma key.

CTDM Compressed time division multiplexed chrominance recording; part of the Betacam method of recording.

Cue A particular lighting condition or an indication for action to start, i.e. actor to start performing or lighting change to start.

Cursor A vertical or horizontal line that can be positioned by the cameraman in the viewfinder as a reminder of a precise frame position or to check a vertical or horizontal visual element.

Cutaway Cutting away from the main subject or master shot to a related shot.

DAT Digital audio tape.

DCC Dynamic contrast control compresses highlights of the picture to allow a greater contrast range to be recorded.

Decibels (dB) A logarithmic ratio of changes in sound intensity similar to the ear's logarithmic response to changes in sound intensity.

218

Depth of field The zone of acceptable focus in the field of view.

Dichroic filter A mixture of glass layers with different refractive indices, designed to reflect one colour whilst allowing others to pass through. Commonly used on battery lamps to convert the colour temperature of tungsten to daylight, and in light splitting blocks.

Diffuser Material which scatters the light to create a softer light source.

Digital A data stream of individual binary numbers representing an unbroken variable value.

Digital injection (DI) A method of directly connecting an audio output from a musical instrument or other audio equipment to a balance audio input.

Digital manipulation Rearranging and recombining small elements (pixels) of an image.

Dimmer An electronic device for controlling the light output from a light source. Usually a thyristor or silicon controller rectifier (SCR) but recent developments have included the transistor dimmer.

Dingle Branches placed in front of a luminaire to create a dapple effect or in front of a lens to create a foreground feature.

Discharge light source Lamps which produce light by ionizing a gas contained in a bulb.

Display mode Selecting particular information about the camera to be displayed in the viewfinder.

Distortion Unwanted damage to an analogue signal that results in the output of a system being different from the original.

Dolby A noise reduction process used in audio recording and playback.

Downlink The signal path between satellite and receiver.

Down stage Moving towards the camera or audience.

Dropout The short loss of a recorded signal due to faulty head-to-tape contact or tape imperfections.

Dry Describes the inability of a performer either to remember or to continue with their presentation.

Dynamic range The relationship of the highest value to the lowest value of sound intensity or picture brightness that can be reproduced.

EBU European Broadcasting Union. Advisory and regulatory body for broadcasting in Europe.

Edited master The final version of edited material that will be seen by the viewer.

EDL Edit decision list created to define the in and out points of an edit sequence.

E-E Electronics to electronics; a VTR facility switch which enables the signal to bypass the recording head.

Effects (Fx) Visual or audio effects.

EFP Electronic field production is the term used to describe single camera location video programme making other than news.

Electronic shutter An electronic method of varying the length of exposure time of the CCD. Can be used to improve the slow motion reproduction of motion.

Encode The technique of combining colour information with a luminance (monochrome) signal.

ENG Electronic news gathering describes the single camera video recording of news events.

Entropy The unpredictable part of a signal which has to be transmitted by a compression system if quality is not to be lost.

Equalization Increase or decrease in the level of chosen audio frequencies.

Establishing shot The master shot which gives the maximum information about the subject.

EVDS Enhanced vertical definition system; a method of reducing motion blur.

Extender An additional lens which can be switched internally in the zoom lens to extend the zoom range of focal lengths.

Eyeline The direction the subject is looking in the frame.

f number A method of indicating how much light is being allowed to pass through the aperture of the lens.

Face tones Signal derived from face tones, typically (average European face) about 0.5 V.

Fader A control for varying the level of an audio or video signal.

Feed Either a video signal or the cable that carries the signal.

Field One top-to-bottom scanning of an image. Two fields interlaced make up one frame.

Field integration A technique connected with the read-out of a CCD where adjacent lines are averaged.

Fill light A light source used to make shadows transparent, i.e. reduce the contrast.

Filter wheels Filter holders of colour correction, neutral density or effects filters that are arranged within the camera to allow for the quick selection, by rotating the wheel, of the required filter combination.

First generation The acquisition medium on which the video signal was first recorded.

Flange back The distance from the flange surface of the lens mount to the image plane of the pick-up sensor commonly known as the back focus.

Flight kit A portable set of location lamps and stands able to be packed in a compact container for easy transportation.

Focal length of a compound lens The distance from the principal point of a compound lens (e.g. a zoom lens) to the point at which rays from an object at infinity form the most sharply defined image.

Focus pull Moving the zone of sharpest focus to another subject.

Foldback A feed to allow artists to hear selected sound sources on loudspeakers or headphones.

Foot candle Unit of illuminance in imperial units, 1 lumen/ft^2 = 1 foot candle.

Format The method of recording the image (e.g. DVCPro; S-VHS; Betacam, etc.).

Frame One complete television picture comprising of two interlaced fields or a single film image.

Frame integration A technique connected with the read-out of a CCD where vertical resolution is improved at the expense of motion blur.

Frame interline transfer (FIT) A method of transferring the CCD charge to eliminate vertical smear.

Frame store An electronic device for storing individual video frames.

Frame transfer (FT) The method of transferring the charge vertically from the CCD pixels exposed to the subject, to a duplicate set of pixels.

Free run Frame identification by timecode which is set to the actual time of day when the frame was recorded.

Frequency The number of complete cycles per second.

Frequency response The range of frequencies that a particular system can reproduce without distortion.

Fresnel Stepped lens used in the fresnel spotlight.

Fundamental The original or lowest frequency of a complex signal.

Gain The amplification of a video or audio signal calibrated in dBs (e.g. +6 dB of video gain is the equivalent of opening the lens iris by 1 stop).

Gaffer The chief lighting electrician.

Gamma The law of the transfer characteristic of a system, i.e. relationship between input and output signals.

GEO Geosynchronous orbit satellite that revolves at the same rotational speed as the earth and appears stationary from the earth's surface.

Gobo Stainless steel stencil used in profile projectors to create effects, e.g. windows, abstract pattern, moon, etc.

Grads An abbreviation of graduated applied to front-of-lens filters which progressively filter or colour the picture vertically.

Graticule Engraved calibration scale on the front of waveform monitors and vectorscopes.

Grid area The structure above a studio floor.

Grip Supporting equipment for lighting or camera equipment. Also the name of the technicians responsible for handling grip equipment, e.g. camera trucks and dollies.

GV General view; this is a long shot of the subject.

HAD Hole accumulated diode is a CCD sensor which increases the proportion of the sensor that can collect light without decreasing resolution.

Hand-held Operating a portable camera without a camera mounting.

Hard light Any light source that casts a well-defined shadow.

Harmonic A range of frequencies that are multiples of the fundamental that make up a complex waveform.

Hertz Unit of frequency, 1 Hertz = 1 cycle/second.

High angle Any lens height above eye height.

High key Picture with predominance of light tones and thin shadows.

HMI A discharge lamp producing light by ionizing a gas contained in the bulb.

Hot head A remotely controlled camera pan/tilt head often on the end of a jib arm.

Hue The dominant wavelength, colour describing what we see, e.g. red.

Hyper HAD Increasing the sensitivity of the HAD CCD by the use of a micro lens with each pixel.

Illuminance (illumination) (E) A unit of light measurement for incident light, lumens/m^2 = lux.

Image size The image formed by the lens on the face of the CCD.

Insert edit The adding of video, audio or timecode, out of sequence, to a pre-recorded tape.

Insert point An input/output in a system allowing the connection of other equipment.

Interlace A method of scanning separate parts of an image in two passes (fields) in order to reduce the bandwidth required for transmission.

Interline transfer (IT) A method of transferring a charge from the pixels exposed to the subject to an adjacent duplicate set of pixels.

Inverse square law A fundamental law in lighting and sound where the intensity of light and sound falls off as the inverse of the distance squared.

Invisible technique Production method which emphasizes the content of the shot rather than the production technique.

Iris Variable circular aperture in the camera used to control exposure, calculated in *f* stops.

ISDN Integrated Services Digital Network is a system that allows the transfer of audio or other data via a telephone line.

Isoed Recording the (isolated) output of an individual camera or cameras in a multi-camera shoot in addition to the main recording.

JPEG The Joint Photographic Experts Group, which identifies a standard for the data compression of still pictures.

Kelvin (K) A unit measurement of heat used to describe colour temperature.

Key Mood of a picture, i.e. high key/low key.

Key Keying signal for chroma key operations.

Keylight or key The main source of light illuminating the subject.

Kicker Light used at eye level from upstage, at eye level to 'kick' the side of the artiste's head.

Knee Modified part of the transfer characteristic of a camera designed to progressively compress highlights.

Ku-band The frequency spectrum between 10.7 GHz and 18 GHz.

LCD Liquid display crystal. A reflective or transmissive alphanumeric display.

Level The volume of an audio or video signal.

Line level A reference audio level measured at 1000 Hz.

Linear matrix Involves cross-coupling between R, G and B to help obtain the desirable analysis characteristics essential for faithful colour reproduction.

Live The transmission of an event as it takes place.

Locked-off Applying the locks on a pan and tilt head to ensure that the camera setting remains in a preselected position. Can also be applied to an unmanned camera.

Long lens A lens with a large focal length or using a zoom at or near its narrowest angle of view.

Long shot (LS) A description of a shot when the full length human figure fills the frame.

Look angle The angle of elevation of the signal path above the horizon to a satellite.

Low angle A lens height below eye height.

Low key Picture with a predominance of dark tones and strong shadows.

LTC Longitudinal timecode is recorded with a fixed head on a designated track on the tape.

Lumen Unit of quantity of light flow per second, 'weighted' by the photopic curve.

Luminaire Name given for a complete lighting unit, i.e. light source or lamp plus its casing.

Luminance (L) A measure of the light reflected from a surface. A total flux reflected of 1 lumen/m^2 has a luminance of 1 Apostilb (Imperial measurement 1 lumen/ft^2 = 1 foot lambert).

Luminance signal That part of the video signal which represents the relative brightness points of an image.

Luminous intensity A measure of a lamp's ability to radiate light, measured in candelas (old term, candlepower).

Lux A unit for illuminance, 1 lumen/m^2 = 1 lux.

Macro A switchable facility on a lens that allows focusing on an object placed closer to the lens than the normal minimum object distance (see MOD).

Matrix Electrical circuit for deriving 'mixtures' of signals, e.g. colour difference signals and luminance signals from RGB signals.

Matte box A filter holder and bellows extension for the control of flare, fitted to the front of the lens.

Medium close-up (MCU) A shot description usually describing a framing of a person with the bottom of the frame cutting where a suit breast pocket would normally be.

Medium shot (MS) A description of shot size with the bottom of the frame cutting at the waist when applied to the human figure.

Megahertz (MHz) One million cycles per second.

Metal particle A video tape coating allowing a wider frequency response to be recorded and an improved signal-to-noise ratio compared to oxide tape coating.

Millisecond One thousandth of a second.

Mired Micro reciprocal degree value allows the relationship between a correction filter and the colour temperature shift to be calculated.

MOD Minimum object distance; the closest distance a subject in acceptable focus can be to the lens.

Modelling The action of light revealing contour and texture of a subject.

223

Monitor termination A switchable electronic 'load' (usually 75 Ω) on the back of a monitor inserted at the end of a video cable feed to prevent the signal 'bouncing back'. If several monitors are looped together, termination only occurs at the last monitor.

Monochrome Reproduction of a single colour such as a black and white image.

Movement blur The degradation of the image related to the speed of subject movement during the exposure time of a single picture.

MPEG2 Moving Picture Experts Group 2 is a series of benchmark values specifying different degrees of compression.

Multi-generation Numerous re-recordings of the original recording.

Neutral density filter A filter which reduces the amount of light transmitted without altering the colour temperature.

Ni-Cad Nickel-cadmium is the constituent of rechargeable batteries widely used to power broadcast camcorders and cameras.

Noddies Television jargon for cutaway shots recorded for editing purposes after an interview showing the interviewer listening and 'nodding' at the interviewee's comments.

Noise reduction A method of reducing the noise on recorded or transmitted analogue audio.

NTSC National Television System Committee. Usually signifies an American method of encoding colour.

OB Abbreviation for outside broadcast. Usually a multi-camera production from a non-studio venue using a mobile control room.

Off-line editing Low-quality images that are used to produce edit lists or a non-transmittable edited guide tape.

Off-shot Describes the camera when its output is not selected at the vision mixing panel to be fed 'to line'.

On-line editing Any system that produces a final edited broadcast quality programme.

On-shot Describes the camera when its output is selected at the vision mixing panel to be fed 'to line'.

Opacity The reciprocal of transmission of light through a film or filter.

Oscillator Equipment to produce pure tone (sine wave) used for lining-up and calibrating systems.

Oscilloscope Cathode ray oscilloscope used to provide a visual display of video signals.

Oxide tape Tape coating used in the first generation of the beta format cameras.

Pad A circuit used to reduce or attenuate the signal level.

PAL Phase alternating Line. A European development of the American NTSC system of encoding colour.

Pan-pot Pan(oramic) pot(entiometer); this adjusts the apparent position of a sound source in a stereo image.

Peak programme meter (PPM) This measures sound by averaging the peaks of intensity over a specified period and rapidly responds to high level transients.

Peak white Either 100 per cent video signal level or 60 per cent reflectance neutral grey surface.

Peak white clipper A 'gain limiting' circuit set to the same level in each colour channel of the camera that restricts any signal to a maximum level.

Perspective The apparent position of closeness of sound in an image. Also the optical methods used to assess or construct image depth.

Phantom power The DC supply to some types of condenser microphone using the signal cable.

Phase A time delay between two signals. It is expressed in degrees as the actual time will vary with frequency.

Picture monitor Good quality viewing monitor, similar to a receiver but without RF and sound sections.

Pink noise A random signal that appears to the human ear to contain an equal level of frequencies.

Pistol grip Hand grip controlling zoom movement that may be attached to a lightweight lens when operating the camera 'hand-held' or attached to a pan bar.

Pixel Abbreviation for picture cell – a single point in an electronic image.

Playback Replaying a recorded shot or sequence of shots or audio.

Point-of-view shot A shot from a lens position that seeks to duplicate the viewpoint of a subject depicted on screen.

Polecat Adjustable spring loaded aluminium tubes with rubber feet that can be used vertically or horizontally to support lightweight luminaires.

Post production Editing and other work carried on pre-recorded material.

Practical An in-shot light source, e.g. wall light.

Prime lens A fixed focal length lens.

Print-through The transfer of magnetic information from one layer of tape to another when stored on a reel.

Production control rooms Production areas on outside broadcasts (see Scanner), or adjacent to studios used by production staff, lighting and audio.

Prompters A coated piece of glass positioned in front of the lens to reflect text displayed on a TV monitor below the lens.

PSC The production method of recording material on a portable single video camera.

Pulse coded modulated (PCM) Digital transmission system.

Purity In a monitor, the ability of the red gun only to hit red phosphors, etc.

Quantize In a digital system, allocation of 'sample' level prior to coding.

Real time (1) Timecode which changes in step with the actual time of day.

Real time (2) The actual running time of an event as opposed to 'screen time' – the compression of time achievable by editing.

Recces The inspection of a location by production staff to assess the practicalities involved in its use as a setting for a programme or programme insert.

Record run Timecode which increases only when a recording is made. Record run only records a frame identification when the camera is recording.

Recorded-as-live A continuous recording with no recording breaks.

Redhead A 800 W portable lightweight lamp.

Redundancy When compressing a signal, the part which can be predicted from the signal already received and therefore need not be sent. It is redundant.

Reflector Any white or silvered surface that can be used to reflect a light source.

Reverberation The gradual decay of reflected sound.

Reverse angle When applied to a standard two person interview, a camera repositioned 180° to the immediate shot being recorded to provide a complementary shot of the opposite subject.

Robotic camera A camera with a remotely controlled camera head, e.g. pan/tilt, zoom and focus. May also include camera position and height.

Rocking focus Moving the focus zone in front of and behind the selected subject in order to determine sharpest focus.

Sampling rate The number of measurement points over time that describes a continuously variable voltage.

Saturation A measure of the purity of a colour, e.g. pale red or deep red.

Scanner The production control rooms of an outside broadcast production.

Scene file A removable data storage chip from the camera that contains memorized settings.

SECAM (Sequential Couleur à Memoire) A French developed method of encoding colour.

Shooting off Including in the shot more than the planned setting or scenery.

Shot number A number assigned to a specific shot as detailed in a camera script or camera rehearsal.

Shuttling Rapidly reviewing video tape to determine content or edit point.

Signal to noise The level difference, in dB, between the wanted signal and the unwanted background system noise.

Simple PAL Monitor mode which enables the eye to average out colour errors, i.e. no delay line used. Also enables phase errors to be seen.

Single shot technique The single camera discontinuous recording of a number of shots that are later edited in post-production.

Slo-mo replay Replaying a pre-recording at a slower speed than normal transmission.

SNG (satellite news gathering) The technique of relaying video location news reports or news material via a satellite to a base station.

SOC (satellite operation centre) The control centre of the owner/operator of a satellite.

Soft light A light source that produces a soft-edged shadow.

S/PDIF A consumer version of the AES/EBU digital interface.

SPL Sound pressure level expressed in dB where the reference is the threshold of human hearing.

Spot effects Sounds that relate to short actions, usually in vision.

Star quad A four core sound cable designed to reduce unwanted interference pick-up.

Stereo Usually understood to mean a system of reproducing a wide sound image using two channels.

Stop Either the *f* number the lens is set to or the unit change between two standard *f* numbers.

Switcher See Vision mixer. Note that job titles vary from country to country.

T number Indicates the amount of light transmitted by a lens at a specific iris setting. Unlike *f* numbers, identical T numbers on lenses will transmit the same amount of light independent of lens design.

T piece Small BNC connectors to allow teeing of video connectors, e.g. connect two video cables to one video socket.

Talkback Inter-communication by microphone and headset between a television control room and other operational areas and technicians.

Termination 75 Ω resistor included across the video cable at the end of a transmission chain. Inclusion of 75 Ω termination ensures no reflection of energy, and ensures the signal level is correct.

The narrow end of the lens The longest focal length of the zoom that can be selected.

Tight lens A long focal length primary lens or zoom lens setting.

Timecode Enables every recorded frame of video to be numbered.

Transformer A device made with two coils wound around a magnetizable core to isolate a signal or to change its voltage.

Transient A fast changing signal.

Transient response The ability of equipment to follow fast changes in level.

Translucent Semi-transparent; usually some form of light diffuser.

Tungsten The filament material in a lamp producing light by heat.

Turtle Very low lighting stand for rigging luminaires at floor level.

Tweak Term used for small adjustments to lighting rig or operational settings, e.g. black level or iris setting.

Tx Abbreviation for transmission.

Uplink The signal path from an earth station to a satellite.

Upstage Moving further away from the camera or audience.

User-bit A programmable identification code compiled by the 'user' of the camera which is recorded as part of the timecode on each video frame. User-bit allows up to nine numbers and an A to F code to be programmed into the code word which is recorded on every frame.

VCA Voltage controlled amplifier.

Vectorscope Special oscilloscope designed to display the chrominance information in an easily recognizable way, i.e. hue and saturation.

Video barrel A small in-line adaptor designed to connect two BNC video cables together.

Video contrast range The relationship between the brightest part of the scene and the darkest part.

Video wall A number of individual TV screens often stacked in a rectangle displaying multiple, individual or composite images.

Vignette The shading of the edges of the picture area.

Virtual reality System of chroma key where the background is computer generated. The size and positioning of the background is controlled by the foreground camera movements.

Vision control The person who adjusts camera exposure, colour, gamma, etc., in a multi-camera production. Also applied to the area where they perform this function.

Vision mixer The person who switches between video sources. Also applied to the equipment they use to perform this function.

VITC (vertical interval timecode) These are timecode numbers recorded in one or more of the unused lines in the TV signal and can be read when the tape is in still frame.

Voice-over A commentary mixed with effects or music as part of a sound track.

Vox pops (vox populi) The voice of the people, usually consists of a series of impromptu interviews recorded in the street with members of the public.

VTR Video tape recorder.

VU meter Volume meter indicates average level of sound.

Waveform monitor Oscilloscope with appropriate time-base for displaying the television waveform. Usually includes a face-plate graticule to indicate sync level, black level, peak white and percentage signal level.

Wavelength The length between adjacent peaks of a signal.

White balance The electronic process of defining a reference white lit by a light source of a specific colour temperature.

White noise Random noise containing an equal level of the audio frequency spectrum

Wide angle The horizontal field of view of a lens greater than approximately 40°.

Wide shot (WS) A description of shot size which includes objects greater than the size of the human figure.

Working-as-live Continuous recording with no opportunity for recording breaks or retakes.

Working behind the camera Operating the camera using remoted lens controls attached to pan bars and a non-monocular viewfinder.

Wow and flutter Variations in speed of a mechanical system, audible as frequency variations in an analogue recording.

Zebra exposure indicator A black and white striped pattern that appears in the viewfinder at points in the picture corresponding to a pre-set video level. Used as an aid to manual exposure.

Zero level voltage A standard reference audio signal of 0.775 V at 1000 Hz used for audio equipment line-up.

Zoom A variable focal length lens achieved by internally moving elements of the lens.

Zoom ratio The ratio of the longest focal length to the shortest focal length a specific zoom lens can achieve.

Zoom tracking A lens pre-focused on a distant subject will stay in a focus for the whole of its zoom movement towards (or away) from that subject providing the back focus (flange back) has been correctly aligned.